Michael Heinlein, Cordula Kropp, Judith Neumer,
Angelika Poferl, Regina Römhild (eds.)
Futures of Modernity

Sociology

MICHAEL HEINLEIN, CORDULA KROPP, JUDITH NEUMER,
ANGELIKA POFERL, REGINA RÖMHILD (EDS.)

Futures of Modernity

Challenges for Cosmopolitical Thought and Practice

[transcript]

Bibliographic information published by the Deutsche Nationalbibliothek
The Deutsche Nationalbibliothek lists this publication in the Deutsche Nationalbibliografie; detailed bibliographic data are available in the Internet at http://dnb.d-nb.de

© 2012 transcript Verlag, Bielefeld

All rights reserved. No part of this book may be reprinted or reproduced or utilized in any form or by any electronic, mechanical, or other means, now known or hereafter invented, including photocopying and recording, or in any information storage or retrieval system, without permission in writing from the publisher.

Cover layout: Kordula Röckenhaus, Bielefeld
Cover illustration: Ulrike Beck, 2bex Design & Konzept
Typeset by Harry Adler
Printed by Aalexx Buchproduktion GmbH, Großburgwedel
ISBN 978-3-8376-2076-4

Table of Content

Futures of Modernity: An Introduction
Michael Heinlein, Cordula Kropp, Judith Neumer,
Angelika Poferl and Regina Römhild | 7

COSMOPOLITANIZING EUROPEAN MODERNITY

Thinking beyond Trajectorism
Arjun Appadurai | 25

Cosmopolitan Hope. A Comment
Natan Sznaider | 33

Ironic Politics – Politics of the Future?
Wolf Lepenies | 37

The Triple Challenge
Zygmunt Bauman | 43

WORLD RISK SOCIETY – CLIMATE CHANGE IN A COSMOPOLITICAL VIEW

**Ordinary Catastrophe:
Outsourcing Risk in Supply-Chain Capitalism**
Anna Tsing | 51

**Reflexive Modernity Brings us back to Earth.
A Tribute to Ulrich Beck**
Bruno Latour | 65

**Living the Winter of Discontent:
Reflections of a Deliberative Practitioner**
Maarten Hajer | 77

The Political Contradictions of Second Modernity
Ted Nordhaus and Michael Shellenberger | 95

INEQUALITY AND GOVERNANCE IN THE GLOBAL AGE

Global Inequality and Human Rights:
A Cosmopolitan Perspective
Ulrich Beck | 109

The Politicization of Europe. A Cosmopolitan Project
Edgar Grande | 129

The Future of Global Inequality
Anja Weiß | 141

A Good Job Well Done:
Richard Sennett and the Politics of Creative Labour
Angela McRobbie | 155

INDIVIDUALIZATION COSMOPOLITANIZED

Of the Individual and Individualization:
The Striving Individual in China and the Theoretical Implications
Yunxiang Yan | 177

Individualisation, Migration and Gender Relations
Elisabeth Beck-Gernsheim | 195

Inequality: From Natural »Facts« to Injustice –
On the Political Sensibility of the Individualized Human
Ronald Hitzler | 201

Cosmopolitan Individualization. Twelve Theses on Ulrich Beck:
A God of One's Own. Religion's Capacity for Peace
and Potential for Violence
Hans-Georg Soeffner | 215

Notes on Editors and Contributors | 231

Futures of Modernity: An Introduction

MICHAEL HEINLEIN, CORDULA KROPP, JUDITH NEUMER,
ANGELIKA POFERL AND REGINA RÖMHILD

The controversy prompted by the thought and writings of Ulrich Beck over the multifaceted dynamics of the fundamental transformation that modernity is undergoing under conditions of globalization raises new kinds of challenges for politics and everyday life worldwide, but especially for a social science that deals with these issues. At issue is what conclusions should be drawn from the recognition that, neither in the West nor at the level of global pluralism, are modern societies the normatively integrated formations developing in linear ways as which they were characterized and described, for example, by the long-dominant structural functionalism (see Schwinn 2006). The plural, contingent present of global modernities points, on the contrary, to worldwide processes of reflexive modernization and to the interrelation between successfully enforced goals of modernity and the dynamic of unintended side effects. These very side effects of the process of modernization represent the driving force of an epochal transformation that is changing the coordinates of this transformation itself toward a *modernization of modernity* (Beck and Bonß 2001; Beck and Lau 2004) and is directing it into new, hitherto unexplored channels. The authors of this book have made it their task to survey this other modernity that is overlooked and concealed by linear conceptions of modernization and to address the production of uncertain social futures in the present.

MULTIPLE FUTURES

The contours of a ›world risk society‹ (Beck 2009) that are beginning to take shape can no longer be described and explained in terms of the categories of social science that take their orientation from the framework of the industrialized nation state and the apparent exclusivity of European or Western modernity. Global risks – such as, for example, climate change and terrorism – the question of global social inequality, the increasing plurality, multi-directionality, and transnationality of global mobility and communication, and the confrontation between diverse cultural outlooks and paths of modernization unfolding at different levels call for the development of further perspectives on emerging social realities and the associated opportunities and problems. Beyond that, however, the fundamental question of a further pluralization and globalization of modernity is acquiring a new explosive quality in both social practice and scientific theory. With the increase in transnational interdependencies and interrelations, complex forms of *internal globalization* of local societies are developing in which the actors, ideas, and products of a worldwide constellation of »multiple« (Shmuel Eisenstadt), »interwoven« (Shalini Randeria), or »global« (Arjun Appadurai) modernities are confronting each other simultaneously and directly in social action: A process of ›cosmopolitization‹ (Beck 2000, 2002, 2004, 2006; Beck/Sznaider 2006; Römhild 2010; Poferl 2012) is occurring that, with unexpected radicality, is both localizing »the global« and, conversely, globalizing »the local« and is converting them into distinctive social and cultural configurations.

A major consequence of these developments, which is central to this book, is the opening up of new spaces of possibility that, as will be shown below, point to *multiple futures* of reflexive, cosmopolitan modernization. The traditional conceptions of the future associated with the Western, industrial modernity of the nation state were decisively shaped by a conception of the linearity of social experience and its continuation into the future. On this conception, modernization was a continuous, unchanging process whose social (symbolic and material) counterpart was a largely unfailing trust in an unknown future. Hence, the future that had still to be decided could be imagined within the framework of a dynamic of change geared to continuity as a »not-yet-present« from which the practices of the social production of the future – politics and economics, in particular, though also institutionalized life plans and individual decisions – could take their orientation and acquire stability (see Adam 2010). The institutions and premises of modern societies were regarded accordingly as »future-resistant,« as it were: an institutional framework that, although in need of reform, was largely stable made possible substantive connections between decisions and associated practical consequences, on the one hand, and new requirements and opportunities of action, on the other. The ineluctable openness of the future could be transformed, notwithstanding irritations, into a feeling of *future security*.

However, the consequences of social and political action – in particular through the interdependence with the decisions and actions of »global others« previously regarded as distant – which are increasingly perceived as uncontrollable, are undermining this feeling of security and challenging the associated social practices of the production of the future. The teleological understanding of modernity that associates time and history with purposeful »progress« is profoundly unsettled (see the contributions of Appadurai, Sznaider, Tsing, and Latour in this volume). The institutional arrangements of the First Modernity founded on this understanding are increasingly powerless to meet, let alone master, the new kinds of challenges posed by a globalized or cosmopolitanized present. The formerly socially de-problematized decision-making contexts now exhibit potentially highly risky features at the level of both institutions and the individual conduct of life. Whether it is a matter of personal decisions concerning reproduction, of work and relationships, the production and negotiation of gender and cultural identities, the consumption of goods, the organization of leisure time, social commitment or other things – almost all areas of human life have been gripped by an insecurity engendered by modernity itself. The claim of industrial modernity to shape and master the future is proving to be a peculiarly transitory and eurocentric project, a presumptuous illusion of knowledge and control that is prone to uncertainty, and it is becoming problematic in concrete decision-making situations within a tension-laden context of knowledge and ignorance (Braun and Kropp 2010). The place of a fundamental confidence in the similarity between the past and the future is being taken by risky multiple futures that are anchored in a society of different presents where they have to be negotiated in the face of extremely diverse claims and outlooks. The quality of the »futures of modernity« consists in their (epochal?) new openness that is leading to an equally novel form of politicization of the future: The social imagination and production of our futures points to pluralist perspectives and interests and to highly diverse constellations of actors, to politics »from above« and »from below.« It is controversial, contradictory, and ambivalent. It can exhibit quite different features – whether this occurs in the form of mere practical responses to cosmopolitanized presents or, in addition, also issues in reflective cosmopolitan action. Moreover, which institutions and which normative positions can and must be activated or developed for this purpose remains open.

REFLEXIVE MODERNIZATIONS

The relationship between uncertainty and the future is increasingly being integrated into the decision-making processes of contemporary societies. With reference to reflexive modernizations this means that, in addition to the structural *reflexivity* of the unintended side effects emphasized by Ulrich Beck – that is, the massive influence they exert back on the principles and institutions of modernity (see Beck, Giddens, and Lash 1994) – future-related, »reflexively prompted« *reflection* is increasingly becoming the sign of our times.

The current variety of »modernization stories« and the thematization of their side effects specific to localities not only lead to a tension-laden, competitive form of coexistence. As Anna Tsing shows (in this volume) using the example of the modern, postcolonial treatment of the Indonesian rainforest, the disastrous consequences of the capitalist modernization project, which is characterized as »progress« from a Western perspective, are increasingly coming to light. However, this holds equally for the anticapitalist modernization projects of the socialist East, of the »second world« in the tripartite world of the Cold War; they, too, were presented to the »third world« as emancipatory development aid (see Chari and Verdery 2009; Boatcă 2007), based on a different ideological foundation, but in a similar colonial attitude. In particular, the promise made by both capitalist and real socialist modernization projects that economic and social progress would reinforce each other has proven to be fragile. The global hopes for social security and equality inspired by modernization are being replaced by global disappointments. This is also shown by the ethnographic analysis of Yunxiang Yan (in this volume) which discusses individualization processes under Chinese conditions. The example of educational aspirations clearly reveals the ambivalence of these processes: liberating Chinese individuals from the constraints of the previous all-encompassing social categories of the family, kinship, and socialist work, shifting the meaning of personal achievement to the individual and now resulting in »striving individuals« (Yan) driven by an urge to succeed (in materialistic terms) or a fear of failure, – but unless Western individuals without any underpinning emancipation politics.

In many cases, a contrary downward spiral at odds with the logic of development is taking shape: The ecological impacts of these processes of modernization not only affect an apparently separate »nature,« but also react back with full ferocity on the social and economic foundations of modernized societies – which once again reveals their fundamental dependence on ultimately uncontrollable »natural« resources. The risks of reflexive modernization are not isolated; on the contrary, because of their conspicuous interconnections they develop an equally conspicuous internal dynamic. In this context, strategies for managing risk in one place can lead to all the more catastrophic accumulations of risks at another place, as not only Ulrich Beck makes clear in his contribution. Thus, one can already predict that the consequences of climate change and an increasingly unbridled exploitation of resources have long since gone beyond posing a threat only to living conditions in the regions viewed as »peripheral« from a Western perspective. With the new migration figure of the ›climate refugee‹ (Biermann and Boas 2010; Klepp and Herbeck 2012), with foodstuffs tainted with radioactivity or poisons that point to distant industrial catastrophes, with the crises of whole production sectors and associated financial markets, and with the economics of global organ trafficking, the side effects imminent in development have long since also reached the »centers« of modernization – long before the apocalyptic scenarios displaced into an indefinite future that dominate the discourse on world risk society have been realized.

In this process of mutually entangled reflexive modernizations and the »everyday catastrophes« that already have to be managed and discussed today (Latour and Hajer in this volume), the logics rooted in colonialism and in industrial modernity are increasingly becoming targets of criticism. This criticism is aimed in part against the ideas of modernity as still unfulfilled promises, in part against the practices of its self-declared authors and custodians. In the wake of the Cold War, Western-style modernization seemed to undergo a new upswing and to be getting ready for its final victory march in the socialist societies undergoing upheaval. However, the faith in this victory march had long since been definitively shaken in the postcolonial societies because of their long history of involvement with the Western capitalist modernization project (Ziegler 2008). Critical voices are being raised in these countries that call for a decentering of the Western dominance in the project of modernity. In his book, *Provincializing Europe*, Dipesh Chakrabarty (2000) connects this with the proposal for a renewal of modernity by its »others« who formerly were understood only as addressees but not as co-creators:

›European thought is at once both indispensable and inadequate in helping us to think through the experiences of political modernity in non-Western nations, and provincializing Europe becomes the task of exploring how this thought – which is now everybody's heritage and which affects us all – may be renewed from and for the margins‹ (Chakrabarty 2000, 16).

However, this renewal, which Chakrabarty understands primarily as an intellectual project, is also opening up an (indirect) route through the cosmopolitanized constellations and practices that are emerging at the interfaces between reflexively interwoven modernizations (see Beck in this volume). That surprising opportunities are opening up in the very ruins of the impacts of modernization is shown by Anna Tsing using the example of the subcontractor business that is developing around the cultivation of a gourmet mushroom on desolate former rainforest land (in this volume). Such precarious spaces of opportunity, which wrest an existence founded upon the failure of the modern past from this very failure, arise when people have to act at the interstice of no-longer-verified modern knowledge and an unknown future – hence practically everywhere.

Unlike in the present-fixated First Modernity in which the future was conceived as the progress of the present and was as a result neglected, decision-making processes in contemporary societies are increasingly contingent on a continuous imagining, gauging, and negotiating of (im)possible futures. As a result, the available social stores of knowledge and their legitimation, central modern institutions and their myths of origin, are unavoidably becoming embroiled in multifarious debates, as all of the texts in this volume illustrate. The fact that it is becoming increasingly impossible in these debates to ignore the interrelations between diverse modern presents and pasts could facilitate an active, cosmopolitical reflection on the foundations and consequences of reflexive modernizations. However, this would require a global dialogue »among equals« (see Beck and Grande 2010) that includes all experiences with modernity and evaluates them in a (self-)critical fashion. In the Western centers of the modern production of knowledge, in particular, this is connected with an opening towards the outlook of the »others« and a »provincialization« of the epistemological foundations and the universal assumptions of the Western theorem of modernization, as this has long been called for in German-speaking, European social science (see, among others, Reuter and Villa 2010; Gutiérrez Rodríguez et al. 2010; Conrad et al. 2012). In this connection, the repudiation of the teleological phantasm of progress and the insight that the unfinished project of modernity could learn from other genealogies could prepare the ground for a reflective approach to the interwoven simultaneity of uncertain futures.

UNCERTAIN HOPES

Do we stand at the beginning of a »world society« with planetary networks of reorganization of the social, as certain columnists interpret the so-called Arab Spring? Or is the triumph of a »cosmopolitanism,« for which the humanists repeatedly hoped, and thus the triumph of a united »world bourgeoisie« with globally shared values and norms? Or is at least the isomorphic spread of Western institutions and legitimacy myths as a universally valid standard imminent (Meyer 2005)? Scarcely! The respects in which Western history turns out to be just *Western* history, not just with a fading aura but also with declining legitimacy, are too diverse. The international power and exchange relations, which operate essentially according to the modality of differentiation and exploitation, are too contradictory. The »cultures,« which cannot be described as nation states and then be united, are too heterogeneous. Finally, the living conditions, the involvements, and the room for creativity – but also the self-thematizations of successful and threatened societies alike, are too unequal. Underlying all of those notions of completion, as Arjun Appadurai shows, is ultimately a eurocentric, expansionist, imperialist ›trajectorism‹ – namely, ›a deeper epistemological and ontological habit, which always assumes that there is a cumulative journey from here to there, more exactly from now to then.‹ Trajectorism is based, implicitly or explicitly, on a ›project of conversion and conquest‹ – ›playing out on a global terrain of its own demons, divisions and unresolved anxieties‹ (Appadurai in this volume). As Natan Sznaider (in this volume) adds: ›This is not Kant's world of »eternal peace« but a world of eternal risk and negotiation.‹

The world includes incomparably more (and more fruitful) standpoints, it is likewise irrevocably networked, it is connected and entangled in more than one exchange relation, though it is also structured in local and particularistic ways. It is no longer possible for anyone to close him or herself off from the everywhere articulated, but different, perspectives on the future. While cosmopolitanism is propounded as a norm and an uncertain hope, Ulrich Beck speaks of *cosmo-*

politization as the – often coerced – inclusion of the excluded Other, as at once idea and reality of the ›enmeshment with the cultural Other‹ (Beck 2006 and in this volume). Microcosm and macrocosm are inseparable in this regard. But if even simple questions – what is a family? what is a culture? – can no longer be answered in a globalized, cosmopolitanized context, who can be surprised that perceptions of risk (Hajer), conceptions of individuality (Yan), notions of gender relations, family, and partnership (Beck-Gernsheim), of (in)justice (Hitzler), of good work (McRobbie), or of political-institutional integration (Grande) are not shared, but that in their various ways they challenge identity and universality, truth and knowledge, tradition and future. The question of the significance of religion that is often neglected by theories of modernization (Soeffner) must also be discussed in new ways in this context. And who would be surprised that such ›entangled cosmologies‹ (Latour in this volume) do not end on the earth but also include the heavens and the skies and other forms of life. For climate change also means establishing an indissoluble connection between human activities and global environmental change – in short, of doing cosmo-politics ›in the sense of altering the associations [...] that all beings establish with all other beings‹ (Latour in this volume). Therefore, climate change challenges us, as the anthropologist Kirsten Hastrup (2012) also believes, to re-examine the anthropocentrism of the modern (self-)understanding beyond the eurocentrism of modernizations. If debates over the ›gradual composition of the common world‹ (ibid.), decisions over the worlds in which we want to live, become necessary for the futures of modernity, then the barrier between science and politics also collapses.

AN OUTLOOK ON FUTURES OF MODERNITY

The present volume is devoted to exploring possible Futures of Modernity, their acknowledged and concealed traditions and origins, their horizons of possibility and criteria of validity to be negotiated under entirely novel, cosmopolitanized conditions, and, last but not least, to the search for instruments and categories of a critical social science that has repudiated the nation state framework no less than the problematized routines of differentiation and trajectorisms. Based on the social scientific thought of Ulrich Beck, the volume brings together an avant-garde of critical thinkers to offer their interpretations of the coming challenges and their social dynamics and political implications. In what follows, we offer brief presentations of the four sections of the book.

1. COSMOPOLITANIZING EUROPEAN MODERNITY

The Europe of today has become the major arena in which the hegemony of a Western modernity and its economic, political, and cultural claims to global dominance are being fundamentally contested. Not only global crises, but also transnational movements – of people within, outside, and across European borders, and of goods and risks, ideas and histories, extending from the »periphery« to the »center« – are putting the national, but also the Europeanized, will to political control under pressure. As a result, they are proving to be a major force in cosmopolitanizing European societies and the modern traditions on which they can rely less and less. Ultimately, these processes raise the question of how to acknowledge both theoretically and practically the simultaneous presence of »other« modernities within a truly global, cosmopolitan project of Reflexive Modernity that transcends Eurocentric restrictions.

One of the first, and fundamental, steps in this direction, according to *Arjun Appadurai*, would be to critically re-examine the »trajectorism« of Western projects of modernization, which means their obsessive ideology of predictable, controllable directions, goals, and outcomes of history. What is required is the risky, but necessary revision of an ominously successful, imperial cosmopolitanism of modern world domination, which can succeed only with the help of and in dialogue with those who are excluded in this imperial modernity, alternative cosmopolitanisms of other societies and civilization.

But, one could ask further with *Natan Sznaider*, weren't these alternatives already a major theme of the eighteenth-century Enlightenment, which always also involved a self-critical fascination with the »noble savage« and a corresponding reflexive perspective on the Western societies and their path to modernity? Couldn't the twenty-first century gain a new approach to this age of not-yet-lost epistemological innocence – and in so doing effect a post-imperial cosmopolitanization of the Enlightenment, which would then have to be understood, entirely in keeping with Dipesh Chakrabarty, not as just a Western but also a global heritage and as an unfinished project involving global responsibility?

The willingness and ability to problematize oneself are forerunners of reflexive modernization since the Enlightenment, as *Wolf Lepenies* observes. Can cosmopolitan traces of the constant confrontation with the possibility of the other be detected here and in the associated capacity for (self-)irony, for an »ironic politics« – traces on which a contemporary political revision of modernist-imperial arrogance could draw directly?

Zygmunt Bauman directs attention back to the observation of a fundamental convulsion of the Western ideology of modern »trajectorism.« As he sees it, this ideology and the certainty that it once imparted confront a threefold challenge: 1. in the experience of an »interregnum,« hence of a transition in which the old order is no longer valid but in which a new order is not yet really visible, let alone established; 2. in the closely related experience of fundamental insecurity; and 3. in the disparity among institutional arrangements that leads to a drifting apart of (global) power and (local) politics. We should start from this latter discrepancy, according to Bauman, by »complementing« the »negative« consequences of globalization with »positive« opportunities (for instance, forms of global political representation). However, this calls – and with this we could link up again with Appadurai – for a global confrontation with the »Other,« with the repressed of the European history of modernization; for a global politics that is shared by all can be developed only in an awareness of a shared history of interwoven modernities (Conrad and Randeria 2002).

2. WORLD RISK SOCIETY – CLIMATE CHANGE IN A COSMOPOLITICAL VIEW

Contemporary societies are confronted with the problem of global environmental change – but not all in the same way. The thematization of climate change still largely conforms to those rigid Western, industrial preconceptions that played and continue to play a decisive role in its emergence. The claim to knowledge and control that was unleashed in the Enlightenment and has frequently been criticized as technocratic remains intact and not only permits unintended side effects to proliferate in its shadow but also management fantasies and authoritative discourses of constraint and political necessity. Moreover, to date those who claim to be able to specify what is good and bad for all places and relations from an ecological vantage point still scarcely bother to make sure that global comparisons among the criteria of judgment are possible. But climate change is a tricky business that assumes different guises for different publics and is represented in equally diverse ways. And, yet, the belief that an exact science that will make breakthroughs to clear and hence »true« statements, offers »one best way« problem solutions remains unshaken, notwithstanding all setbacks. Against this background, the following four contributions offer more than inspiring proof of the relevance of cosmopolitan reflections.

Anna Tsing situates her observations on the outsourcing of risk in supply-chain capitalism, on the one hand, in the global, but unequal, contexts of the displacement not only of goods but also, on an at least equal scale, of bads. On the other hand, she touches on the sore point of risk management that under Western capitalist hegemony has less the effect of avoiding risks than of ›shipping environmental consequences elsewhere‹ (ibid.), even if these in the next moment – in the shape of ordinary catastrophes – blithely escape the security cordons. In doing so, the ethnologist shows the extent to which the underlying thought patterns can already be found in Western literature and that, for example, Captain Ahab is part of that Western thought fixated on progress for which the outsourcing of disaster – elsewhere and into the future – counted as smart fragmentation and positive accomplishment.

Bruno Latour pursues this line of thought and in his diagnosis takes a further step back. He recounts the shock of the first astronauts, in spite of the most advanced technologies, not at conquering new terrain, but, when looking back from the barren moon at the precious Earth, at finally recognizing the need to protect its life-sustaining atmosphere and its continuation in spacesuits: ›And our condition on »biosphere one« is much worse than in the international space station, for learned astronauts, experimenters, can always turn to the motherland and say in a confident male voice: »Houston we have a problem.« But us here, on the blue planet, we've got no base to turn to,‹ according to Bruno Latour. In this world of ›entangled cosmologies‹, controversies over the correct knowledge, the correct practice, the correct epistemology, and, of course, the correct risk management become questions that decide over the future that have long since ceased to halt at the boundaries of science and politics, propaganda or proof, values or facts, but instead call for cosmopolitics.

The same problem is also addressed by *Maarten Hajer* who was assigned the complex task of placing the scientific and science-policy foundations of the most recent IPCC Reports on a less contestable footing from a constructivist perspective favorable to democracy, after its ›expert authority was problematized, directly and with outrage in the media‹ – the well-known climategate affair. Hajer takes up the challenge and strives – as reconstructed for us step by step in the text – to restore the claim to advise politics from the perspective of deliberative theory and thereby provides the tools for tomorrow to those familiar with the scientific and political scene. How is authoritative governance possible – in spite of the contingencies of modern futures?

Ted Nordhaus and *Michael Shellenberger* relate such considerations back to Ulrich Beck's interpretation of climate change as the quintessential global risk and social contradiction that undermines modernist institutions, especially the nation state. However, the two activists from California contradict the over-optimistic expectation that ›global norms can be created through cosmopolitan moments‹ (Beck 2008: 13). Instead they regard ›the rise of neo-liberalism [as] a second modernity phenomena, closely related to changing notions of the state, the economy, and modernity itself‹ and consequently explore whether explicit and direct state and collective responses to the crises of Second Modernity are even possible in a world in which the modern state has become simultaneously ubiquitous, intertwined with virtually every part of modern life, and at the same time virtually invisible to its citizenry. Either way, the big challenge facing the social sciences is arguably to overcome industrial mindsets and norms that cannot guide evaluations and decision-making any longer, and instead to invent ways, methods, and formats of reflexive, cosmopolitan thinking required to address the dramatic challenge of climate change.

3. INEQUALITY, POWER AND GOVERNANCE IN THE GLOBAL AGE

One of the most troubling aspects of the »global age« is the supposed decline of the nation state as the principle of internal and external order. This means that the dimensions of inequality, power, and governance – which in modern societies are typically tied to nation state boundaries, and thus are supposed to be processed at the national level – can no longer be grasped from nationally shaped perspectives. Thus, the question is: How can we think about these issues from a cosmopolitan perspective?

In his contribution, *Ulrich Beck* uses these questions as an occasion to connect the analysis of global inequalities with the issue of human rights against the background of a methodological cosmopolitanism. His starting point is that ›cosmopolitization means the global Other is no longer out there, not only near us but ›in‹ us.‹ It seems all the more urgent that the social sciences as well as politics should overcome the constraints of the national outlook – for it is also the case that ›cosmopolitization enforces an enmeshment with the global Other, which opens up spaces and perspectives for the implementation of human rights regimes.‹ Thus, cosmopolitization itself provides the opportunity of confronting global inequalities with a cosmopolitan inflection of human rights.

In his contribution, *Edgar Grande* draws attention to the European context by throwing light on the process of European integration against the background of its increasing politicization. His central thesis is ›that the political foundations of the process of European integration and the conditions governing how the political system of the EU functions have undergone a fundamental transformation.‹ This transformation is made possible by the emergence of novel, and in their outcomes contrary, economic, cultural, and political conflicts that problematize cosmopolitan Europe itself: ›the political conditions for the further development of a cosmopolitan Europe have changed fundamentally‹ – in particular, as Edgar Grande shows, in highly paradoxical ways.

Anja Weiss deals with the future of global inequalities in her contribution. Taking her lead from the story of Barack Obama's childhood, she develops a comparison between different perspectives in social science, philosophy, and political science on how to conceptualize the globalization and cosmopolitization of inequality. Her diagnosis concerning the toolkit of social science for dealing with global inequality proves to be a sobering one: ›Currently, the strength of sociological analyses is not in the conceptual debate about global justice or in empirical analyses on a world scale.‹ An exception for Anja Weiss, however, is the study of contemporary reflexive-modern institutional change that results in ›moral economies transcending national container states.‹ This also prompts her plea for a sociology that should be more devoted to the institutions ›which go beyond the nation state.‹ Anja Weiss can be interpreted as arguing that only then will a critical confrontation with global inequality that also generates political effects become possible.

Finally, in her contribution *Angela McRobbie* addresses working lives in the new creative sector. Drawing on Richard Sennett's reflections on the flexibilization of work, the city, and craft, McRobbie develops a perspective that is able ›to think in new ways about the creative industries.‹ The result is ›a vocabulary which refuses hyperbole, glamour and excitement and which brings into play topics such as under-employment, craft, dedication, public-mindedness, social care and the retrieval of time and space from the speeded-up creativity-machine.‹ This paints a haunting picture of life and work in the creative sector that exposes the manifold risks, inequalities, and precarities in a domain is marked more than almost any other by new cosmopolitan populations in large urban environments.

4. INDIVIDUALIZATION COSMOPOLITANIZED

Individualization is both releasing individuals from traditional structures and re-embedding them in new social relations, giving rise to a paradoxical »force to freedom.« However, individualization is not confined to European borders or the Western World. Rather, we have to consider simultaneous varieties and complexities of individualization that interact in different ways in a global world. This is why we have to understand and define individualization and its ambivalences in a cosmopolitan perspective, why we have to ask for divergent as well as for convergent developments, and why we have to identify historically and culturally specific meanings, conditions, and challenges.

Yunxiang Yan opens the series of contributions with an analysis of social processes of individualization in the Chinese context. He works out the peculiarities of the Chinese path of individualization and its political-economic and historical background from a vantage point informed by social and cultural anthropology and devotes particular attention to the distinction between macro-social, institutional, and biographical-subjective dimensions of individualization and their contingencies. In this way, the varying role of the individual in the process of individualization acquires importance in the comparison between China and Western Europe; but, on the other hand, different influences of individualization on the production of the ›new individual‹ depending on social settings are also apparent.

Elisabeth Beck-Gernsheim draws on recent research on transnationalization to exhibit distinctive features of gender-specific differences in individualization. In doing so, she concentrates on the connection between individualization and migration that remained a ›blank spot‹ into the 1990s in research on trends towards change in modern societies. The discussion of individualization is not an exception when it comes to this deficit either, according to Beck-Gernsheim. Today it must be assumed that migration represents an important driving force of individualization, contradicting the stereotype of a migration population primarily wedded to tradition. Moreover, striking similarities between the mainstream society and immigrants crystallize out in typically »male« and »female« patterns of individualization.

Ronald Hitzler takes up the broad and explosive issue of the relation between social inequality, injustice, and natural »facts.« His starting point is the diversity of human beings, which, despite all social imprinting – and notwithstanding omnipresent processes of social construction – has an individual aspect that is largely excluded from traditional models of class and social strata. A multiplication of experiences of inequality can also be established under conditions of individualization, among which are, for example, deprivation according to age, gender, and bodily and mental capability. Hitzler argues that inequality can develop its political conflict potential only when it is evaluated as – more or less illegitimate – ›injustice‹ by society. The question he raises is what status individual, »natural« injustice can assume in this dynamic.

Hans-Georg Soeffner deals with the religious presuppositions of social individualization and with the associated development of types of individuality specific to (European) modernity. The range of explanations in the sociology of culture and the sociology of religion extends from the anthropological foundation of the experience of limits and of overcoming limits, which is at the source of human religiosity, through the structurally imposed individuality in modern societies with its over-elevation of the individual, up to the idea of *A God of one's own* developed by Ulrich Beck (2010) and its cosmopolitical potential. According to Soeffner, a heroic optimism of reflexive (theory of) modernization appears in the hope for a ›polytheistic baldachin‹ of cosmopolitan individualization. Only the further course of history can demonstrate its chances of realization – and with this, the question of the futures of modernity concludes not only the discussion of individualization but also this volume as a whole.

The contributions to this volume originated in a symposium in honor of Ulrich Beck organized by the editors that took place at the Ludwig Maximilian University of Munich in July 2009. We would like to thank all of the authors for their willingness to confront the question of the »Futures of Modernity« in productive ways on that occasion and in their contributions to this book. Furthermore, we would like to thank the German Research Foundation (DFG), the Allianz Kulturstiftung and the Institut für Soziologie of the LMU Munich for their generous support of the symposium, without which this book would not have been possible either.

Translation by Ciaran Cronin

References

Adam, Barbara (2010). History of the Future: Paradoxes and Challenges. In: *Rethinking History* 14 (3): 361–378

Beck, Ulrich (2000). The Cosmopolitan Perspective: Sociology of the Second Age of Modernity. In: *British Journal of Sociology* 51 (1): 79–105

Beck, Ulrich (2002). The Cosmopolitan Society and its Enemies. In: *Theory, Culture & Society* 19 (1-2): 17–44

Beck, Ulrich (2004). Cosmopolitical Realism: On the Distinction Between Cosmopolitanism in Philosophy and the Social Sciences. In: *Global Networks* 4 (2): 131–156

Beck, Ulrich (2006). *The Cosmopolitan Vision*. Cambridge, Malden: Polity Press

Beck, Ulrich (2009). *World at Risk*. Cambridge, Malden: Polity Press

Beck, Ulrich (2008). *Risk Society's ›Cosmopolitan Moment‹*. Lecture at Harvard University, November 12, 2008; http://www.labjor.unicamp.br/comciencia/files/risco/AR-UlrichBeck-Harvard.pdf

Beck, Ulrich (2010). *A God of One's Own: Religion's Capacity for Peace and Potential for Violence*. Cambridge, Malden: Polity Press

Beck, Ulrich and Wolfgang Bonß (eds.) (2001). *Die Modernisierung der Moderne*. Frankfurt/M: Suhrkamp

Beck, Ulrich; Anthony Giddens and Scott Lash (1994). *Reflexive Modernisation*. Cambridge, Malden: Polity Press

Beck, Ulrich and Edgar Grande (eds.) (2010). Varieties of Second Modernity: Extra-European and European Experiences and Perspectives. Special Issue, *British Journal of Sociology* 61 (3)

Beck, Ulrich and Christoph Lau (eds.) (2004). *Entgrenzung und Entscheidung: Was ist neu an der Theorie reflexiver Modernisierung?* Frankfurt/M: Suhrkamp

Beck, Ulrich and Natan Sznaider (2006). Unpacking Cosmopolitanism for the Social Sciences: A Research Agenda. In: *British Journal of Sociology* 37 (1): 618–624

Biermann, Frank and Ingrid Boas (2010). Preparing for a Warmer World: Towards a Global Governance System to Protect Climate Refugees. In: *Global Environmental Politics* 10 (1): 60–88

Boatcă, Manuela (2007). The Eastern Margins of Empire: Coloniality in 19th Century Romania. In: *Cultural Studies* 21 (2): 368–384

Braun, Kathrin and Cordula Kropp (2010). Beyond Speaking Truth? Institutional Responses to Uncertainty in Scientific Governance. In. *Science, Technology, & Human Values* (35): 771–782

Chakrabarty, Dipresh (2000). *Provincializing Europe: Postcolonial Thought and Historical Difference*. Princeton, Oxford: Princeton University Press

Chari, Sharad and Katherine Verdery (2009). Thinking between the Posts: Postcolonialism, Postsocialism, and Ethnography after the Cold War. In: *Comparative Studies in Society and History 51* (1): 6–34

Conrad, Sebastian and Shalini Randeria (2002). Geteilte Geschichten – Europa in einer post-kolonialen Welt. In: Sebastian Conrad and Shalini Randeria (eds.) *Jenseits des Eurozentrismus: Postkoloniale Perspektiven in den Geschichts- und Kulturwissenschaften.* Frankfurt/ M: Campus

Conrad, Sebastian; Shalini Randeria and Regina Römhild (eds.) (2012), forthcoming. *Jenseits des Eurozentrismus: Postkoloniale Perspektiven in den Kultur- und Geschichtswissenschaften.* 2nd expanded edition. Frankfurt/M: Campus

Gutiérrez Rodríguez, Encarnación; Manuela Boatcă and Sérgio Costa (eds.) (2010). *Decolonizing European Sociology: Transdisciplinary Approaches.* Farnham, Burlington: Ashgate

Hastrup, Kirsten (2012), forthcoming. Auf dem Weg zu einer globalen Imagination? Klimawandel und das Ende einer Ära in den Sozialwissenschaften. In: Regina Römhild et al. (eds.) *Europa dezentrieren: Postkoloniale, multipolare Perspektiven einer reflexiven Anthropologie.* Bielefeld: transcript

Klepp, Silja and Johannes Herbeck (2012), forthcoming. Decentering Climate Change: Aushandlungen um Klimawandel und Migration in Europa und Ozeanien. In: Regina Römhild et al. (eds.) *Europa dezentrieren: Postkoloniale, multipolare Perspektiven einer reflexiven Anthropologie.* Bielefeld: transcript

Meyer, John W. (2005). *Weltkultur. Wie die westlichen Prinzipien die Welt durchdringen.* Frankfurt/M: Suhrkamp

Poferl, Angelika (2012), forthcoming. ›Gender‹ und die Soziologie der Kosmopolitisierung. In: Heike Kahlert and Christine Weinbach (eds.) *Zeitgenössische Gesellschaftstheorien und Genderforschung: Einladung zum Dialog.* Wiesbaden: Springer VS

Reuter, Julia and Paula-Irene Villa (eds.) (2010). *Postkoloniale Soziologie: Empirische Befunde, theoretische Anschlüsse, politische Intervention.* Bielefeld: transcript

Römhild, Regina (2010). Aus der Perspektive der Migration: Die Kosmopolitisierung Europas. In: *Das Argument 52* (1): 50–59

Schwinn, Thomas (ed.) (2006). *Die Vielfalt und Einheit der Moderne: Kultur- und strukturvergleichende Analysen.* Wiesbaden: VS Verlag für Sozialwissenschaften

Ziegler, Jean (2008). *La haine de l'Occident.* Paris: Albin Michel

Cosmopolitanizing European Modernity

Thinking beyond Trajectorism[1]

ARJUN APPADURAI

There is no shortage of traps for contemporary social science. One is the illusion that we have become modern. To guard against this trap, we have Bruno Latour's elegant demonstration that we have never been modern, an insight that shocked sociology and gave a new lease on life to anthropology. Another is the illusion that we are now secular, an error that has been corrected by many scholars, perhaps most forcefully by Charles Taylor (2007) and Peter van der Veer (2001), who have shown why this claim is not true empirically and could hardly ever have been true normatively. Al-Qaeda and many less dramatic social movements have also forced us to retreat from this trap. We continue to hope that we have become more scientific, but Foucault, and many others since then, have shown us the problem with any simple story of the victory of science, especially since they have shown that science is itself an historical fragile set of practices and institutions. We also keep seeking to avoid the trap of determinism, without becoming worshippers of sheer contingency. We constantly waver between the Scylla of exception and the Charybdis of false legality. We have become suspicious of all universalisms but are rightly reluctant to celebrate relativism, especially when it acquires a sinister tone and requires us to celebrate female circumcision, gender violence or cultural totalitarianism. In short, we have become masters of the strategic avoidance of some of the bigger traps into which even our Masters, such as Comte, Marx, Durkheim, and Weber sometimes fell, even if they fell with much more elegance and reluctance than their many lesser followers. In my case, the biggest seduction was the modernization theory of the 1960's and 1970's, the opiate of the technocrats of developmentalism, which combined the logic of many of these deeper traps.

But there are traps, and then there are meta-traps. I would like to discuss one such meta-trap. And that is the trap of thinking within the optic of »trajectories« or what we may call in a rather inelegant way, the meta-trap of »trajectorism«. Trajectorism has on old history in the West, traceable at least to the Bible with its

---

[1] | A fuller version of this argument appears in Chapter 12 of Arjun Appadurai, The Future as a Cultural Fact: Essays on the Global Condition (Verso, forthcoming, 2012).

ideas about the journey from sin to salvation, from this world to the other, from blindness to redemption, all exemplified in the life of Jesus at one level, and in the road to Damascus, at another level. The Greeks were not exempt from this way of thinking and Plato's famous allegory of the Cave is an early version of the journey from darkness to light, from shadow to substance. And ever since, the idea of a trajectory has formed and framed and Western thought, even to the extent of creating a retrospective narrative of the inevitability of the West itself, constructed out of the bits and pieces of Greek philosophy, Biblical mythology, Roman law, Gothic architecture, Renaissance humanism, and many more minor elements, constantly composed into retrospect story of »rise and fall«, of progress and stasis, of dark and bright episodes, all framed in a grand trajectory which we still see, with remarkable lack of distance, as the story of the West. But the story of the West is no more than one version of the idea of a Trajectory. And this is the meta-trap which social science inherited most powerfully from its great prior ancestors in religion and pre-industrial humanism.

I should add that trajectorism is not the same as evolutionism, triumphalism, predestinationism, the myth of progress, growth or convergent modernization, though each of them relies on the hidden ontology of trajectorism. Trajectorism is a deeper epistemological and ontological habit, which always assumes that there is a cumulative journey from here to there, more exactly from now to then, in human affairs, as natural as a river and as all-encompassing as the sky. Trajectorism is the idea that time's arrow inevitably has a telos, and in that telos are to be found all the significant patterns of change, process and history. Modern social science inherits this telos and turns it into a method for the study of humanity.

In other places, such as China, India, Africa and the Islamic Belt, not to speak of the islands and forests of Anthropology, the trap of the Trajectory never become the framing conceptual trap, although its presence can sometimes be detected, especially in Islam. These places have their own meta-traps, such as the idea of the nothingness of the world, or the myth of eternal return, or the idea of multiple births, or some other driving meta-narrative. But »trajectorism« is the great narrative trap of the West and is also, like all great myths, the secret of its successes in industry, empire and world conquest.

So what does this have to do with today's cosmopolitanisms and today's forms of cosmopolitanization, in the world of risk, emergency and exception, which Ulrich Beck has done so much to illuminate?

Trajectories in Time and Space

So far, I have perhaps conveyed the assumption that trajectorism is mainly an episteme about time's arrow and has to do with sequence, cause, duration and chronology, the normal hallmarks of our current scientific assumptions about temporality. This is true but it is not the most important truth for my purposes today.

Let me back up. One of the persistent puzzles about the European world journey has been the question of the link between the universalism of the Enlightenment (which argued for the necessity of world-wide equality through the spread of knowledge, among its other key arguments) AND the European imperial project, a project of spatial dominion which ended up also as a project of world-conquest. In spite of some efforts to cast light on this inner affinity between the project of Enlightenment and the project of world-dominion, by authors like Edward Said (1978), Valentin Mudimbe (1988), and others, we have made no real progress on this problem. Foucault, who might have had something to say on this matter, did not speak much of the French imperial project and even the great Max Weber did not elect to link the global journey of capitalist ethics to the project of empire.

Suffice it to say that it does not seem likely that journey from Renaissance humanism to Kantian universalism, roughly from the sixteenth to the eighteenth centuries in Europe, could not have been connected to the project of Vasco da Gama and his many maritime successors to find the New World in searching for the Old World and also vice versa. Well before the age of industrial capitalism and the imperial adventure of Europe in the nineteenth century, the Iberian sailors and conquistadors had connected the projects of conquest, conversion and economic plunder in the New World, a connection touched upon in the work of writers like Anthony Pagden (1983) and Peter Hulme(1992).

Perhaps this is not the first time in human history that a project of ethical universalism is tied to a project of conversion and conquest: two large earlier examples are the Roman Empire and the early history of Islamic expansion. But there is something special about the European understanding of its ethical universalism (rooted in Enlightenment ideas of knowledge, education and common humanity) and the urge to world exploration and global expansion that characterizes the Dutch, English and French projects after 1800 and later the German, Belgian and Italian adventures, especially in Africa. What is this special quality?

I propose that this quality has something to do with the post-Renaissance European idea of modernity, which requires *complete global expansion for its own inner logic to be revealed and justified*. In both the Roman and Islamic examples, the ethical project was self-standing and conquest was a secondary extension of this project. But European modernity could not regard itself as complete without covering the surface of the globe. Naturally this proposal does not pretend to address the myriad ways in which ethical visions seeped into mercantile, military and political ambitions, sometimes of the most violent and greedy varieties. Another way to put this proposition is that the idea of the cosmopolis as it took shape in the 17th century in Europe (see, for example, Stephen Toulmin's useful overview of this process), was in some ways integrally linked to the imperial vision (Toulmin 1990).

Till very recently, European cosmopolitan impulses, whether expressed in travel, adventure, mapping, surveying, trading or warfare, were characterized by an inner contradiction between the urge to translate and interpret other worlds, and the urge to colonize and to convert, often by means of violence.

What I have called trajectorism is thus not only a parochial vision of temporal processes, it is in addition a problematic ideology of spatial expansion. Empire, specifically European imperialism of the last three centuries is a transverse spatial enactment of a defective vision of temporality in which time's arrow always has a single direction and a known destination. That destination is the world written in the image of Europe. Europe, in this mode of thinking is unthinkable except as the singular expression of time's arrow and this arrow is so conceived as to require its dominion over the globe. Thus the world and the globe become one and the same, and each is seen as Europe's tomorrow and Europe's elsewhere.

COSMOPOLITANISM TO COSMOPOLITANIZATION

If this view of European trajectorism has any validity, it follows that the European cosmopolitanism of the last three centuries is in fact a narrower ideology than it at first appears to be. Put starkly, it is more parochial than cosmopolitan. Now this may appear to be yet another effort to »provincialize« Europe in Dipesh Chakrabarty's eloquent image (Chakrabarty 2000)), to demystify its claims to a universal ethics, to cast doubt on the generosity of its ethical motives, and to revisit Edward Said, and many subsequent analysts, who have sought to put Europe in its place, as one among many visions of the common good, which won the world through the accidents of economic innovation and strategic good fortune, and perhaps the helping hand of Calvin's God. But I am not concerned to repeat these eloquent denunciations.

My further observation is that the sort of cosmopolitanism to which European trajectorism gave birth after the enlightenment had a parochializing effect on the European imagination itself. So we must return to the scene of the crime and ask how Europe diminished its own ethical possibilities in the mistaken idea that it was bringing its own best values to the world. In what way did Europe thus limit its own possibilities?

THE INNER DIALECTIC OF EUROPEAN COSMOPOLITANISM

The inner problem of European cosmopolitanism, in the past three centuries has something to do with its contradictory and alternative genealogies. We must recognize, to start with, that contrary to the dominant meta-narrative of Western modernity, it is not itself a cumulative, predictable or inevitable outcome of any discernible history. This meta-narrative is itself an expression of a trajectorist ideology, which tends to see Europe itself as a logical outcome of ideas which led from one phase or idea to the next, in some sort of destinarian manner.

The fact that the self-construction of Europe, itself a selective later image of certain possibilities in the idea of Western Christendom, is a product of continuous triage and selective retrospective historicization. Parts of Europe's special mix of confidence, ethnocentrism and world-adventure comes surely out of the modern debt to the missionizing logic of Western Christendom, a genealogy which is still visible in current debates over the future of secularization. Other parts owe themselves to a conscious orientation to the Roman vision of the world, which centers on law, technology and military force as key elements of the relevant past. Yet other parts favor the classical Greek heritage, notably those modern self-images of Europe in which reason and its empire take precedence over all other forms of argument and imagination. Still other images are deliberately shortsighted and see in modern Europe a history which most importantly begins in the Renaissance and its ideas of humanism, individual expression and a highly aestheticized vision of what is properly Europe's real past. There are, of course, many other streams of European self-fashioning, which stress more obscure referents in the past, ranging from its early scientific traditions to more obscure poetic, mystical and political moments and texts in its past. Thus the idea of Europe, in the modern period, always builds the meta-narrative of the European trajectory from a varied and sometimes contradictory archive, a rearview mirror which is continuously adjusted as different classes, estates and regions seek to see in their own claims a larger unfolding of the European story.

Thus when the Enlightenment becomes the dominant ideology of the political present in Europe, it never fully displaces alternative images of the European trajectory. The battle between the variety of trajectorist meta-narratives never really abates and we can see this in a series of debates, sometimes strictly intellectual, sometimes bloody struggles for power and place among groups and classes in Europe. Thus when the idea of the cosmopolis takes shape in Europe after the 17th century, what it exports to the rest of the world is less a unified value system or world-picture and more a series of efforts to paper over the cracks in the European meta-narrative, the struggle between its contradictory trajectorist narratives. The battle between church and state, the struggle between private property and various visions of collective ownership, the tension between the rule of law and the rule of the masses, the opposition of this and otherworldly impulses in European religiosity, these are all examples of the unresolved contradictions which Europe played out in the imperial project, in which these deep conflicts encountered societies and ideologies which contained their own, often very different visions of these very matters. For cosmopolitanism is ultimately a matter of ideas and what Europe exported in its imperial projects was the playing out on a global terrain of its own demons, divisions and unresolved anxieties.

This is the most serious problem with European ethnocentrism as it played out in the colonies of Africa, Asia and the Islamic world in the age of empire: not its clarity or arrogance but its numerous contradictions, all of which found their genealogies in different versions of trajectorism. In a word, European cosmopolitanism – as spread throughout the world through books, speeches, icons, images and narratives – imposed profound European conflicts unto an unpredictable series of colonial spaces, each of which had their own forms of intellectual culture and world-imaging. In short, European cosmopolitanism was not primarily an effort to impose some European consensus on the rest of the world, it was an effort to find consensus by the staging of unresolved European debates on a world which had not invited this engagement. What do we do with this troubled project of cosmopolis?

A RISK WORTH TAKING

Ulrich Beck's recent work points us to make a useful distinction between cosmopolitanism and cosmopolitanization (2002), though he may well wish to disassociate myself from my reading of this important distinction!

What we have today is an opportunity for Europe to take risks of a different type than those entailed by the Enlightenment project in its 18th century form or its imperial project of world-dominion. To continue on that model in today's world of global dependencies, mass migration, democratization and mass mediation leads directly to the policies of Fortress Europe, a direction which is as far from any cosmopolitan ideal as we are likely to get.

The risk that Europe, and Europeans, might better be advised to take, has two sides. One is the risk of re-examining the sources of Europe's trajectorist ideologies – from missionization to modernization and development – so as to achieve a deeper and more critical understanding of Europe's self-formation in the mirror of a mistaken imperial project. This risk, the downside of which is self-flagellation which is normally followed by self-congratulation, has an upside which is the potential of discovering alternative sources of the always evolving European self, sources which might be more congenial to dialogue rather than dominion as a world strategy. The other, even more worthy risk, is to make a more sympathetic effort to explore the alternative ways in which other societies and civilizations have imagined cosmopolis[2], since these other

---

2 | A monumental example of such an alternative cosmopolis is to be found in Sheldon Pollock's path breaking study of the politics and poetics of the Sanskrit cosmopolis in pre-modern South and South-East Asia: *The Language of the Gods in the World of Men:*

images and imaginaries might yield deeper grounds for exchange, criticism and political conviviality in the realities of European society today. The downside risk here is that we may discover that the European archive has indeed, after a thousand years of world-ascendancy, finally run dry and has nothing new to offer in our struggles to achieve equity, sustainability and conviviality in our cities and countries. But the upside is also clear: and this is the possibility that in separating cosmopolis from empire and seeking an actual encounter between alternative images of cosmopolis, Europe might discover untold riches in its own multiple genealogies. This would be good for Europe. And also for the world that Europe once ruled.

References

Beck, Ulrich (2002). The Cosmopolitan Society and Its Enemies. In: *Theory, Culture & Society*, 19(1-2): 17–44
Chakrabarty, Dipesh (2000). *Provincializing Europe: Postcolonial Thought and Historical Difference*. Princeton: Princeton University Press
Hulme, Peter (1992). *Colonial Encounters: Europe and the Native Caribbean, 1495–1797*. Oxford: Routledge
Mudimbe, Valentin (1988). *The Invention of Africa. Gnosis, Philosophy, and the Order of Knowledge*. Bloomington, Indiana: University Press
Pagden, Anthony (1983). The Savage Critic: Some European Images of the Primitive. In: *The Yearbook of English Studies*, Vol.13: 32–45
Pollock, Sheldon (2006). *The Language of the Gods in the World of Men: Sanskrit, Power and Culture in Premodern India*. Berkeley: University of California Press
Said, Edward (1978). *Orientalism*. New York: Pantheon Books
Taylor, Charles (2007). *A Secular Age*. Cambridge: Belknap of Harvard University Press
Toulmin, Stephen (1990). *Cosmopolis: The Hidden Agenda of Modernity*. New York: Free Press
Van der Veer, Peter (2001). *Imperial Encounters: Religion and Modernity in India and Britain*. Princeton: Princeton University Press

Sanskrit, Power and Culture in Premodern India. Berkeley: University of California Press (2006).

Cosmopolitan Hope
A Comment

Natan Sznaider

›Weep, wretched natives of Tahiti, weep. But let it be for the coming and not the leaving of these ambitious, wicked men.‹ (Denis Diderot, Supplement to the Voyage of Bougainville).

The 18th century was the age of modern cosmopolitanism better known as the Enlightenment. Historically, there are many things we can learn from this period, especially the way one looks and understands others. Montesquieu was a great teacher of a gaze not of our own. French readers where put into the shoes of two Persians, Usbek and Rica, who were like French pretending to be Persians pretending to be French looking at French and European society with awe and amazement. Diderot looked at Tahiti looking back at France through the voyage of Bougainville and Rousseau being Rousseau looked into his heart in order to search for lost civilizations. The Enlightenment was not only abstract philosophy alone. Everybody was supposed to have a little Usbek and Rica in them. It was a cosmopolitan way of looking at the world. Since that time, the Western gaze on non-Western societies is packed with longing for a lost innocence, and is at the same time filled with nostalgia for authenticity and even more with guilt for colonial violence and brutality. All of a sudden, Montesquieu and his friends were just guilty of shameless Orientalism. We do not just look at the so-called Other, but we admire him, elevate him to a pedestal, denigrate everything Western and modern. Nothing betrays cosmopolitanism more than this fraud gaze we supposedly inherited from the 18th century. Thus, let's leave Tahiti for a moment, or actually don't leave it, but let's take a cosmopolitan look at it without neither nostalgia nor guilt. The 21st Century tried to reconnect to the Cosmopolitanism of the Enlightenment. It does not do so out of spite, but it needs to in order to understand the world we live in.

The purpose of my following remarks are to show that methodological cosmopolitanism asks to break up the process through which the national perspective of politics and society, as well as the methodological nationalism of political science, sociology, history, and law, confirm and strengthen each other in their definitions of reality. This is what we inherited from the 19th century. Sociology is a child of that national gaze, more than that, it provided the tools of understanding and legitimizing the nation. The cosmopolitan plea of the Enlightenment was silenced by the voiced who asked to be free under the guidance of the nation. Nation and society became one. This issue, which connects to an entire intellectual project of cosmopolitan sociology challenges this nation state centred view of society. At the same time, and this is another point I ask to make in my comments, this kind of sociology challenges something dear to the Enlightenment, namely universalism. Cosmopolitan sociology does not want to be a universal sociology. It is not philosophy. Cosmopolitan sociology wants to give credit to the particular gaze while keeping a universal horizon. It wants to live in a cosmos and a polis at the same time.

And this is exactly what cosmopolitans want to accomplish. No easy task for readers versed in classical sociological thinking. Tahiti is no paradise; there is no stable nature in Persia or in France. Our 18th century cosmopolitans like Diderot and Montesquieu knew it. This is no nostalgia for primitivism, which would be just another form of anti-cosmopolitanism. This is not just about recognizing the other, not about othering, sociologists and philosophers have done this more than enough and we all in the business about recognizing the other and have, of course, no idea what it really means. Thus, we have to look elsewhere. Another 18th century Cosmopolitan, Immanuel Kant asked his readers at to enlarge their judgment. In his *Critique of Judgment*, he demands *enlarged thought* as the condition for cosmopolitanism. What does this mean? It sounds simple enough. It means disregard for the subjective private conditions of our own judgment. It does never mean to give up judgment at all. Just the opposite is true. The Cosmopolitan condition means to place ourselves at the standpoint of others without giving up ours. Judging means horizons of knowledge. Without them we cannot judge. Our thinking is encompassed in the plurality of meanings. Not West or Non-West, but both. Not neither-nor, but and-and as one of the battle cries of a cosmopolitan perspective tells us. You make present in your own person others than yourself, which is the meaning of a common world. This is the problem of cosmopolitanism, you don't become the other, you remain what you are, but you have the imagination to know what that kind of feeling might be for others through their words and thoughts. This is not Kant's world of "eternal peace" but a world of eternal risk and negotiation. Their project tries to redefine what it means to be European. Looking from the outside in redefines the inside, challenges both European and non-European ways of looking at the other.

Thus, in the end, the new cosmopolitan project we encountered in this conference wants to reconnect ours to the 18th century, to jump over the nation-state bound conception of society, jump back and forward beyond the profession's boundaries, which was founded on the rejection of the Enlightenment. Sociology has finally come home to its own roots and modern day cosmopolitans push this project a big step forward. Thus, we visit unfamiliar places and try to familiarize ourselves and our readers with them. Cosmopolitans are a bit like readers of travel literature, like accidental tourists who makes familiar by making things look close, which are actually far away. »Caution: Objects in this mirror may be closer than they appear«, is the starting sentence of Jean Baudrillard's account of the foreign place called America. Is this risky or a chance or both? There are risks involved in looking at unfamiliar places with a familiar language. We look outside Europe and we think we know these places, which do indeed look closer than they appear. Sociologically, these places do not behave like we are used to. Thus, it is time for taking cosmopolitan sociology for a ride outside of Europe and explore with its meaning for other contexts than the ones most of us sociologists are familiar with. Different intra-national contexts have been explored in the past (like gender and minorities). They were first steps, but still part of a nationalized sociology. Cosmopolitan thinking tries to save globalization from those who see it as an inevitable process of history determined by some obscure laws. Social scientists don't like this too much. Sociologists are used to think in structures. But structure means that there exists a relative duration. No structure without time. But with increased acceleration, in compressed modernity, there may be neither duration nor structure. In the old days, acceleration signaled the coming of the apocalypse. Now acceleration (and maybe even the apocalypse) is part of our everyday life. Is there a hidden hand in history? Is there meaning in history? And those who thought that all this meant the End, invented conspiracy theory.

Thus a cosmopolitan sociology needs to arrest time for a moment and tell stories about people's lives. This is the reason why until now cosmopolitan sociology has lagged behind cosmopolitan literature, but it is slowly beginning to catch up. Telling stories about people's lives prevents the search for abstract theory which was characteristic for sociology for such a long time. But telling stories does not mean to get lost in the private worlds of individual narratives. The cosmos is always there. In the end it is about sociological hope. And hope is precisely what you need when you don't know what the future will be and a world order collapse. If you know the future, there is no need for hope. as social scientists have become masters of avoidance of the dilemmas of modernity. On the one hand, many of us feel attracted to universalism, secularism, scientism you name it, on the other hand, we feel actually quite sophisticated to buy into these promises. So, we become critical. And what does that mean? Should we turn into relativists and celebrate the beauty or ugliness of particularism? Probably not.

Thus, it seems to be true that cosmopolitanism relates to a pre-modern ambivalence towards a dual identity and a dual loyalty. But clearly more is at stake here. Following the historical route of the cosmopolitan tradition from Hellenism via Christianity to the modern Western world makes the idea of cosmopolitanism open to criticism from outside the Western traditions. And what is that tradition, after all? Who are the heroes of Western Universalism? Do they exist at all? Thus, the concept of cosmopolitanism itself is being criticized as geographically and philosophically challenged. Thus, the concepts and the traditions of cosmopolitanism originates in the Western tradition – if it all exists – can be cosmopolitanized from without. Thus, we need a new sociological starting-point, one which continues the sociological tradition, but also one which recreates it and understands its newness by constantly negotiating the particular with the universal. In addition to understand newness does not mean to give up the old. Universalism obliges us to respect others as equals as a matter of principle. That is indeed an old principle. Yet for that very reason there is the constant risk and even danger that it does not involve any requirement that would arouse curiosity or respect for what makes others different. On the contrary, the particularity of others is sacrificed to an assumption of universal equality. And this is exactly what cosmopolitans have to avoid.

The relation of the universal and the particular is one of mutual constitution and inner connection rather than mutual opposition. This is an old philosophical cliché and most authors of good literature know it intuitively. Sociologists usually don't. This is a crucial point in the cosmopolitan enterprise. In methodological cosmopolitanism, the universal means what it does because the particulars are its background, and where the particulars mean what they do because the universal is their background. So that when one changes, the other changes – but where neither disappears. Universalism and particularism need to be thought out together. Sometimes, sociological language acts like a screen. You can only see what the curtain is letting through. But there is no choice, only silence or a hopeless cultural relativism would be the alternatives. Clearly, we don't go far enough but what needs to be done is to cosmopolitanize cosmopolitanism. We still see the neat correspondence between nation, territory, society and culture. Maybe this is not such a bad thing after all. In the end, one sees that the distinctions between West and non-West really don't make that much sense anymore when you think in cosmopolitan terms. Maybe we pay too much tribute to such dichotomies and our criticism of this becomes part of the problem we investigate. And this is true for other sociological categories as well. The nation-state may be the source of all evil for some, but it may also be the last resort of protection for others and we need to hold off its burial for another moment.

Ironic Politics – Politics of the Future?

WOLF LEPENIES

›When I see my friend after a long time, my first question is, Has anything become clear to you?‹ (Emerson 1847) Would Ralph Waldo Emerson also have asked Ulrich Beck this question? Ulrich Beck has helped us to achieve clarity about one thing, at any rate: Direct and indirect self-problematization are hallmarks of reflexive modernization. Irony, which is inseparable from self-irony, is one guise assumed by this problematization. If Western democracy has slid into a »phase of reflexivity«, isn't it time for an ironic politics?

›Most unusually for an American politician [...] he has a sense of historical irony – and is willing to articulate it‹ (Tomasky 2006: 16). This is how an American commentator in 2006 characterized the forty-three-year-old Senator from Illinois Barack Obama. If any author fostered the development of this sense of historical irony in Obama, then it was Reinhold Niebuhr. The American President is beholden to this Protestant theologian – there is an Obama-Niebuhr connection. At its center is Niebuhr's 1952 essay *The Irony of American History*. To the present-day reader it reads like a prophecy of recent and current events.

Half a century ago the issue was the threat posed to the United States by a fundamentalist movement, namely Communism. Today Niebuhr's warning to democracy not to resort to fundamentalist means when combating fundamentalism has regained its relevance. The point, in the words of Ulrich Beck, is to avoid the ›elemental fundamentalism of self-righteousness and indoctrination‹ (Beck 1997: 161). One avoidance strategy consists in practicing irony and self-irony. Showing this in the case of American society, which is marked by a high level of resistance to irony, is a challenge. To quote a book entitled *Irony and Consciousness*: ›To be American seems to be equivalent to not being ironic. As people become American they cease to have the characteristics that induce ironic behavior‹ (Reinitz 1980: 175). *The Irony of American History*: an un-American book.

For Niebuhr, history is shaped by pathos, tragedy, and irony. Natural disasters inspire pathos: in the face of nature, the question of why remains meaningless. Those historical situations are tragic in which evil is knowingly done in order to accomplish something good: The use of atomic weapons to enforce peace was the cautionary example in this regard. To Niebuhr, the ironic element appears to be the most important feature of history: Overweening virtue breeds vice, strength becomes weakness through overconfidence, and an excessive striving for security aggravates the general sense of insecurity.

The perilous irony of American history consisted in the fact that over time an »innocent nation« – to invoke the self-understanding of the Pilgrim Fathers – became the most powerful empire on God's earth. Many American politicians are convinced that the United States came to be the superpower almost against its will, at any rate rather haphazardly and always with noble intentions. »Empire by Invitation« is the technical term among historians. It's a kind of »taxi theory« of imperialism: America supposedly rushed to the focal points of world events only because it was called. Reinhold Niebuhr refuted this taxi theory. He showed that, from the founding period on, American politics was the expression of an emphatic will to power and bore imperial features.

The Cold War decades, during which the USA and the USSR held each other in check through fear of a nuclear strike by the enemy, were for the USA merely an interruption of its imperial policy. »Ironic ambiguity,« according to Niebuhr, shaped America's relationship to Communism. The USA met the self-righteousness of its opponent with a hardening of its own self-righteousness. There is, however, as Niebuhr wrote, ›a hidden kinship between the vices of the most vicious and the virtues of even the most upright‹ (Niehbur 1952: 147). The United States should not adopt an *ideological politics* when faced with the threat posed by a fundamentalist movement, according to Niebuhr. On the contrary, the point was to pursue a determined *interest-driven politics* – but without missionary zeal. Democratic nations also have a legitimate right to impose their interests by violent means if necessary, according to Niebuhr, but they must do so in an awareness of their fallibility. Every exercise of power under democracy should be accompanied by a twinge of conscience. This was Niebuhr's plea for an ironic – that is, forceful – politics that was nevertheless mindful of its limits. It would involve a combination of self-confidence and reasonable self-doubt.

Niebuhr was in turn indebted to an »unpolitical« German for pointers in formulating this idea of an ironic politics. Ten years earlier, the theologian had published a review of *Order of the Day*, a collection of Thomas Mann's political essays in English translation. Niebuhr regarded the fact that history had compelled Thomas Mann to take a stance on current political issues from a democratic standpoint as an appropriate punishment for the sin of contempt for the political that the author had incurred from an early age. Niebuhr was alluding to Mann's book *Betrachtungen eines Unpolitischen (Reflections of a Non-Political Man)* that appeared in 1918. And it seems plausible that the author of *The Irony of American History* was influenced by the closing chapter of Thomas Mann's wide-ranging polemic entitled ›Irony and Radicalism‹. Here Thomas Mann discovers Kant as a representative of political irony: ›It is possible‹, Thomas Mann admits,

›that I see [irony] where other people do not see it; but it just seems to me that one cannot grasp this concept comprehensively enough, that it should never be taken too ethically and too politically. When Kant, after a terrible and only too successful epistemological campaign, reintroduced everything again under the name of ›Postulates of Practical Reason‹, and made possible again what he had just critically crushed [...] then I see political irony in this‹ (Mann 1983: 429).

Gently, almost emotionally, Thomas Mann, who was ruthlessly unpolitical in resisting of parliamentary democracy, arrives at a stance that he describes in terms of »domestic« as opposed to »foreign policy«:

›Irony as modesty, as skepticism turned backward, is a form of morality, is personal ethics, is ›domestic policy‹. But all politics, in the civic sense as well as in the sense of the intellectual man of action, of the activist, is foreign policy‹ (Mann 1983: 425).

›If one asks us Germans for our admission ticket into the democratic age, although we cannot point to a French, an American or an English Revolution, we can – thanks to Kant! – point to Immanuel Kant‹ (Beck et al.: 1996: 77).

Thus wrote Ulrich Beck. »Reflexive modernization« – in the democratic age that also means an invitation to political irony. To follow this invitation with Kant can be especially instructive.

On June 8, 2001, Charles Krauthammer wrote in the *Washington Post* that the time had come for a new, forceful and power-aware US foreign policy exclusively oriented to American interests:

›The new unilateralism seeks to strengthen American power and unashamedly deploy it on behalf of *self-defined* global ends [...] After a decade of Prometheus playing pygmy, the first task of the new administration is precisely to reassert American freedom of action.‹

Prometheus who wanted to stop acting like a pygmy [...] Was the author aware of the tragic fate of the fabled Prometheus when he depicted America's future self-image in this way? Soon, at any rate, there was nothing more to be heard of Prometheus while the »pygmies« thrived. For from now on this was how those who were supposedly too cowardly to participate in the »War against Terror«, or who were allegedly too unsure of their own convictions to impose them by force, were described. This held especially for the Old Europeans. France and Germany, above all, seemed to be »political« or »moral pygmies« because they refused – according to the official Washington usage – to combat evil in the world with military force. The vocabulary was infectious. In the end, even the then Secretary-General of NATO, Lord Robertson, warned the European allies against continuing to act like »military pygmies« – and called for a sharp increase in national military budgets.

An even more effective slogan for sharpening the scorn poured over the European weaklings by Americans loyal to the government was coined by Robert Kagan, Director of the *Carnegie Endowment for International Peace*, with his famous saying that Americans are from Mars, Europeans from Venus. The Americans, according to Kagan, lived in the Hobbesian world of realpolitik in which contracts are without force and power is everything, whereas the Europeans were taking refuge with Kant in the dream of perpetual peace.

Kagan implied that it was time for a fresh reading of Hobbes and Kant. And lo and behold: Hobbes was no more a mere cynic of power who denied the necessity of contracts than Kant was a quixotic dreamer. On the contrary, in his writings on politics and the philosophy of history, in particular, Kant shows himself to be an ironist. Irony accompanied his attempt to combine anthropological skepticism with hope in the philosophy of history. The ›achievement of a civil society universally administering right‹ (Kant 1968: 39) is not nourished by illusions concerning human nature – quite the contrary. The human being is made of crooked timber from which nothing straight can be fabricated, he is an animal in need of a master, he is driven by ›ambition, tyranny, and greed‹ (Kant 1968: 38). Antagonism and strife are part of the nature of *homo sapiens*; they are indispensable preconditions of human progress. Kant sounds – like Hobbes. The establishment of a great »federation of nations« is anthropologically improbable – but this is precisely why we must take our orientation from this regulative idea, even if the »treatment of history proper, that is written merely *empirically*« remains far removed from it. Kant exhibits irony when he places his own writings in proximity to novels and speaks of daydreams. Finally, the title of his memorandum *Zum Ewigen Frieden (On Perpetual Peace)* is ironic. »Zum Ewigen Frieden« was a pun on the name of a Dutch inn: »The House of Perpetual Peace.« On the sign above the entrance was a depiction of a graveyard. Kant knew that perpetual peace is reserved for the dead. The living were supposed to aspire to it.

When, some years after Kant had published his essay *Idea for a Universal History with a Cosmopolitan Aim* in the *Berlinische Monatsschrift*, war again broke out in Europe, the publisher Carl Spener made a request to the philosopher to write a revised and expanded edition of his work that would take account of the changed historical circumstances. Kant turned him down: ›If the powerful of this world are in a drunken fit,‹ he wrote, ›then one must strongly advise a pygmy who values his skin to stay out of their fight‹ (Cassirer 1921: 198 [Kant 1793]). Kant's prudence consisted in keeping his distance from a politics that was showing clear signs of intoxication and was not amenable to sober rational considerations. It sounded like a premonition of Reinhold Niebuhr's warning not to respond to the threat posed by fundamentalism with fundamentalist means.

How difficult this is to accomplish would become clear to a friend of Reinhold Niebuhr's almost sixty years later – namely, George F. Kennan, who once described Niebuhr as »the father of us all.« Kennan wanted his strategy of containing Communism to be understood, entirely in Niebuhr's spirit, as sober and skeptical interest-driven politics – and had to stand by and witness how it turned into a political ideology under Secretary of State John Foster Dulles. Apparently it was not possible to respond to the irony of history with an ironic politics.

During the 1990s, »irony« became a slogan of choice in debates over the American *zeitgeist*. In September 1991, exactly 10 years before 9/11, an issue of the journal *Esquire* appeared with the cover story: ›Forget Irony – Have a Nice Decade!‹ It was an exhortation to embrace a new seriousness and to break with the blasé mentality and timidity in the face of any commitment. In 1998, Richard Rorty, a long-standing proponent of »liberal irony,« outlined the project of a patriotism for the American Left in his book *Achieving Our Country* (German: *Stolz auf unser Land*). Rorty thereby gives expression to the yearning for a »better irony« that should shape American politics in the future. Its hallmarks would be upstanding commitment combined with rejection of ideological arrogance.

On September 11, 2001, the »nice decade« came to an abrupt end. Since then, the debate has erupted not only in the United States but in the whole of the democratic West over whether the murderous ideology of Islamist fundamentalism must be combated with ideological means, or whether the survival of the West can be assured by the sober, but self-confident, defense of its own interests alone. One article which dealt with the feasibility of an ironic politics in America during the 1990s quoted from Thomas Mann: ›The intellectual must choose between irony and radicalism; a third choice is not decently possible.‹

The fact that, with Barack Obama, a Democrat was elected American president who is distinguished by his sense for the irony of history is itself an ironic state of affairs. Let me repeat the statement already quoted above that ›to be American seems to be equivalent to not being ironic‹ (Reinitz 1980: 175). There are assertions to the contrary, but they tend to stem from outsiders or rebels against American society. Thus, an American who became a European, and hence potentially an ironist – namely, T. S. Eliot – formulated his plea for an ironic attitude as a generous skepticism because he believed uncertainty to be intrinsic. This conviction must also find favor with the author of *Risk Society*.

›Perhaps skepticism, enriched with irony [...] is the existential form in which modernity will cast off the megalomaniacal presumptions of the industrial era,‹ wrote Ulrich Beck (1997: 162) in his book *The Reinvention of Politics*. Can one speak of ironic politics in this context? Isn't it just a matter of a politics that is aware of the ironic potential of history? In any case, it is a matter of an attitude that should be the distinguishing feature politicians in an era of great uncertainties, and one which by no means condemns them to practical inaction. Once again in the words of Thomas Mann: ›Irony as modesty, as skepticism turned

backward, is a form of morality, is personal ethics, is ›domestic policy‹« (Mann 1983: 425).
›When I see my friend after a long time, my first question is, Has anything become clear to you?‹ Ulrich Beck has done much to make the preconditions and possibilities of this »domestic policy« clear to us, the ideal of an attitude that is not only valid for politicians. We are grateful to Ulrich Beck, as an in the best sense turbulent spirit, for his liberal patience. I am thereby thinking of a distinction made by Friedrich Naumann who said that conservative patience has a sense for what has become whereas liberal patience creates space for that which wants to become.

Translation by Ciaran Cronin

References

Beck, Ulrich (1997). *The Reinvention of Politics*. Cambridge: Polity Press
Beck, Ulrich; Anthony Giddens and Scott Lash (1996). *Reflexive Modernisierung. Eine Kontroverse*. Frankfurt am Main: Suhrkamp
Emerson, Ralph Waldo (1847). *The Journals and Miscellaneous Notebooks X*. Cambridge: Belknap of Harvard University Press
Kant, Immanuel (1921 [1793]). Brief an Karl Spener, 22. März 1793. In: Ernst Cassirer (ed.). *Immanuel Kants Werke, Bd. X, Zweiter Teil: 1790–1803*. Berlin: B. Cassirer
Kant, Immanuel(1968). Idee zu einer allgemeinen Geschichte in weltbürgerlicher Absicht. In: Wilhelm Weischedel (ed.). *Kant. Schriften zur Anthropologie, Geschichtsphilosophie, Politik und Pädagogik. Band 9*. Darmstadt: Wissenschaftliche Buchgesellschaft
Mann, Thomas (1983). *Reflections of a Nonpolitical Man*. New York: Frederick Ungar
Niebuhr, Reinhold (1952). *The Irony of American History*. New York: Charles Scribner's Sons
Reinitz, Richard (1980). *Irony and Consciousness: American Historiography and Reinhold Niebuhr's Vision*. Lewisburg: Bucknell University Press
Tomasky, Michael (2006). »The Phenomenon«. Review of Barack Obama's book The Audacity of Hope. In: *The New York Review of Books*, 53(19): 14–18

The Triple Challenge

ZYGMUNT BAUMAN

Like the Holy Trinity known from the Scriptures, the challenge which humanity is currently facing and which, once complemented by the responses it may eventually evoke or fail to evoke, is bound to shape the future of the planet, is triple yet *triune* (»three in one«, or »both three and one at the same time«). It is made of three parts: interregnum, uncertainty, and institutional disparity; yet each part conditions the other two, while being inseparable from them.

INTERREGNUM

Sometime in the late 20s or early 30s of the last Century Antonio Gramsci recorded in one of the many notebooks he filled during his long incarceration in the Turi prison[1]: ›The crisis consists precisely in the fact that the old is dying and the new cannot be born; in this interregnum a great variety of morbid symptoms appear.‹

The term ›interregnum‹ was originally used to denote a time-gap separating the death of one royal sovereign from the enthronement of the successor: these used to be the main occasions on which the past generations experienced (and customatily expected) a rupture in the otherwise monotonous continuity of government, law and social order. Roman law put an official stamp on such understanding of the term (and its referent) when accompanying interregnum with proclamation of *justitium*, that is (as Giorgio Agamben reminded us in his 2003 study of the *Lo stato di eccezione*) an admittedly temporary suspension of laws heretofore binding (presumably in anticipation of new and different laws being possibly proclaimed). Gramsci however infused the concept of ›interregnum‹ with a new meaning, embracing wider spectrum of the socio-political-legal order, while simultaneously reaching deeper into the socio-cultural condition. Or rather (taking a leaf from Lenin's memorable definition of the »revolutionary situation« as a condition in which the rulers no longer *can* rule while the ruled

---

1 | *Quaderni del carcere;* here quoted after Gramsci 1971: 276.

no longer wish to be ruled), Gramsci detached the idea of ›interregnum‹ from its habitual association with the interlude of (routine) transmission of hereditary or electable power, and attached to the extraordinary situations in which the extant legal frame of social order loses its grip and can hold no longer, whereas a new frame, made to the measure of newly emerged conditions responsible for making the old frame useless, is still at the designing stage, has not yet been fully assembled, or not strong enough to be put in its place.

I propose (following recent Keith Tester's (2009) suggestion) to recognize the present-day planetary condition as a case of interregnum. Indeed, just as Gramsci postulated, ›the old is dying‹. The old order founded until recently on a similarly »triune« principle of territory, state, and nation as the key to the planetary distribution of sovereignty, and on power wedded seemingly forever to the politics of the territorial nation-state as its sole operating agency, is by now dying. Sovereignty is no longer glued to either of the elements of the triune principle and entities; at the utmost, it is tied to them but loosely and in portions much reduced in size and contents. The allegedly unbreakable marriage of power and politics is, on the other hand, ending in separation with a prospect of divorce.

Sovereignty is nowadays, so to speak, un-anchored and free-floating. Criteria of its allocation tend to be hotly contested, while the customary sequence of the principle of allocation and its application is in a great number of cases reversed (i.e., that principle tends to be retrospectively articulated in the aftermath of the allocating decision, or deduced from the already accomplished state of affairs). Nation-states find themselves sharing the conflict-ridden and quarrelsome company of actual, aspiring or pretending, but always pugnaciously competitive sovereign subjects, with entities successfully evading the application of the heretofore binding triune principle of allocation, and all too often explicitly ignoring or stealthily sapping and impairing its designated objects. Ever rising number of competitors for sovereignty outgrow already, even if not singly then surely severally, the power of an average nation state (multinational financial, industrial and trade companies account now, according to John Gray (2009: 231), ›for about a third of world output and two-thirds of world trade‹). Sovereignty, that right to deciding the laws as well as exceptions to their application, and the power to render both decisions binding and effective, is for any given territory and any given aspect of life-setting scattered between multiplicity of centres – and for that reason eminently questionable and open to contest; while no decision-making agency is able to plea full (that is unconstrained, indivisible, unshared) sovereingty, let alone to claim it credibly and effectively.

Uncertainty

Risk, says Ulrich Beck, the pioneer of its contemporary exploration and still its leading and most proficient theorist[2], from the beginning of modernity ›amalgamates knowledge with non-knowing within the semantic horizon of probability‹.

›The history od science dates the birth of the probability calculus, the first attempt to bring the unpredictable under control – developed in the correspondence between Pierre Fermat and Blaise Pascal – to the year 1651‹.

Since then, through the category of risk, ›the arrogant assumption of controllability‹, Beck adds, ›can increase in influence‹.

With the benefit of retrospect, from the perspective of the admittedly liquidized sequel to the compulsively liquidizing yet solidity-obsessed early modernity, we may say that the category of risk was an attempt to reconcile the two pillars of modern consciousness – the awareness of contingency and randomness of the world on one hand, and the »we can«-type confidence on the other. More exactly, the category of »risk« was an attempt to salvage the second, despite the obtrusive, resented and feared company with the first. The category of »risk« promised that even if the natural setting as well as the human-made additions to that setting are bound to stop short from unconditional regularity and so away from the ideal of full predictability, humans may still come quite close to the condition of certainty through gathering and storing knowledge and flexing its practical, technological arm. The category of »risk« did not promise foolproof security from dangers: but it promised the ability to *calculate their probability and likely volume* – and so, obliquely, the possibility of calculating and applying the optimal distribution of resources meant to render the intended undertakings effective and successful.

Even if not explicitly, the semantics of »risk« needed to assume, axiomatically, a »structured« (»structuring«: manipulation and the resulting differentiation of probabilities), essentially rule-abiding environment: a universe in which the probabilities of events are predetermined, can be scrutinized, made known and assessed. But however far may the »calculation of risk« stop from a flawless and infallible certainty, and thus from the prospects of pre-determining the future, its distance may seem small and insignificant in comparison with the unbridgeable categorial abyss separating »semantic horizon of probability« (and so also the hoped-for risk calculation) from the premonition of uncertainty saturating and haunting contemporary liquid-modern consciousness. As John Gray

---

2 | Ulrich Beck, *Weltrisikogesellschaft* (2007). Here quoted after Ciaran Cronin's translation *World at Risk* (2009, 4f.).

pointed out already a dozen years ago (Gray 2009: 236), ›the governments of sovereign states do not know in advance how markets will react [...] National governments in the 1990s are flying blind‹. Gray does not expect the future to usher into a markedly different condition; like in the past, we may expect ›a succession of contingencies, catastrophes and occasional lapses into peace and civilization‹ (Gray, 2009: 223) – all of them let me add, unexpected, unprevisible, and more often than not catching their victims as well as their beneficiaries unawares and unprepared ...

It seems ever more likely that the discovery and announcement of the centrality of »risk horizon« in modern mentality followed the eternal habit of the Owl of Minerva, known to spread its wings at the end of the day and just before the nightfall; or the yet more common proclivity of objects, as noted by Heidegger, to be transported from the state of »hiding in the light«, of staying immersed in the obscure condition of *zuhanden*, to the dazzling visibility of *vorhanden* no earlier than they go bust, fall out of routine, or otherwise frustrate the (only half-conscious and tacit, as a rule) expectations; in other words, things become known thanks to their disappearance or shocking change. Indeed, we have become acutely conscious of the awesome role which the categories of ›risk‹, ›risk calculation‹ and »risk taking« played in our modern history, only at the moment when the term »risk« lost much of its former utility and called to be used (as Jacques Derrida would suggest) sous rature, having turned (to use Beck's own vocabulary) into a »zombie concept«. When, in other words, the time has arrived to replace the concept of *Risikogesellschaft* with that of *Unsicherheitglobalschaft* ... Our dangers differ from those which the category of ›risk‹ strove to have captured and brought to light by being un-named before striking, un-predictable and in-calculable. And the setting withing which our dangers are born and from which they emerge is no longer framed by the *Gesellschaft* – unless the »*Gesellschaft*« is coterminous with the population of the planet.

INSTITUTIONAL DISPARITY

I've already mentioned the progressive separation leaning uncomfortably close towards a divorce between power and politics – the two seemingly inseparable partners residing for the last two centuries, or believed and postulated to reside, inside the territorial nation-state. That separation has resulted in the mismatch between intitutions of power and those of politics. Power has evaporated from the level of nation-state into the politics-free »space of flows« (to borrow Manuel Castells' expression), leaving the politics ensconced as before in the previously shared abode, now degraded to the »space of places«.

The growing volume of power that matters (that is, the power having if not the final say, then at least the major, and in the end decisive, influence on the setting of options open to the agents‹ choice) has already turned global; politics has remained however as local as before. Accordingly, the presently most relevant powers stay beyond the reach of extant political institutions, whereas the frame for maneouvre in the inner-state politics continues to shrink. The planetary state of affairs is now buffeted by ad-hoc assemblies of discordant powers unconstrained by political control due to the increasing powerlessness of the extant political institutions. The latter are thereby forced to severely limit their ambitions and to »hive off«, »outsource«, or »contract out« the growing number of functions traditionally entrusted to the governance of national governments to the non-political agencies. The emaciation of the political sphere (in its institutionalized orthodox meaning) is self-propelling, as the loss of relevance of the successive segments of national politics rebounds in the erosion of the citizens' interest in institutionalized politics, and in the widespread tendency to replacing it with the drive to experiment with »free floating«, electronically mediated quasi-or-inchoate/incipient politics – eminent for its expeditiousness, but also for its ad-hocness, short-termism, one-issuesness, fragility, and staunch resistance, or perhaps even immunity, to institutionalization (all those qualities mutually dependent and reinforcing).

***

To sum up: facing the triune challenge, and finding an exit from the state of interregnum and chronic as well as unredeemable uncertainty, would require *the restoration of the commensurability of power and politics*. The present-day uncertainty being rooted in the global space, that task can be performed solely at the global level, and solely by (alas not as yet existing) global law-making, executive, and juridical institutions. This challenge translates as the postulate to complement the heretofore almost wholly »negative« globalization (i.e., globalization of forces intrinsically hostile to institutionalized politics – as capitals, finances, commodity trade, information, criminality, drug-and-arms traffic etc.) by its »positive« counterpart (as, for instance, globalization of political representation, law and jurisdiction) which has not yet started in earnest.

REFERENCES

Beck, Ulrich (2009). *World at Risk*. Cambridge: Polity Press
Gramsci, Antonio (1971). *Selections from the Prison Notebooks*, ed. and trans. Quintin Hoare and Geoffrey Nowell-Smith. London: Lawrence & Wishart
Gray, John (2009). *Gray's Anatomy: Selected Writings*. Allen Lane
Tester, Keith (2009). Pleasure, Reality, the Novel and Pathology. In: *Journal of Anthropological Psychology*, 21: 23–26

World Risk Society –
Climate Change in a Cosmopolitical View

Ordinary Catastrophe: Outsourcing Risk in Supply-Chain Capitalism

ANNA TSING

In our times, it seems, the chickens come home to roost. Several centuries of planned and unplanned environmental damage have taken their toll, and suddenly we see that our species has created a livability problem on a global, multispecies scale. Will living things other than bacteria survive human destructiveness? The answer is frighteningly unclear. Yet the most powerful response continues to be: »Shoo those problems elsewhere, away from me.«[1]

How have we arrived at this place? Most commentators begin with the tools and the toys (internal combustion engines, nuclear power plants), and indeed they must be part of the story – as long as we pay attention to how they have been deployed. Ulrich Beck's concept of »risk society« is useful to tell *that* tale (see, for example, Beck 2007) Watching risk management illuminates the process in which fractured, uneven landscapes are created. Risk management ships environmental consequences elsewhere, away from the worlds of risk managers. Risk management thus contributes to the structured inequalities of the world's environmental landscape. Everyone knows that segregating environmental spaces to cordon off danger does not work; contamination slips through every barrier. Yet the process of fracturing environmental space to outsource risk has only become more pervasive, if more contested, in response to this knowledge.

In this essay, I offer a few thoughts about the fracturing of environmental space in relation to the current elite plan to organize the global economy: subcontracting and allied forms. I call this plan »supply-chain capitalism« to locate my comments in the awkward catch that separates that term used by critics of exploitation, on the one hand, and that used by business boosters, on the other; supply chains, the darlings of contemporary business managers, deserve to be

---

1 | I am grateful to Cordula Kropp for drawing me into this writing project, which began at a conference in Munich in 2009 honoring the work of Professor Ulrich Beck. The participants at that conference, including Professor Beck, were generous and thoughtful in their remarks on the talk I gave, which became this essay.

studied with the structural tools of anti-capitalist critique.[2] Supply-chain capitalism has emerged with the dominance of financial capital over production, which has encouraged leading firms around the world to increase their attractiveness to finance by outsourcing just about everything, and certainly everything involving the ordinary, long-established risks of labor recruitment, training, and discipline, natural resource management, and environmental degradation. Where outsourcing was once a matter of particular commodity sectors and national economic histories, it has become the global standard. Nation states must now work hard to position themselves advantageously on global outsourcing chains. When I spent a semester in Denmark in 2009, for example, the government was trying to position the whole country as a site for design and innovation, leaving all production to India and China. Indians and Chinese, of course, disagree, as they compete by outsourcing to disadvantaged regions and classes within the nation.

Cascades of outsourcing fragment the global landscape, showing the lie of we're-all-one-planet-now discourse. Yet most experts bury awareness of these expectable fragments, whether in the high drama of potentially planet-wide disaster or the imagined safety of business-as-usual. This essay considers how the architecture of supply-chain capitalism shapes the niche-organized landscape of *ordinary catastrophe*, that is, the planned devastation and makeshift, rubble economies that form an expectable feature of global supply chains.

Ordinary catastrophe, in this sense, is not new. To trace the history of risk management is also to trace the making of ordinary catastrophe. Consider, as an example, the invention of stocks by the Dutch East India Company at the beginning of the 17th century. The joint-stock company was a form of risk management for the company's directors, who otherwise stood to lose personally when their ships' long-distance voyages failed. But this was not just about weather. The Dutch ships that sailed to the Indies were heavily armed to break into what once had been a non-European Indian Ocean and China Sea trade. Dutch ships fought off other traders to declare an armed monopoly on the spices so valued in Europe. Lots of money was needed to guarantee these war-as-trade adventures, and stocks made that possible. Of course, such adventures were not a pleasure for the people who lived in the Indies, who were doing fine without the Dutch. They did not need this monopoly trade, and many suffered for it. But for the directors, and those who celebrated their deeds, this was »progress,« that is, the outsourcing of disaster onto others.[3]

---

2 | I use the term supply-chain capitalism to refer to the recent reorganization of the global economy around supply chains. In this usage, supply chains are one particular, contemporary form of commodity chains, which have existed since the beginning of human trade. See Tsing 2009 for more discussion of supply-chain capitalism. For an introduction to recent literature on commodity chains, see Bair 2010.
3 | I take my lead here from Pomerantz and Topik 2006: 163 ff.

The issue of progress is important here, because it is progress that allows us to define the outsourcing of disaster as a positive accomplishment. Progress is a time frame in which a singular timeline stretches into the future, inexorably carrying us along. Progress takes the achievements of elites as the achievements of time itself. Those outside those achievements are »left behind« even as they still exist in experientially coeval time. Risk management is a tool for achieving this effect because it narrows the field of who counts on the timeline of progress. Risk managers and their confederates roll forward from achievement to achievement by casting out disaster to the poor. Elite achievements stand in for global achievements – because they show us progress. Progress is that frame that makes the making of uneven social and environmental landscapes look good.

Progress has also seemed to show us hope. For the last several centuries, social reformers and political visionaries of every persuasion have tied their programs to progress. Karl Marx was a great celebrator of progress. So was Adam Smith. In the 20th century, anti-colonial rebels nurtured dreams of progress. So did great corporations. Yet we have entered a strange time for thinking about progress. While boosters still promote the world-changing charms of the coming future, their claims now sound increasingly hollow. In the 20th century, joint projects of states and corporations tied elite achievements to popular welfare, at least rhetorically. Nation states, whether communist or anti-communist, were supposed to create public wellbeing through progress. Since the late 20th century, state programs with this goal have been in the process of being dismantled. In policy circles, »entitlements« is the latest swear word; funding the disadvantaged is anathema. There seems less and less reason to connect advances in science, technology, or corporate profitability to popular hopes. Without this tie, claims of progress are only for the few; rather than building universal hopes, they only add to our awareness of the fragmentation of social and environmental space. Instead of a singular timeline toward the future, we see multiple competing rhythms; rather than a spatial vortex with its center pointed toward the future, its peripheries lagging behind, we see coeval patches, with their competing claims. Global supply chains are part of this fragmentation.

To find ourselves both becalmed and buffeted, without the sure straight winds of progress, is not the same as looking backward to a romantic past. Instead, the world becomes historical: Contingencies, unexpected alliances, and the productive »friction« of intertwined trajectories matter (see Tsing 2004). We can't just wait for the future to draw us along its expected course, and many possibilities beckon. Progress was always a kind of partial blindness; there are some advantages of learning to see without its erasures. Hopeful alternatives as well as nightmares approach us with a new vividness. This is one reason to pay attention to global supply chains. Even as they structure exploitation and environmental disaster, they also structure potential alliances and common projects of refusal. And consider the alternative: »Green capitalism« is that set of commercial activities that propose to fix the environment while hiding the sins of their own supply chains. In making environmental products for the rich, they send their disasters of pollution and exploitation to places currently out-of-sight and out-of-mind. Since they disavow social and environmental activism, imagining a world saved by markets, green capitalists can only try to hide the ordinary catastrophes caused by their own activities. Such practices cause more problems than they solve; those catastrophes come back to haunt us all. Outsourcing catastrophe is not good enough.

How do global supply chains guide us into niche landscapes of ordinary catastrophe? Consider what it means for a leading firm to outsource risks involving labor and the environment. A less advantaged set of entrepreneurs must pick up the contracts. Depending on their position, they may be able to outsource again to even less advantaged entrepreneurs. At the supply end of the chain, entrepreneurs must cut costs. The ones to survive are most often those who work outside the regulatory apparatus, either by engaging in illegal activities or by finding spaces outside of regulation. Indeed, supply chain architectures feed from the retreat of regulation into the enclosed sphere of market contracts, that is, away from issues of labor, natural resource management, and the environment. Market contracts, furthermore, have become increasingly focused on the single issue of outsourcing risk. As one standard California contract states, in part (quoted in Ross 2004: 129):

›5. Contractor acknowledges that it is an independent contractor and not an employee of MANUFACTURER [...]
9. In the event that contractor is found in violation of any City, County, State, or Federal law, contractor agrees to indemnify, hold harmless and defend MANUFACTURER from any liability that may be imposed on MANUFACTURER as a result of such violation [...]
14. Contractor agrees to indemnify, hold harmless and defend MANUFACTURER from any liability that may be imposed on MANUFACTURER arising out of any claim made by an employee of contractor against the MANUFACTURER.‹

To stay in business, subcontractors, that is, disadvantaged entrepreneurs, must find ways to operate around and beyond the costs of fulfilling contracts and minding regulations. This is only possible by locating required activities in the boundaries and gaps of what we have come to imagine as capitalist modernity. Sometimes this results in the worst possible working conditions, such as those reported from garment sweatshops, where women toil for almost nothing and without any assurances of safety. Other species may also be crowded, segregated, and subjugated to inhumane conditions: Thus, farm subcontractors stuff warehouses full of maimed and crippled chickens, following cost-cutting poultry industry standards.[4] It is important to remember these terrors. But there are more

---

4 | For garment sweatshops, see Ross 2004. For chicken subcontracting, see Watts 2004.

possibilities in this conceptual terrain. Without progress as our blinding guide, we can see nonmodern and noncapitalist forms of labor and nature bleeding into the modern and the capitalist. These are not »premodern« or »precapitalist.« The imagined timeline of progress is inappropriate in discussing supply-chain capitalism. Supply-chain niches are not linked to a singular timeline. We might find them simultaneously modern and nonmodern, capitalist and noncapitalist. All kinds of diverse arrangements thus become visible.

Violence is one kind of labor management; so too is ethnic particularism and indigenous revitalization. Rather than clear separations between modern and nonmodern, capitalist and noncapitalist, we see the internal boundaries of capitalism and modernity unravel. Here we see Hmong refugees in California who pick strawberries for entrepreneurial clansmen, working without wages for dreams of future assistance with bridewealth. Working the highway verges, they undercut Mexican migrants, who expect some wages, however meager. On this modern-nonmodern terrain too are Dayak tribesmen who carry mining pumps to the heart of the Kalimantan rainforest, at home in their intimate foraging landscapes, spreading mining poisons and clearing the global trail for profits in precious ores. In these spaces, what we imagine as the nonmodern and the noncapitalist become central to the contemporary possibilities of capitalism and modernity.[5]

Biological and cultural diversity and resilience are tapped for global profits. Supply chains could not produce without the gifts of diversity as labor and natural resources. But this is a two-way street: Capital accumulation becomes entangled with the vagaries of biological and cultural diversity. Diversity proves too much for modernist planning. This is why we find, among the predictable nightmares, shards of hope and even minor miracles.

The situation is reminiscent in some ways of the global extraction economy of the 19th century, with its greed and violence, its diversity and instability. Finance capital, then too, was running high, charging around the globe. Indeed, it was the fear of this unbridled finance that allowed world leaders to mobilize the great 20th century modernization projects, in which labor and nature would be tamed by the will of big government and big business, working together for uniform natural resource management, uniform labor, uniform education, uniform science. Those modernization projects set the standards we have come to naturalize as capitalism and modernity. Even where they unravel, we hardly know how to look forward without assuming their frames. When we propose regulation, for example, we assume the presence of governance projects that make regulations stick. 20th century modernization projects created governance

---

5 | Hmong strawberrry pickers: Lue Vang, personal communication, 2009; Dayak miners: Tsing 2005.

standards that seemed capable of ruling the world. But what if the world is once again becoming unmanageably diverse?

Contemporary supply-chain capitalism is more similar to 19th century extraction economies than to 20th century modernization projects. Thus, images from the 19th century economy may help us think about today's situation. Famous 19th century novels that describe global supply chains put today's dilemmas of supply-chain architecture in sharp relief. In Joseph Conrad's *Heart of Darkness*, violence breeds violence in the contact zone that produces Congo rubber. In contrast, Herman Melville's *Moby-Dick* highlights the rowdy cosmopolitanism of supply chains. A ship of independent contractors, the diverse native harpooners facilitating Yankee profits, chases whales across the globe for industrial oil.[6] Are Conrad's fort and Melville's ship modern capitalist factories or stews of non-modern fragments? Today's supply-chain capitalism shows the advantages of arguing: »Both.«

Industrial whaling brought whales close to extinction, but this is not part of Melville's story; nor is deforestation in the Congo part of Conrad's. In contrast to the 19th century, it is no longer possible to imagine nature as infinitely resourceful. Stories of supply chains need to be told again, with attention to their environmental consequences. In the rest of this essay, I tell a Conrad story and a Melville story, each in 21st century settings in which environmental threats are clear. Through their contrasts as well as their common themes, these stories re-present the range of supply-chain landscapes to explore their environmental effects.

First, Conrad: In *Heart of Darkness*, mimetic violence destroys both Europeans and Africans. The chain of trade is also a chain of terror. Today we watch in horror too as supply-chain violence destroys other species besides our own. It is easy to find contemporary supply chains that offer just this string of tragedies. In my earlier research in Kalimantan, Indonesia, I watched the consequences of Japanese wood-products supply chains, as they directed the deforestation of the island of Borneo in the last quarter of the 20th century, and with it the expectable extermination of many species and the indigenous cultures that depended on them. Japanese trading companies directed deforestation by taking no responsibility as the rainforest was overrun with destruction. The traders were prescient and self-conscious about outsourcing environmental and political risk; they wanted no trouble, and they were willing to work with strange bedfellows to get that. No Japanese cut down trees in Kalimantan. They advanced loans, technology, and market standards to loggers from other countries; they offered

---

6 | Conrad 1990 [1899]; Melville 1981 [1851]. Beck argues that the modern novel describes the human condition within the social project of risk management (2007: 5 f.). The novels I have chosen portray not only that general condition but also the role of supply-chain niches within it.

trading agreements. The Indonesian army cleared out earlier resource claims with force. Elite Indonesians, Koreans, Malaysians, and Filipinos directed the logging (see Dauvergne 1997; Ross 2001; Tsing 2004).

Or at least the legal logging. Official violence opened the doors to illegality, and from the first, the industry took advantage of cooperation among legal and illegal sectors. Illegal loggers were further subcontractors, selling their logs to the legal loggers after hours. Illegal loggers helped the big companies get around market standards, on the one hand, and environmental regulations on the other. There were always those physically or politically hard-to-get trees, where the legally required equipment couldn't go. When Indonesia enacted tough watershed protection laws, and the legal loggers were not to take trees from steep slopes, illegal loggers could get those trees to sell them to the legal loggers late at night. And what was the difference between legal and illegal anyway? Both needed well-oiled permissions, although the first paid only in Jakarta while the latter offered district officers and local army men their share. The army men worked hard to disempower local residents. Without rights, local indigenous groups were hard pressed to fight the tide of frontier fever sweeping across the land; migrants flowed in to reap the newly freed spoils. Working together, legal and illegal loggers cleared the hills and valleys, leaving deeply eroded hillsides, no longer potential sites for foraging or farming. In this way, supply chains can spread disaster, as businessmen at each link look the other way while products are passed to them. By the turn of the century, the generations' old landscape of indigenous agroforestry, with its extraordinary biodiversity, lay in ruins (Obidzinski 2003; Tsing 2004).

These were not planned industrial forests. Indonesia had industrial teak and pine on the island of Java, where the Dutch planted them, and these had been the source of colonial and postcolonial modernization dreams. From the colonial period, the tropical rainforests of the Outer Islands were considered junk forests, useful only as the site of future plantations of other species. The greatest trees of the rainforest, the dipterocarps, may have been tall and imposing, but their wood is soft and brittle, quite useless for building the things of progress, such as ships and railroad ties. Besides, in the Kalimantan rainforests, there are just too many species. The loggers sent by Japanese trading companies worked in lands considered waste by the state. They had found a use for light, brittle wood: one-use-only disposable plywood and disposable chopsticks. As I make a comparison later to gourmet wild mushrooms, it seems important to note that Kalimantan's forests were felled not for necessity, but for luxury. Japanese consumers wanted chopsticks that had never touched other lips. Builders wanted plywood for construction molds that could be thrown away after a single use. As with mushrooms, too, the traders found their product in the wastelands of industrial forestry, beyond the modernist standards of its central places. This was salvage: the quintessential working mode of supply-chain capitalism.

The usual global environmental assessments – with their calls for more »progress« of the 20th century variety – hardly begin to grasp the contours of the problem. First, through much of this period Indonesia had quite robust environmental laws – and a strong national environmental movement. Second, all this was happening at the height of the international mobilization to save rainforests. Third, green energy and development initiatives were booming, and considerable green technology had been acquired in the plywood sector.[7] Regulations, social movements, green capitalism: None of this made a whit of difference in the destruction of the rainforests. Why? I am urging you to look at the architecture of supply chains, in which powerful trading companies passed off risk and responsibility, sponsoring others to do the dirty work of producing their commodities. Trading companies passed the work to legal loggers who passed it on to illegal loggers, all of them looking away from the mess they were making. This is ordinary catastrophe, an absolutely expectable landscape of destruction made possible by the links of supply-chain capitalism.

Risk management, through its very logic, divides us: There will be elite decision makers who take or allay risks and, then, collateral damage, that is, those who bear the burdens of those distant decisions (Beck 2007: 160 ff.). Ordinary catastrophe is the landscape of collateral damage. In the mudslides of Kalimantan, we find it in one of its most planned, expectable forms: the result of decisions to outsource all activities that might affect the environment – because of their risk. Let others do that killing work, do it elsewhere, and do it badly. After all, the plywood arrives cheaply, and the forests of Japan are still intact.

Or are they? Noboru and Mayumi Ishikawa have studied the links between the unfortunate state of Japanese forests and the Japan-directed deforestation of Southeast Asia (Ishikawa 2007; 2009. See also Iwai 2002). In the 1950s and 1960s, tree plantations were created through much of Japan in response to the government's dream of domestic self-sufficiency in timber. Mixed forests were cut down to make way for timber monocrops. Rural labor was plentiful then, and the price of wood was high. Planners imagined this situation as continuing into the future; trees were planted in close rows and on steep slopes. Lots of handwork would be required. But with the opening of Japan to cheap Southeast Asian timber, the price of domestic wood plummeted. Soon enough, it was no longer worthwhile to thin or even harvest Japanese trees. The planted forests, so recently created, declined into overcrowded and pestilent places, neither sites of biodiversity nor of rural livelihood. People's allergies to the pollen of the timber trees kept out even recreation. The cost-cutting destructiveness of supply chains had reverberated closer to home. Outsourcing catastrophe rarely keeps it away for long.

---

7 | Environmental mobilizations: Hurst and Warren 1998; green technology: Sonnenfeld 1999.

One result of the conversion of mixed forests to plantations was the loss of traditional forest products. One of those was the aromatic mushroom called matsutake, a favorite food of the autumn season – and, for some, a symbol of Japanese culture. Matsutake grow with pine trees, and in Japan pines are a part of the peasant complex of mixed forests. Until the 1970s, Japan's forests produced plenty of matsutake. But pine trees were disappearing in central Japan in the 1970s – from the conversion of mixed forest to plantations; from the abandonment of remaining peasant forests as peasants moved to the city; and from an invasive nematode pest imported earlier from North America. With the decline of pines, matsutake disappeared. But this was still the Japanese boom period, and matsutake were in high demand, especially as expensive perks for business partners. In the 1980s, importers began to bring matsutake from foreign countries, where it had been found growing in other kinds of human-disturbed forests. By the early 21st century, Japanese were importing matsutake from forests around the northern hemisphere, including forests in China, Korea, Sweden, Finland, Turkey, Mexico, Canada, and the U.S. Pacific Northwest. My recent collaborative research has studied matsutake supply chains to examine the formation of social and ecological links and discontinuities.[8] This research is also the inspiration for my invocation of Melville's *Moby-Dick*.

My Melville example thus continues with Japanese supply chains, but with a less familiar commodity: matsutake. It shows where one might look for the possibilities beyond rather than just the terrors of supply-chain capitalism. Because supply chains draw people of many different backgrounds and circumstances into the same system of links, the architecture of supply chains can also sponsor the pleasures and dangers of a rowdy cosmopolitanism, full of cultures in motion. These links extend, indeed, beyond humans to other-than-human species, and it becomes possible to imagine alliances for survival across species and ecologies as well as cultural barriers. Still, there is nothing utopian about the promise of such alliances; through its cost-saving logic, supply-chain capitalism places them in the cracks and ruins of earlier projects of modernity and progress, where most everyone, human and not human, is damaged.

Alliances for survival build on our varied histories of damage in fragile collaborations that may at least continue life. Where extinction is at stake, perhaps that isn't so bad. It is a place to begin thinking about threatened lives in common, and the common lifeworlds to which they might contribute. The matsutake commodity chain is useful for thinking about such possibilities because, in many supply areas, matsutake are foraged by refugees, minorities, or indig-

---

8 | The Matsutake Worlds Research Group includes Timothy Choy, Lieba Faier, Michael Hathaway, Miyako Inoue, Shiho Satsuka, and myself. We are grateful to support from the University of California Pacific Rim Initiative and the Toyota Foundation. See Tsing 2009a for a sense of the project.

enous people – that is, the people who don't mind finding their livelihood in the forest. Furthermore, these vulnerable and often displaced people have found their way into vulnerable and disturbed forests, themselves ruins of the projects of progress.

In the US Pacific Northwest, matsutake foraging exemplifies a rubble economy in a rubble ecology. The matsutake area was once a center of U.S. industrial forestry. It was the place where loggers and scientists came to mutually agreeable terms on what industrial forestry would look like. It is hotly debated whether the plan or the execution was the problem. In either case, the industrial forest lies in ruins (Robbins 2004; Hirt 1994; Langston 1995).

Consider the eastern Cascades: When white settlers first arrived, the eastern Cascades was a great ponderosa pine forest, with thick, tall, widely spaced boles in an open park-like setting. From the first, the settlers saw the forest as potential timber. But once cut down, that open forest did not return. The dominance of ponderosa pine had been maintained by forest fires that discouraged more flammable trees, and by the 20th century, foresters had suppressed those fires. A much more flammable, smaller tree grew up in the ponderosa forests: lodgepole pine. As it name suggests, the boles of lodgepole are more useful for poles than boards; this was not a favored timber species. By the late 20th century, most of the timber industry had moved away, and the lodgepole forests were crowded, slow growing, and full of pests. These are the ruins, the wastelands of modern capitalist resource management. Amazingly, in this ruined terrain, the world's most expensive mushroom flourishes. After the modern project destroyed the area, a fragile matsutake economy unfurled in the rubble.

Who wants to make a living picking mushrooms in an abandoned forest? The rubble economy is an odd assortment of independent and self-motivated labor: white Vietnam veterans and out-of-work loggers; SE Asian refugees from U.S. wars in Indochina and their aftermath. Racist white vets wander the forest with Hmong and Mien tribesmen, Lao Buddhist monks, and Khmer amputees. This is not a scene of wage labor: Every mushroom picker works for his or her own purposes. Everyone is an independent contractor, an imagined entrepreneur at the end of a long supply chain that sends mushrooms to Japan. Everyone is armed, wary, dressed in camouflage, remembering old wars. But what they share across conflicts is a wild enthusiasm about the forest and its secret places. To find matsutake requires close observation and familiarity. It takes several years to achieve any success as a forager. Most successful foragers draw on their histories of jungle fighting to learn their way around the forest – and to delve into its secrets (Tsing in press).

Perhaps at another historical period, these displaced warriors might not be making a living foraging in the forest. But when the Southeast Asian refugees arrived in the United States, washed up from their experiences fighting both American and civil wars, the institutional capacities of U.S. welfare state were being dismantled. Welfare was cut. Bilingual education and affirmative action were drawn back. Most of these refugees had few of the resources required to assimilate without government assistance. Without communal guarantees, they were forced to look for a living on their own, using the resources of ethnicity, kinship, and what skills they had gathered to survive war. That they found themselves a self-made living in the forests is a product of this moment in U.S. history. There they joined white Americans who had been displaced through war trauma or through unemployment. The cosmopolitanism of the matsutake forests is a heterogeneous and shifting formation of the dispossessed.

What does any of this have to do with *Moby-Dick*? First, like the whaling ship Pequod with its motley crew, the matsutake forests of the U.S. Pacific Northwest offer a rowdy cosmopolitanism in which friendships and alliances sometimes reach across all kinds of barriers. In all their particularities and vulnerabilities, matsutake foragers were pressed together into the volatile world of supply chains. The Pequod's harpooners, a Polynesian, a Native American, an African, and a South Asian, were similarly displaced – and then thrown together with the Yankee sailors. One might argue that this cosmopolitanism is »reflexive« in the sense that Beck uses the term, that is, an unselfconscious »reflex« of social worlding processes (Beck 2007: 119 ff.). The rowdy cosmopolitanism of both 19th century American whaling and 21st century American matsutake foraging develops from the architecture of supply-chain salvage, which pulls all kinds of displaced people into close contact. *Moby-Dick* is an anthem to this kind of rowdy cosmopolitanism.

Second, mushrooms, like whales, inspire passion and awe among their hunters. Like whales, they tell their hunters about the global diversity and interdependence of nature. Like whaling, commercial mushroom foraging inspires a practical and intimate study of more-than-human lifeways. Much of *Moby-Dick* is devoted to the loving description of awe and curiosity about whales, as well as whalers' commercial motives – and killing obsessions. Similarly, matsutake foragers, in all their varied cultural peculiarities, devote themselves to the study of the multispecies forest. To find the mushrooms, they must know the forests' processes and niches: its histories of seasonality; its varied plants and animals; the hidden interconnections among living things. I was struck by the detailed and nuanced knowledge of matsutake foragers. Sometimes, across all barriers, there is begrudging respect. Might one see in this respect the possibilities of living in common at a time when destruction seems all around?

Of course, mushrooms and whales make a telling contrast. In the 19th century, whales could be imagined as symbols as the infinite grandeur of nature, wild and powerful without end. Mushrooms are a humbler organism for more challenged times. Those that grow in ruined places, making something of damage and destruction, tell us not of nature's grandeur but of small acts of resilience. Mychorrizal mushrooms make it possible for trees to live in places where the ground seems barren and unpromising. Mushrooms mop up many of modernity's mistakes – radioactivity, heavy metals – and feed those back to us in other forms. They draw us into multispecies worlds of unregulated survival, good and bad. They make something of the ordinary catastrophes of our times. We might attend to the worlding processes they show us.

Let me return to my main points. *Supply-chain capitalism creates niche landscapes of ordinary catastrophe by outsourcing environmental risks.* Supply-chain capitalism makes use of the waste spaces of capitalism and modernity. Outside of regulations and standards, it is possible to tap the world's cultural and biological diversity as labor and natural resources for the pursuit of profit. It is easy, too, to destroy just about everything, human and nonhuman, since no one at the top need take responsibility. Ordinary catastrophes are produced as outsourcing distributes environmental risks to out-of-the-way places.

Too often we recognize as ›global‹ only that which seems most perceptible to elites. But such forms of globality are only an incitement to elites to hide dirty things. The rise of fears about environmental degradation and destruction has thus itself reshaped the global environment by encouraging the outsourcing of environmental messes. One reason to pay attention to global commodity chains is to refuse to allow those messes to stay out of sight. Each concrete wall made with disposable plywood should remind us of an eroding hillside in Kalimantan, an ordinary catastrophe of the supply chain.

Supply-chain capitalism has increasingly shaped the fate of global cultural and biological diversity. No place on earth is too remote. But diversity thus, too, characterizes supply chains. Another reason to pay attention to them is that they are varied in every way – and thus pregnant with radical alternatives. The matsutake supply chain offers a livelihood to a few dispossessed warriors ... who have opened themselves to the awe of the forest. If all of us must – as it seems we must – watch the horrors of unfolding environmental damage, we might as well watch with the mushrooms on the mountain.

REFERENCES

Bair, Jennifer (2009). *Frontiers of commodity chain research.* Stanford: Stanford University Press

Beck, Ulrich (2009). *World at risk.* Cambridge: Polity Press

Conrad, Joseph (1990 [1899]). *Heart of darkness.* New York: Dover Publications

Dauvergne, Peter (1997). *Shadows in the forest: Japan and the politics of timber in Southeast Asia.* Cambridge: MIT Press

Hirt, Paul (1994). *Conspiracy of optimism: management of the national forests since World War II.* Lincoln: University of Nebraska Press

Hurst, Philip and Carol Warren (eds.) (1998). *The politics of environment in Southeast Asia: resources and resistance.* London: Routledge

Ishikawa Mayumi (2007). *From Bornean Rainforest to Japanese Living Room: Timber and Global Connections,* a lecture for UNESCO Post-Graduate Inter-University Course in Biotechnology 2006–2007, UNESCO-Japan Program for Development of Human Resources and Research Network in Natural Sciences and Technology, September 10, Osaka University, Japan

Ishikawa, Mayumi (2009). *Timber Networks linking Japan and Southeast Asia: Sociological Studies of Global Connections,* School of Human Sciences, Osaka University

Iwai, Yoshiha (2002). *Forestry and the Forest Industry in Japan.* Vancouver: UBC Press

Langston, Nancy (1995). *Forest dreams, forest nightmares.* Seattle: University of Washington Press

Melville, Herman (1981 [1851]). *Moby-Dick.* New York: Bantam

Obidzinski, Krystof (2003). *Logging in East Kalimantan, Indonesia: the historical expedience of illegality.* Ph.D. Thesis, University of Amsterdam

Pomerantz, Kenneth and Steven Topik (2006). *The world that trade created.* Armonk: M.E. Sharp

Robbins, William (2004). *Landscapes of conflict: the Oregon story, 1940–2000.* Seattle: University of Washington Press

Ross, Michael (2001). *Timber booms and institutional breakdown in Southeast Asia.* Cambridge: Cambridge University Press

Ross, Robert (2004). *Slaves to fashion: poverty and abuse in the new sweatshops.* Ann Arbor: University of Michigan Press

Sonnenfeld, David (1999). Vikings and Tigers: Finland, Sweden, and adoption of environmental technologies in Southeast Asia's pulp and paper industries. In: *Journal of World-Systems Research,* 5(1): 26–47

Tsing, Anna (2004). *Friction: an ethnography of global connection.* Princeton: Princeton University Press

Tsing, Anna (2009). Supply chains and the human condition. In: *Rethinking Marxism,* 21(2): 148–176

Tsing, Anna, for the Matsutake Worlds Research Group. (2009a). Beyond economic and ecological standardization. In: *The Australian Journal of Anthropology* 20(3): 347–368

Tsing, Anna. In press. Free in the forest: popular neoliberalism and the aftermath of war in the U.S. Pacific Northwest. In: Zeyneb Gambetti and Marcial Godoy-Anativia (eds.). *States of insecurity.* New York: New York University Press

Watts, Michael J. (2004). Are hogs like chickens? Enclosure and mechanization in two ›white meat‹ filieres. In Alex Hughes and Susan Reimer (eds.). *Geographies of commodity chains.* New York: Routledge

Reflexive Modernity Brings us back to Earth
A Tribute to Ulrich Beck

BRUNO LATOUR

ENTANGLED COSMOLOGIES

We're right to talk about »the heavens« or »the skies«, rather than »heaven« or »the sky« because we've got several above us. I'm not only thinking of »Our Father, who art in Heaven« who, since the 17th century, is not quite sure exactly where he should be seated to hear our prayers. He's surely pretty uneasy, for even if he has a place (and even, according to some, a throne) in Heaven, he certainly no longer has one in the sky. No, I'm actually thinking mainly about the numerous orbs, vaults, circles, globes and milieus in which we are simultaneously immersed, we, the children of the industrialized societies of the 21st century, and which we all refer to with the same word, »sky«. When ethnologists systematically frame the way of thinking of a people or a culture, they never fail to describe the *cosmos* in which their informers are situated – a cosmology that is sometimes of a vertiginous complexity. But, so complex is the cosmology of industrialized societies, that ethnologists would have difficulty depicting it.

When they turn to look at the sky, most of them are wondering »what the weather will be like tomorrow«. For them, it is the sky of meteorites, agitation, rain and good weather, climatic phenomena: in short, meteorology. But of course they are no longer looking outside at the azure-blue sky or the blackness of the night. No, what they look at attentively is the TV screen for the weather forecast, or the alerts sent to their mobile phones by the national meteorological service. So *where* is this sky, the one of the countless Mr Weatherman or Ms Weatherwoman dancing on our screens? There is no easy answer, for while it is indeed outside, the sky is also *inside* networks of satellite observation and weather stations. If there's a strike at the meteorological service, the weather forecast sky disappears as surely as the Sky of »Our Father who art in Heaven«.

Moreover, many of those who watch the weather forecast check with the same close attention the astrological Sky described to them by other, somewhat more heretical, specialists. Oh, how strange, we'd departed from that Sky three centuries ago? Yes, but it's still there. Seriously, or not? Difficult to say; floating, intriguing, vigorously contested by some, accepted with amused condescendence by many. We're nevertheless steeped in it, and the same informer can talk to you about tomorrow's weather, angels and the attention that ought to be paid to Jupiter or Venus, without really believing in any of it.

If she really tries, the ethnologist will find informers for whom the sky is *space* and even, taking things a bit further, the universe. Perhaps they've read Koyré's book, *From the Closed World to the Infinite Universe* or Brecht's play on Galileo, or Koestler's *Sleepwalkers*. In any case, they know that the blue dome that others are watching is no more than a tiny fraction of the infinity of space. They seem, moreover, to be very comfortable with this off-centredness, and to have no difficulty taking the point of view of Sirius, which enables them to grasp the Earth from the Sun, or even from other clusters of galaxies. If the »Father in Heaven« has no more throne, the observer of the infinite sky does have his own seat. Obviously, things become complicated if we start to wonder *where* he is comfortably seated and what he is looking at so attentively in order to be so sure of what he's saying about this universe. For, with a sudden return to Earth, there he is well and truly situated somewhere in an observatory, in front of a globe, facing a blackboard, surrounded by peers, and busy moving about in the infinite space of finite thought. »But where is he really?«, anxiously wonders the ethnologist, responsible for representing this cosmology: infinitely distant or infinitely close?

He remembers that ancient cosmology distinguished between the *sub-lunar* world – that of earthly corruption – and the *supra-lunar* world – that of the growing perfection of spheres –, a difference that the new cosmology, that of the sky as an infinite space, no longer recognizes at all. He knows this, and yet he can't prevent himself from finding a rift between the infinite space of the astronomer and the narrow stool on which that same astronomer is perched, shivering in the cold night behind his telescope.

The question is all the more overwhelming in so far as other informers, other scholars in white coats poring over other models, seem to be becoming interested in a very different sky, far greater than that of meteorology but equally variable, and which they call the *climate*. And the shock is all the greater for the observer, in so far as this climate seems to vary in relation to the collective action of humans ... What they learn to decipher is no longer the influence of Jupiter on humans' romantic adventures, but that of humans' industrial adventures on the destiny of the clouds and the air and oceanic currents. What a strange reversal. And this sky seems to encapsulate humans in a fragile bubble from which there is no escape. When she was young, long before seeing Neil Armstrong take his first small step, she dreamed, like so many others, of breaking free of it to all go and walk on the Moon. Ah, but those were the days of the infinite universe and the »conquest of space«. Have those times disappeared?

Photo by NASA/flickr

Have we gone back to space *under* the Moon, to being entrapped in Gaia – and perhaps even threatened by Her?

What a strange cosmology, this one of the Moderns. It seems to have no outer space, while in certain closed places – laboratories – it has crossed the universe from the furthest bounds of the Big Bang. And in other places, by lifting their eyes to the sky, some seem to see in it meteors, about which they can do nothing, and also the boomerang effect of their own actions carried out on the Earth, while others wait for the »Father in Heaven« to reappear in the clouds, and yet others – although they are sometimes the same ones – hope that the planets will finally sort out their lives. All this while attentive engineers, somewhere in Houston or in the forest of Kourou, tighten the last nuts and bolts of the engines that they're getting ready to send *into* space. Indeed, these are widely diverse skies for a tightly entangled cosmology.

Here's a picture so often contemplated: astronauts floating in space. They've donned their space suits, their movements are slow, practised thousands of times in a swimming pool. They're being watched by the space ship, as closely and surely as the ship itself is being watched by Houston, and behind them, in the background, the Earth is unrolling its continents.

But have you noticed this strange reversal? When Louis Bleriot crossed the Channel a century ago, no one imagined that his grandchildren would travel in an Airbus or a Boeing just a few decades later, without even finding it surprising. When the first astronauts landed on the Moon fifty years ago, all of humanity saw Neil Armstrong as a new Bleriot: there was no doubt, space travel was going to happen.

Yet that's not at all how things have turned out. While pioneer aviators were soon replaced by commercial aviation firms, astronauts have remained »those magnificent men in their flying machines«. Fifty years after the first moon landing, we're still waiting to see the industrial machines that will turn space travel into mass transport. And it's not the brief excursions offered to millionaire tourists that are going to revive our dreams. While in aviation museums we incredulously witness the stupefying transformation of motorized kites into giants of the air – how was such a quick metamorphosis possible? –, in space museums we see, with equal incredulity, the canned foods of the Apollo programme. For what mysterious reason did these chrysalises not turn into the giants of space that we read about in science fiction novels and that the genius of Professor Calculus had already picked up in Syldavia? And it's not for want of having dreamed about them taking off. How we envied those athletes capable of escaping gravity and seeing entire continents at a glance through narrow portholes, from the incessant noise and discomfort of their cramped cabins – despite our niggling doubt as to their real capabilities when it came to initiative and steering: were they really latter-day hero conquistadors, or anthropomorphic appendages to the machine?

But if we really did envy them, it was above all because they sometimes were able to describe to us the »blue planet«, by finally, really and truly occupying the global point of view that poets had imagined and mathematicians had calculated. The globe under their eyes, and therefore under ours, rolled through space, but it wasn't the globe of geographers and schools, it was the one they came from, Mother Earth, from which they couldn't be separated for an instant for fear of death. It was in this sense that they bore so little resemblance to aviators, to those who tamed that which was heavier than air. Far from revealing the other worlds seen thousands of times already through telescopes or the embedded eyes of probes, it was our own world that they were bringing infinitely closer to us.

That's probably what condemned them, those unfortunate astronauts: this blue planet, too vast, that they rolled out at our feet. We'd sent them to »conquer space« but it was the old earthly homeland that they revealed to us. A strange paradox of these »pioneers« that no one has followed: we found them heroic only when there were disasters that cost them their lives. (In research offices there are even some murmurs that, for all future missions, robots would do just as well and would cost a great deal less.) That's because their greatness was elsewhere. Those tiny spaceships or, better still, the spacesuits worn on space walks – that conquest within the conquest, that intensification of audacity – enabled us to understand that, from then on, survival was *equipped*. Survival in the space suit, first, then in the cabin, but also, and above all – and this was the great turnaround, the complete surprise – survival on earth, in the motherland.

»There's no outside. We can't go out. We're always *inside*«. This was the great lesson that the engineers had to learn in »explicating« every detail of life »in«

space, that the astronauts had to repeat countless times before risking space walks in those fragile suits, and that they taught to the inhabitants of the blue planet. We thought we were sending them »outside«, those astronauts finally delivered from the constraints of the atmosphere and gravity, finally free in their movements, floating above us. But, bang, we're the ones who find ourselves trapped in the delicate machinery of the »Spaceship Earth«. It's as if the miniature version sent off into the distance to enable the planet to dream of its next migration had allowed this old Earth, the scale-one original, to understand that it would never migrate, that there was no evasion possible. A new theology lesson started by Gagarin, »there's no God in space, I saw it myself«, and which continues today: »there's no Earth other than ours where we could live«. The return of the astronauts to Earth. The end of hope in the plurality of worlds habitable by us humans, definitively trapped in our survival equipment. And our condition on »biosphere one« is much worse than in the international space station, for learned astronauts, experimenters, can always turn to the motherland and say in a confident male voice: »Houston we have a problem«. But us here, on the blue planet, we've got no base to turn to. It's not Gaia who sent us, and it's not She who will listen to us. We *do* have a problem.

ADJUSTING TO A NEW WORLD OF CONTROVERSIES

There had already been the question of cigarettes and their link to cancer. We had already witnessed the skilful disinformation of manufacturers and their »experts«, so insistent that it was necessary, to follow it, to invent the paradoxical term »the science of deliberately induced ignorance« or agnatology (Brandt 2008; Proctor and Schiebinger 2008). This is no longer a matter of adding cleverly contrived counter-information to a subject that is starting to disturb the public, as we have always done with propaganda, but rather of going *upstream* to the beginning of the controversy, where positive knowledge starts to be produced, in order to prevent that knowledge from being closed off (Oreskes and Conway 2010).

The trick of this new form of propaganda is that it can be perceived as nothing but the continuation of all the great epistemological virtues that scholars like to recommend to one another: the culture of scepticism and radical doubt, the necessity to redo experiments until complete consensus has been obtained, the haughty distance from political issues, the meticulous attention to the details of experimental protocols, the appeal to the great persecuted figures of the history of science, especially Galileo whose mention in this context can but amuse historians. But the really clever part is that these disinformers manage to hide the fact that this is counter-propaganda of political origin, since they position themselves on supposedly *apolitical* ground which, for their opponents, also has to remain the sacred terrain of science in search of facts only. Here we have a fine example of camouflage, of the kind of mimicry that we see in insects, since it's the most politicized who so marvellously imitate the non-political nature of scholarly production!

Indeed, scientists attacked in this way are caught in their own trap since they too insist on the virtues of doubt and scepticism, on the necessity to stick to the most robust protocols; and they too contend that it is necessary to hold their science as distant as possible from politics, and to mention only the surest facts.

Strangely, scientists tend to be in an uncomfortable position when the consensus becomes too strong. As soon as scientific communities start to agree and to conclude their debates, they risk being seen as an arrogant, absolutist power seeking to impose its points of view on the rest of the world by deliberately concealing areas of uncertainty. It is at this precise point, when consensus is reached, that the lobbies can safely attack scientific results by disguising themselves as ultra-precautious, rationalist and objective scientists. They don't even have to be specialists on the issues they challenge. They simply need to talk »of science« by imitating the serious scientist and occupying the field of facts, while erecting as many epistemological obstacles as are needed to prevent closure of the debate.

That is precisely what cigarette manufacturers have been doing for fifty years, and also what, for the past fifteen or twenty years, many lobbyists have been doing, in whose interests it is to oppose the anthropic cause of global warming – some of the »experts« and other »think-tanks« having moreover switched from the one issue to the other (Hoggan 2009). The result of this camouflage? The »researchers« sent by lobby groups make short work of the voiceless scientists, who are stupefied to see that, without any new research, the consensus in the process of being reached can be attacked. All the statistics show that agnatology is infinitely more effective than counter-propaganda or disinformation. Neither the researchers nor the public seem to have antibodies against those who devour them whole by brandishing the invigorating virtues of scientific doubt.

Agnatology has been so successful here that the cause of global warming, which still received bipartisan support in the United States during the Bush Senior era, has become the touchstone currently defining the difference between Republicans and Democrats. Maximum politicization owing to an attack that apparently concerns only facts which everyone agrees to detach from political issues to the greatest possible degree! And having acquired university degrees is of no help in resisting. On the contrary, precisely because these campaigns of scepticism appeal to what cultivated circles, especially in France, like to put forward the most: respect for science, for doubt, for debate, and for the distance that should always be kept from dirty political questions.

HIDING BEHIND THE MAGINOT LINE OF EPISTEMOLOGY

For those who, like me, have been studying the mechanisms of the production of facts for decades, a whole series of important problems arises with the sudden appearance of these controversies artificially maintained to avoid consensus becoming evident to politicians and the public. How can antibodies be produced to enable scientists to withstand this unfair competition? How can the public, mobilized against its will as an arbitrator in an artificially maintained dispute, be given the means to perceive the spurious nature of this type of arena?

The first strange fact obviously stems from the idea that a state of things whose truth would lead to a radical alteration of the lifestyles of seven billion human beings could be accepted without being questioned by all the parties concerned, just as Pythagoras' theorem or the atomic composition of water are accepted. Here there is really an admirable trust in reason and in the extension of Enlightenment thinking: »Learn unquestionable facts, good people, and the weight of your knowledge will inevitably guide your action.« That the anthropic cause of global warming might be accepted without encountering any opposition, is what should have appeared impossible. On the basis of so many examples in the history of science – from 19th century bacteriology to Aids –, it is for this impossibility that we should probably have prepared ourselves.

Or else it means that no one has grasped the practical consequences. That is probably what happened in the 1980s: agreement was easily reached because we were not yet consciously aware of the immensity of the changes. Believing in the power that facts alone have as a mobilizing force shows trust in rationalism but also a huge dose of political naivety. Any smoker who knows full well that by lighting a cigarette it's his or her lungs that will suffer, will understand this diagnosis. As the saying goes: »If you know but you don't act, you don't really know«. But no, of course, we don't know and will do everything possible not to know. The success of climate-sceptic lobby groups is incomprehensible without the massive support that each of us contributes to *not* knowing, as Clive Hamilton (2010) shows throughout his book. In this respect he is right, »we are all climate sceptics«.

But where does this idea come from, that action inevitably *follows* certain knowledge? The idea is particularly strange in so far as it obviously makes all action fragile. It means that doubt need only be instilled ahead of action, where the consensus that will produce »unquestionable« facts is being reached, in order to suspend a whole series of supposedly ineluctable consequences. That is why Allègre and the climate sceptics are so successful: since their opponents claim to act in the name of a certainty that can no longer be challenged, they simply have to show that there is reasonable doubt on the basis of which action can be completely interrupted. Of course, the hitch in this operation is the idea of an action *following* knowledge. Ask those responsible for nuclear warfare during the Cold War whether they waited to have complete knowledge before taking massive anticipatory measures? They acted pre-emptively against the Soviets, and in so doing they learned, bit by bit, the exact meaning of the threat (which, with hindsight, they realized that they had exaggerated). Action and knowledge go hand in hand, walking in step. Together they explore, through a series of bets constantly made on the future, the uncertainty inherent in every situation.

We're starting to see why the disinformers made short work of the poor scientists: first, by claiming to separate the anthropic causality of global warming from the series of its really revolutionary consequences, and second, by carrying on acting as if certain and complete knowledge had to precede action, they put scientists in the impossible position of defending themselves behind the Maginot Line of rationalism, while they were swamped on all sides by challenges that were beyond them.

But strangest of all was claiming to have protected them from those who were attacking them, by trying, against all evidence, to *maintain* the distinction between science and politics – a distinction that offers such weak protection that it is precisely the sledge-hammer argument of these poor scientists' opponents! So, we always get back to the belief that, if only science and politics could be separated, then, finally, we would have unquestionable facts that would influence the action of educated citizens through a type of educational percolation. And this wonderful dream carries on while the climate-sceptic lobbies use this same argument to try to stop us from »politicizing« climate science and to urge us to limit ourselves to »facts alone«. And it is this inability of the real specialists to respond to this argument that makes the public the inadvertent arbitrator of what it believes to be a war on equal terms to depoliticize science!

From cosmology to cosmopolitics

Can we clarify this preposterous situation a little? I believe we can, provided we modify the word »politics« slightly and ensure that the verb »politicize« is not an accusation that is supposed to stigmatize the opponent. Researchers who establish a causal link between human action and global climate change »do politics« in the sense of altering the associations – and thus directly the »social« – that all beings establish with all other beings. They are thus engaged in a cosmology – a cosmopolitics – involving, in different ways, all the entities that previously did not count in the public understanding of problems. Of course this is not »politics« in the sense of parties and even less so of lobbies, but we could illuminate debates over the »gradual composition of the common world« by recognizing that any alteration of links between the entities inhabiting our world are well and truly part of public life – especially when the subject applies to the entire planet.

Instead of asking them to protect themselves behind the illusory barrier of »total distinction« between science and politics, we would at last enable researchers unfairly attacked to defend themselves by openly asking their opponents to specify *in what world* they would like to live, with whom, and *what interests* they defend. The trick of agnatology, remember, is to turn against scientists the autonomy of a science kept sheltered from all form of politics. By agreeing to play this game, we make the public expression of interests and of cosmology impossible. »In what world do you claim to live? With what support?« Let everyone at least fight under their own flag.

If this is a »war of worlds«, as the rapid transformation of the Republicans into climate-sceptics has shown it to be, then at least let it be one on equal terms. While the slogan »defend science against the damaging invasion of politics« introduces no difference into the debate, since this is what both the real specialists and the governor of Texas, Rick Perry and former cabinet minister Allègre say, the question »in what world do you live, with whom, by means of which instruments do you make it aware, with what degrees of uncertainty are you prepared to compromise?« would enable the public to more easily detect what the most partisan interests are – the only thing, as Walter Lippmann (2009) reminds us, that we can ask of the »phantom public«. While the science against politics debate has never functioned, politics against politics would quickly reveal the miserable positions of the climate-sceptics since, for sure, »their kingdom is not of this world«, at least not of this planet.

By defending themselves on the same terms, researchers would not only clarify what is meant by »politics« but would also give a positive meaning to the extent of their uncertainties. For the moment, in the impossible position in which they are put, asked as they are to give politicians the certainty that would finally allow them to act, any expression of *doubt* plays against them and affords the climate sceptics, by nature positivists, with an opportunity to bore holes in knowledge. This is what happened with »climategate«, when the sceptical lobbies claimed to publicly denounce the scheming of researchers busy groping along as they explored the dreadful complexity of the earth's climate. Of course they are groping; they are researchers... Big deal! It is this idea of doubt and »healthy scepticism« that must also be questioned.

A VERY ORIGINAL TYPE OF SCIENCE

But if climate science has so poorly withstood the accusation of being riddled with uncertainties, at least in the eyes of the media and the public, it is because it has failed to show the extent to which its assurance is grounded on bases other than current epistemology. Positivism can never be used to defend science against criticism, and even less so in the case of climate science, which demands a very new epistemology and in no way resembles the types of certainties on which the philosophy of science has cut its teeth – in short the results of mathematical physics. As we see in the admirable book by Paul Edwards, the simple operation of reviewing each basic »datum« by means of models intensely annoys the positivists. Yet this is precisely the innovativeness of these disciplines that have to collect data, »givens« *(données)* – or more exactly »obtaineds« *(obtenues)* –, produced by all sorts of disciplines, through instruments that would remain incommensurable without standardization. And every effort at standardization implies committees, networks, scholarly societies, non-profit organizations, in short, *institutions*, whose indispensable presence is *never* taken into account by ordinary epistemology. As soon as the real specialists talk, we see the deployment of a type of uncertainty that in no way *undermines* the fabric of the truths being produced, but that, on the contrary, proves *the extension* of the networks of instruments, the care that goes into interpretations, the gradual shortening of intervals of confidence, and the coherence of data obtained more and more independently from one another. This is precisely what positivism, in search of a single all-encompassing fact, will never achieve.

We see that the climate specialists would be more likely to win over the public to their cause by taking seriously their political or rather cosmopolitical role, and not trying to defend themselves with an epistemology that allows a single doubt to overturn the entire web of knowledge, rather than confining themselves behind the Maginot Line of the science/politics distinction and allowing themselves to be bombarded, without any power to react, via the expression of tiny doubts aimed at a science that is impossible to attain.

It is not by disseminating information that we will change the minds of those who fully understood that they were embarking on a »war of worlds« – and who already have a head start. We now have to be able to ensure that researchers do not fight with their hands tied behind their backs, paralyzed by the obligation to respect the epistemology of their opponents. Moreover, the public has to have the means of visualizing these debates in their entirety, without them immediately being framed – as the courts or TV studios do, into a »for« and an »against« – by a false equality that overlooks the immense differences of equipment, knowledge and power. It is precisely these devices, which make it possible to record the uneven distribution of resources, that we have been trying to construct for the past ten years, by means of what we call the »mapping of controversy«. Without a public equipped with new instruments, this change of epistemology would have no chance.

Clive Hamilton (2010: 209 ff.) endeavours to draw our attention to an unexpected obstacle to any ecological policy: hope. Rewriting what is written at the beginning of Dante's Hell, he urges us to: »Abandon all hope ye who enter here« because it is this hope that you cling to that renders you unable to prepare for the Hell waiting for you. I can't help but hope that he is wrong – again this darned hope! – but in any case he is right that we had better entirely give up the hope of a scientific debate finally delivered from any political interference, and the hope of a certainty finally complete, that would enable us to act without going backwards. By jettisoning the fortresses of rationalism, we may eventually find the pathways of a more demanding reason that would, at last, give researchers the leeway they need to fight their opponents on equal terms.

Translation by Liz Carey-Libbrecht

REFERENCES

Brandt, Allan M. (2007): *The Cigarette Century: The Rise, Fall, and Deadly Persistence of the Product that Defined America*. New York: Basic Books

Edwards, Paul N. (2010). *A Vast Machine. Computer Models, Climate Data, and the Politics of Global Warming*. Cambridge: MIT Press

Hamilton, Clive (2010). *Requiem for a Species: Why We Resist the Truth About Climate Change*. London, Washington: Earthscan Publ. Ltd.

Hoggan, James (2009). *Climate Cover-Up. The Crusade to Deny Global Warming*. Vancouver: Greystone Books

Lippmann, Walter (2009 [1993]). *The Phantom Public*. New Jersey: Transaction Publishers

Oreskes, Naomi and Erik M. Conway (2010). *Merchants of Doubt: How a Handful of Scientists Obscured the Truth on Issues from Tobacco Smoke to Global Warming*. London: Bloomsbury Press

Proctor, Robert and Londa Schiebinger (2008). *Agnotology: The Making and Unmaking of Ignorance*. Stanford: Stanford University Press

Living the Winter of Discontent: Reflections of a Deliberative Practitioner

Maarten Hajer

The Authority of Science: On Being a Case Study

When it comes to the science and politics of climate change the winter of 2009 – 2010 may well go down as the winter of discontent. Twenty years of focused institution building through the Intergovernmental Panel on Climate Change (IPCC – the international scientific organization providing assessments of scientific, technical and soio-economic information about the risks of climate change) and the United Nations Framework Convention on Climate Change (UNFCCC – the international environmental treaty to stabilize greenhouse gas emissions) was, quite unexpectedly for most of us, suddenly challenged. First there was the news of the emails from the University of East Anglia (either hacked or leaked, it is still unclear), then the failure to make serious progress at the COP15 at Copenhagen, then the news of »errors« in the IPCC reports. What was at stake was not only the authority of IPCC as an example of an institutional interface between science and politics. The question was whether the very set up of global »science (IPCC) for policy (UNFCCC)« was still credible.

On February 4th, 2010 the international press reported »another error« in the IPCC Fourth Assessment Report of 2007. It followed the error in the meltdown of the Himalayan glaciers (that were reported to melt away by 2035 instead of around 2350). This time it concerned the percentage of the Netherlands that was below sea level. The crucial sentence read:

›The Netherlands is an example of a country highly susceptible to both sea-level rise and river flooding because 55% of its territory is below sea level where 60% of its population lives and 65% of its Gross National Product (GNP) is produced.‹ (IPCC 2007: 547)

This was not correct: only 26% of the country is below sea level. On the other hand: 55% of the country is at risk *of flooding* as next to the 26% of the country that is below sea level, there is another 29% which is susceptible to river flooding. In the Low Countries the water comes from above and below, from the north, the east, the south and the west.[1]

A trivial matter? Perhaps, but a media storm was the result. It was an error that had made it to the IPCC Fourth Assessment Report and now this had been spotted. Only a few hours later I learned that it was my agency, the Netherlands

Flood-prone area

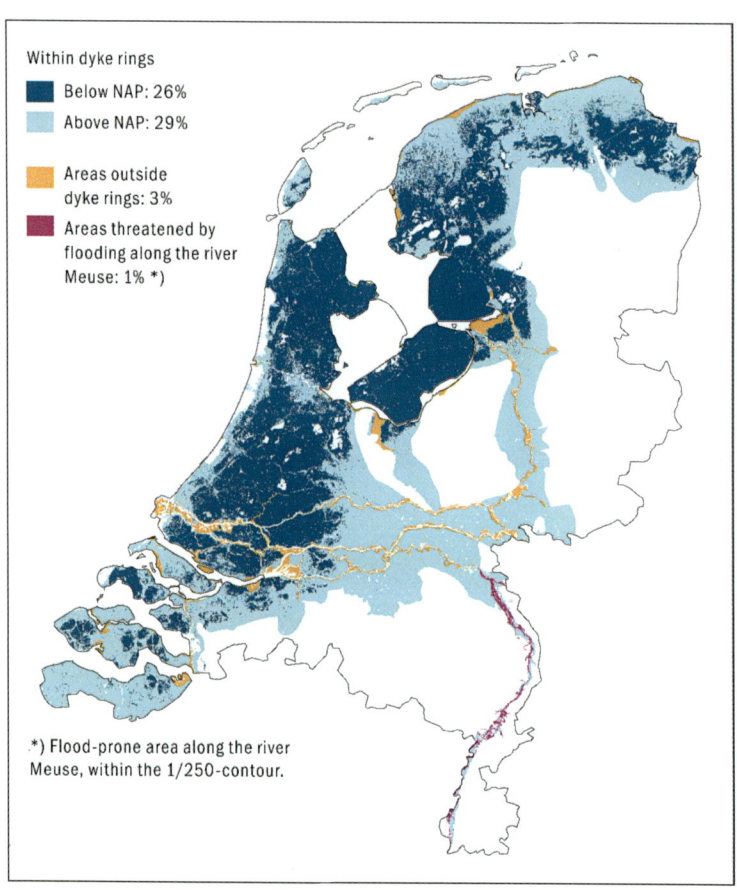

Source: PBL Netherlands Environmental Assessment Agency / Rijkswaterstaat-Waterdienst (2010), PBL website, http://www.pbl.nl.

---

1 | Ironically, the error came to light through the work of a journalist, Tomas van Heste. Van Heste, a graduate of the UvA' STS programme, had simply run a google search on »the Netherlands« in the IPCC' fourth assessment report and this was his first hit. He told me he thought: ›This cannot be true‹ and suddenly he had a scoop that made it to the global media.

Environmental Assessment Agency (PBL), which had been responsible for this particular section of the text of the IPCC report. Welcome in the global risk society. Here was a case in which expert authority was problematized, directly and with outrage in the media.

Here was a case in which the institutions dealing with global environmental change were outflanked. This was not a matter of organizing »risk assessment«, ›risk management‹ and ›risk communication‹ in the orderly linear way that some textbooks would still describe. Here was a case of a mediatized dynamics of risk in which expertise was taken up in the whirlwind of statements and response, of claim and counter claim.

I suddenly found myself in the midst of a political controversy. Rather than studying environmental politics and policy making from a comfortable arm chair in the Department of Political Science of the University of Amsterdam, I was now in the eye of the storm, answering questions from radio stations, newspapers and weeklies – foreign and domestic – and explaining what had happened on the news programs of competing television channels as well as being the object of sardonic criticism in the blogosphere.

Things became even more complicated as Jacqueline Cramer, the Dutch Minister for the Environment and a former academic writing on environment and science (sic), publicly declared she ›would not tolerate any further mistakes‹ from the climate scientists. Under heavy fire from a right wing opposition in Parliament she argued she would commission research to investigate if there were more errors in the IPCC report: ›politics has to know if it can still rely on the science‹. Through an ironic twist it was my agency PBL that was called to conduct this investigation that was published in July 2010.

It provided me with the material for a case study in the dynamics around the authority of science in the global risk society. Here was a case that showed the social explosiveness of risks, be it in a different way than was meant in Beck's original statement. Question was of course if our academic writing on how to deal with risk in a mediatized risk society would provide any guidance. What is more, as we sought to develop and employ a deliberative, or reflexive, or even cosmopolitan repertoire of governance in our investigation it also became a test if such practices would be able to respond to the sudden challenge to credibility that had occurred. Here I will reflect on this period, hopefully avoiding any misguided self-aggrandizement, but in a way that is helpful for thinking about ways in which we can employ scientific expertise in dealing with climate change.

THE USES OF DELIBERATIVE THEORY

Deliberative democracy is a normative political theory. But would a deliberative repertoire prove itself as useful to restore and extent the authority of science and expertise in the midst of a mediatized crisis? Coming from a background as a scholar of public policy I wondered if the work on discursive democracy (e.g. Dryzek 1991), deliberative policy analysis (e.g. Hajer and Wagenaar 2006), frame-reflective policy discourse (Rein and Schon 1986), transparency (Fung et al. 2007), STS (e.g. Jasanoff 1990, 2005) or deliberative democracy, trust and authority (e.g. Warren 1996) could provide guidance as to how to handle our role in the midst of a fierce debate over the authority of climate science and the IPCC.

For me my own analysis of authoritative governance, published only half a year earlier (Hajer 2009) was put to the test. In *Authoritative Governance* I tried to answer the question how authoritative governance is possible in our day and age.[2] It highlighted the central role of the media as a challenge to authority. Central to the argument of the book was that media reinforce the idea of a centre of decision making, an idea that elected politicians help reproduce only too happily (»I just decided that...«). Yet at the same time contemporary sociology points at the emergence of »subpolitics« and empirical work in the field of public policy and government keeps finding that government takes place in shifting networks, often with no obvious centre to decision making. Instead, policy making is conceptualized as a range of interconnected places and situations in which a range of decisions is made. My personal take here is to approach this by reconstructing discourses (what is being said, what vocabularies are employed and to what effect, etc.) and dramaturgy (how is saying it, where and to whom). Taken together this constitutes a theory of policy making as *performance*.

In the book I used Carl Friedrich who recaptured a sense of authority, that ›rests on the ability to issue communications which are capable of reasoned elaboration‹ (1958: 29). Friedrich starts from authority' etymological origins (auctoritas, augere), which stress the importance of reasoning for authority (ibid.; cf. Friedrich 1972: 47f.). Augere, or to augment, leads to an auctoritas which supplements ›a mere act of the will by adding reasons to it‹ (1958: 30). He cites Mommsen, who translated this to mean advice that cannot be disregarded. This may be the root of misunderstanding, as it raises the question why can this advice not be disregarded. Take the example of the expert and the layman. Can expert advice not be disregarded because it is the expert speaking to the layman? Is it the arguments and reasons that the expert can give that make the layman accept his claim? Or is it something in the way an expert speaks to a layman that lends authority to this communication? Or is it a combination of the above?

We know of the traditional way of thinking about authority. An individual can be put »in authority« through a proper and generally accepted procedure, after which people will defer to him or her because they subscribe to these procedures. The most well-known examples of this type of authority are probably the »rational-legal« and the »traditional« forms of authority identified/described

---

2 | The section below substantially draws on Hajer (2009).

by Weber (1978). Yet someone can also be regarded »an authority« because he or she has demonstrated superior powers of judgement or special knowledge (Friedman 1990: 79); this comes close to Weber' »charismatic authority«. In the climate-change case the IPCC was put »in authority« by the UN but – given the political controversy surrounding climate change at the time – this institutional fact was not sufficient to be respected as »an authority«. In bringing together all the relevant science on the theme, it strove to create an »epistemic« authority based on involving the best people with expertise on the subject and on using of peer review as an institutionalized form of ›virtual witnessing‹ (Edwards and Schneider 2001: 233). But this did not, in and of itself, produce an immediate acceptance of its statements as authoritative claims. The IPCC had to establish its authority through an extended contest: until rivals could no longer successfully challenge its claims. Then the IPCC became the authority in the climate-change case. But was this process purely an argumentative one of responding to counter-claims with reasoned rebuttals?

What seems more likely is that the development of authority was also supported by the particular way in which this process was conducted. There was, as Friedman puts it, a ›performative‹ element to authority (Friedman 1990: 79). The IPPC might have been given the status of »being in authority« by the UN General Assembly, but there are situations in which those who have politico-administrative functions cannot rely on the rational-legal authority they derive from the institutional position they have been given. In addition to this *de jure* authority, they have to create *de facto* authority by acting out their role in a sequence of concrete situations. This was the situation that the IPCC faced. Consider the procedural structure of IPCC, for instance. We know the IPCC assessment reports are compiled and reviewed at various stages by leading scientists from relevant disciplines, and that the exact wordings of the politically far more important *Summaries for Policymakers* (SPMs) also have to be agreed upon by delegates from all the participating countries. Whereas some criticize this method as allowing politicians to ultimately decide about what constitutes »scientific consensus«, it is also clear that this very act of translating/expressing science into summary statements crucially contributed to the political importance of the assessment reports, apparently without sacrificing their content (Schrope 2001; Edwards and Schneider 2001). In other words, the claim was regarded as authoritative because of the way in which it was made, where it was made, and by whom it was made. Understanding authority, then, always demands an analysis of the relation between the maker of a claim and the public(s) that need to be persuaded. Authority is always a relational notion. And here the IPCC tinkered with its procedural logic to take into account the fact that »simply« speaking in a scientific language might not be the best way to structure the interface between the scientific community and the political bodies that would work with the IPCC reports.

Authority here stems from a particular practice of reasoning, which developed over time. The success of the IPCC fits with Carl Friedrich's (1958, 1972) account of the process through which authority is gained. While his writings on the topic are not without ambivalence, he theorizes how authority is always related to the person who speaks and the very way in which the message gets expressed (cf. also Herbst 2003):

›[Authoritative] communication[s], whether opinions or commands, are not demonstrated through rational discourse, but they possess the potentiality of reasoned elaboration – they are ›worthy of acceptance.‹ Seen in this perspective, authority is a quality of communication, rather than of persons, and when we speak of the authority of a person, we are using a shorthand expression to indicate that he possesses the capacity to issue authoritative communications [...] The capacity of men to speak in meaningful terms, to say the things which may be thus elaborated, varies enormously. This capacity, I think, is implied when we speak of some of them as authorities.‹ (Friedrich 1958: 35 ff.)

Hence Friedrich not only explicitly links authority to communication; he also appreciates the fact that authority is bolstered by communications that allow for reasoned elaboration. The actually existing, though not necessarily employed, ›potentiality of reasoned elaboration‹ is what determines genuine authority. Authority, then, is not about submission, not about acquiescence, or about ›clenched fists in pockets‹ (Roberto Michels, quoted in Herbst 2003: 481); it is achieved through communication; it is about the development of a way of seeing things that can be, and indeed is, taken up by others and which results in the acceptance of a particular line of thinking and acting. Finally, finding a way to speak in meaningful terms is here taken to mean speaking in different languages to different publics (science, politics). This notion of authority moves away from a foundational understanding of authority and elaborates a discursive model of authority, as Warren (1996) notes. It is a way of thinking about authority that helps us understand its dynamics outside the context of fixed institutions. Viewed in these terms, the IPCC is an example of the new »ad hoc« policy-making practices that, when initiated, characteristically lack any pre-given authority. Whether they can really contribute to helping to address the policy problems depends heavily on their abilities to generate authority.

To sum up, authority is a quality of communication and is therefore contingent. It is something that can be won and lost. If we examine governance in these terms we may, first of all, distinguish certain »repertoires« of governing that might differ in terms of their capacity to generate authority. My claim here is that, in contemporary policy-making, we experience how even familiar and strongly ritualized forms of governance can lose their communicative capacity to generate authority.

HANDLING A CRISIS DELIBERATIVELY

Between February and July 2010 some 35 researchers of PBL contributed to an investigation of the IPCC's fourth assessment report, checking the text for more errors. This assignment nearly split the institute (in total some 250 fte, of which approx. 200 fte researchers). About half the academic staff were convinced this was an assignment that could only do damage to the IPCC and would lead to the demise of PBL as a respected research institute; the other half argued there was no choice and we should act on the parliamentary request in a responsible way. A small subsection of the latter half saw it as a challenge and saw it as an important experiment in an attempt to find a new form of scientific governance.

There was no lack of attention for our investigation. We found ourselves in the line of fire between the climate science community on the one hand and the skeptics on the other. For both we could do no good. The scientific community was deeply suspicious of the PBL investigation and accused us of being irresponsible by taking this on (that there had not been much of a choice once we were mentioned in parliament was quickly forgotten). The skeptics saw us as a clear part of the climate science community: PBL had been involved in the 4th assessment ourselves! They coined two effective phrases: here was a case of »a butcher testing his own meat«, and, locally more effective, they spoke of »WC-eend onderzoek«, or »Toilet Duck research«, after a well known Dutch commercial for a lavatory cleaner in which a laboratory scientist says: ›we from Toilet Duck, advice Toilet Duck!‹

From the outset our strategy was to avoid this »Toilet Duck« effect. Crucial here was to create what we called a »third space«: revert from using any terms that would place us in either camp. Secondly, we aimed to make the investigation an example of how to conduct further climate assessment work: not only being open and transparent, but also making every effort to engage the interested actors in a deliberation on what should be investigated and how to make sense of our results.

A classic take on an investigation into something as sensitive as the case of the errors in the IPCC report would have been to have this taking place behind closed doors. The first news would be the press conference of the report. We decided otherwise. As part of our deliberative approach we sought to create a public sphere for the debate. We invited some of the most eloquent international critics of IPCC to a seminar at PBL. For which we also invited the skeptic bloggers and scientists that had been alienated by the IPCC climate community. Hans von Storch, Mike Hulme and Steve Rayner had all been very critical and agreed to come and speak on the topic of academic quality in IPCC assessment work. It was a stunning experience. Some of the critical voices from within the scientific community were emotional about the fact that they were now finally heard and have their say. An indication to what extent the climate science debate had become politicized and communities had split up.

Another action spoke to the fact that the media framed the IPCC as being a closed community, an ivory tower, a castle. To avoid that PBL would itself also be accused to be elitist and arrogant, I announced in a televised news programme that PBL would open a public website where the public could report all instances of possible errors in the IPCC report. While the critical half of the PBL researchers nearly had a fit and others frantically thought how PBL could deliver on this promise, this communicative act had much bigger effects that we either anticipated or could have hoped for. The website became the symbol of PBL's open assessment procedure. Journalists would always refer to it in their

Basic time line of the PBL investigation of IPCC Fourth Assessment Report

January/February	Errors found
February	Minister commissions PBL to examine IPCC reports
	Various performances in radio and television talk shows
	Announcement of ›public website‹ to help find errors
March	Organization external review
	Seminars with major critics from climate community
	Sceptic bloggers invited to PBL
March/April	Interaction with IPCC authors
	Parliamentary hearings
May	Internal and external reviews
June	Preparing the political ground
4 July	Publication of report

communications (»any news from the website?« »How many people have responded?« »any useful contributions on the website?«). It suggested that it was the alleged arrogance of scientists that enraged the media and the public, while the new commitment to openness at least intrigued.

BLOGGING AS A DELIBERATIVE TOOL

In all of this we profited from an initiative we had taken just months before the investigation started. In the lead up to the Copenhagen conference we had agreed to a blog on the website of the 8 o'clock news. In this blog one of our climate researchers had a weekly exchange with one of the leading and most vocal Dutch climate skeptics, Hans Labohm. Although we had no idea how this would work, it had an important effect. The idea of the blog was that the two protagonists would constantly respond to each other. This led to a deliberative format which cancelled out one feature of the traditional way in which the skeptics communicate: they tend to repeat the same arguments time and again, often for different audiences. This allows skeptics to keep making arguments that have long been refuted by scientists (like the »urban heat island effect«, or the frequent employment of 1998 – a particularly hot year – as a base year). The format of a dialogue exposed this as claims were refuted: »Hey Hans, I noticed you used this graph again in your presentation to parliament. But I had shown you this was wrong, so why did you use it again?«. The format also let to different types of exchanges and even humor slipped in as the two contestants quarreled on a bet whether 2011 would be hotter than average or not and what would be a fair way to measure that.

The fact that we had agreed to this blog was first of all seen as a sign of recognition of the skeptics that above all felt excluded. The irony was that both parties involved were very happy: Labohm with his recognition, and we as it allowed us to communicate the state of climate science to a different audience, one that was not reached at all by our formal reports to the Cabinet and Parliament.

IPCC AND DELIBERATION

Over the twenty years of its existence IPCC had developed its own repertoire. It is a strange mix of positivist »speaking truth to power« elements (»science is now 90% certain that ...«) and deliberative elements like the way in which it agrees on the crucial *Summary for Policy Makers*. The IPCC reports are 3000plus pages of summaries of the state of knowledge on selected topics. They are often referred to as »the bricks«. The summary for policy makers is the digest of the most relevant findings and therefore by far the most important mechanism linking science to politics. The photo below, made by the Chief Scientist of PBL, and member of the Dutch Delegation at the time, Arthur Petersen, shows how IPCC uses the MS Word »track changes« technique in a plenary meeting in which policy makers and scientists agree on the text. Crucial is that they have two competing interests: scientists want a fair representation of the science, policy makers want a statement that their politicians can live with.

This sort of cross over work is on the one hand crucial for the policy process but at the same time easily misunderstood. IPCC is often criticized for not being »purely« scientific but that is missing the point. To judge IPCC by scientific criteria is to miss the essence of the organisational practice and is in itself a political framing. After all, IPCC is an example of »assessment« work. The IPCC does not do research itself and works with selected scientists who, together, are expected to cover a certain theme / knowledge area. Goal is to supply the best available knowledge in support of good political and administrative decision making. This is not at all easy as science chooses its own issues for investigation, its own case studies, which means that the available scientific evidence differs from policy issue to policy issue. In the case of the IPCC it meant that the effects of climate change were far less well researched in some parts of the world (e.g. Africa) than others (North America in particular) with serious consequences, as we can see in the figure below.

Observed changes in biological and physical systems

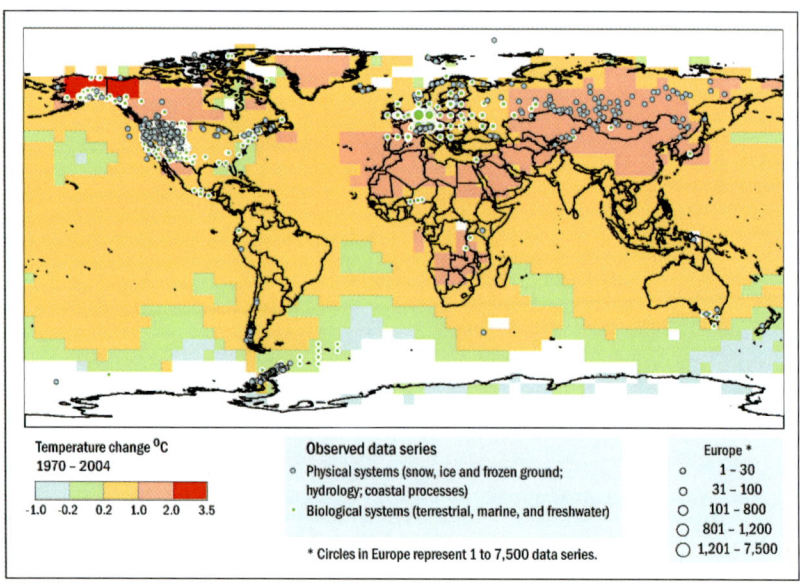

Source: Parry et al. (2007) Climate Change 2007: Figure 1.8.

Assessment should therefore be seen as a specific institutional »practice«, with its own rules, its own »do' & don'ts«. One of our tasks therefore was to explain what IPCC »really« was. Part of the trouble was, after all, that IPCC was judged by a standard that was not applicable to its work as assessment panel.

How facts travel

As it was impossible to reassess 3000 pages of the IPCC's Fourth Assessment Report in three months time we decided to focus on the regional chapters of Working Group II, this being the place were all errors had been found. Inspired by Mary Morgan (2010) we looked how »facts travelled« from academic research to the crucial *Summary for Policy Makers* (SPM). After all, these were the most important, selected facts that were used to underpin the case for action. Starting in the SPM we traced the origin of particular claims all the way to the original reference.

Regional chapter analysis pyramid

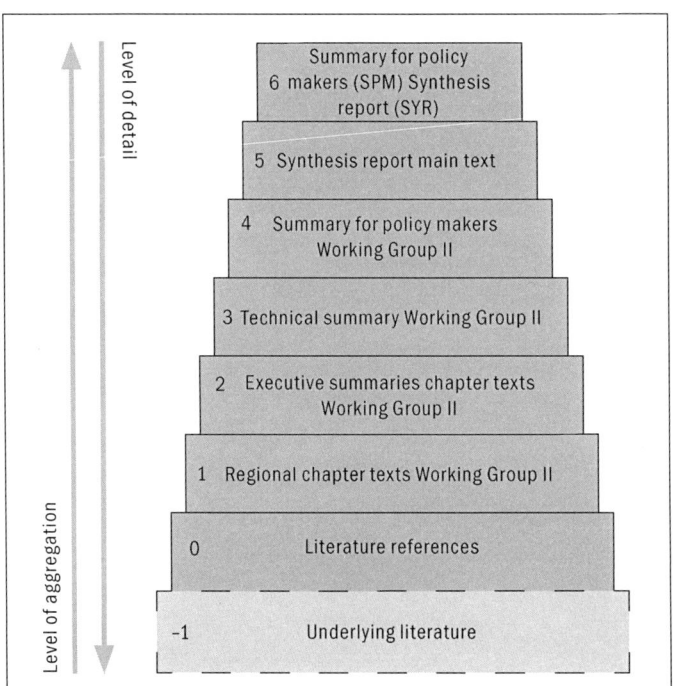

Source: PBL Netherlands Environmental Assessment Agency 2010b

It quickly became obvious that the climate science community was not amused by this undertaking. The confrontation with questions about the origin of claims in the IPCC report was met with outright hostility. Defending the institutional take of IPCC, Joe Alcamo, Chief Scientist of UNEP, let me know in no uncertain terms that this whole investigation was a disaster and that it could only lead to further damage to the case of acting on climate change. He was not the only one. Communication with key players in the 4th assessment was difficult. The fact remained, however, that we found many instances in which it was unclear how IPCC had arrived at its conclusions. Insisting on a deliberative format we approached all relevant IPCC authors and lead authors to get their feedback on our queries.

Expert judgement

It was through the interaction with the IPCC authors that we came to probe the notion of »expert judgement«. It was constantly referred to as a magical formula. In many cases IPCC had come to judgements in the cause of its proceedings yet without spelling out the reasoning that led to a particular stance. Our insistence on a deliberative format, brought out a crucial feature of the IPCC work, in particular of Working Group II, focusing on effects of climate change (Working Group I focusing on the climate system, Working Group III being devoted to possible policy measures): in cases where the existing literature was inconclusive it employed expert judgement to fill gaps.

Structure of the Fourth Assessment Reports

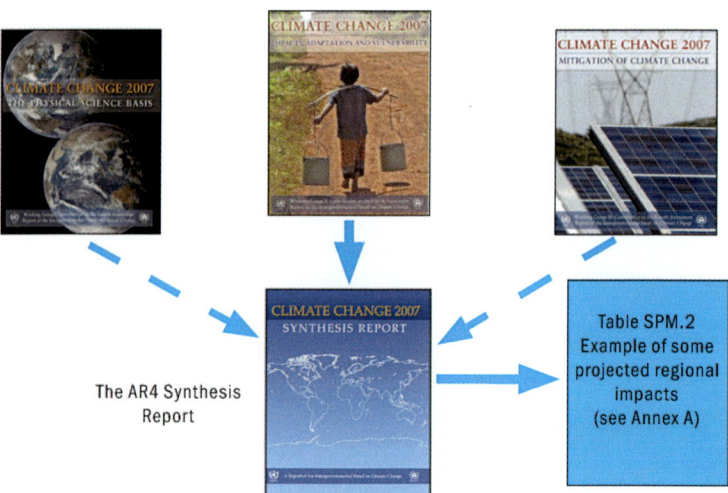

Source: PBL Netherlands Environmental Assessment Agency 2010b

Interestingly, this approach came out to be controversial within IPCC itself. It was very clear that those active in Working Group I (often physicists, meteorologists and climatologists) looked down on the work of Working Group II. The investigation of the possible effects of climate change was taken on mainly by ecologists, biologists, agricultural scientists. They worked with a very different epistemology, did not rely on experiments or theoretical models but much more on field data and observation. This was a long slumbering controversy within IPCC with little appreciation of the difficulty of making regionally specific assessment of what environmental change may have been caused by, or relate to, climate change. Implicit here was the question what sort of science was needed for good policy making.

Crucially, our understanding of the very way in which we should read the IPCC reports came from the direct engagement with the authors. Of particular value here were »in vivo« seminars in which we discussed our preliminary findings. These meetings were, once again, very emotional as some of the scientists felt the PBL investigation as an attack on their academic integrity. The deep engagement in these exchanges created the basis for a good reception of the report as we made sure that whatever we wrote took into account the arguments made, although in several cases we were not persuaded.

»ERRORS« AS FRAME

The very notion of »errors« was, of course, not innocent in itself. That there would be some mistakes in a three volume, 3000 page long assessment report is not in itself necessarily a reason to problematize the quality of the science. The question was also what the IPCC assessment was for. Implicit in the media outrage was the accusation that scientists were »stealth issue advocates« as Roger Piehlke jr (2007) labeled them: scientist working for a political cause but using science as a »fig leaf«. »Errors« were for some »inherent in scientific practice« but for others a clear sign of cheating.

To complete the investigation in a responsible manner we needed to come up with our own idea about the quality of the assessment work and then use our own system of classification. It had to be a system that would do justice to the work of the scientists, speak to the worries of the politicians and at the same time help make a persuasive differentiation between sloppiness, unfounded claims and show where the procedures needed to be reconsidered and redesigned.

The authors of the report, led by Leo Meyer and Arthur Petersen, came up with a classification in which »errors« were redefined and became a subcategory in the overview of findings.

> E1 Inaccurate statement
> E1a Errors that can be corrected by an erratum (5)
> E1b Errors that require a redoing of the assessment of the issue at hand (2)
> E2 Inaccurate referencing (3)
> C1 Insufficiently substantiated attribution (1)
> C2 Insufficiently founded generalization (2)
> C3 Insufficiently transparent expert judgment (10)
> C4 Inconsistency of messages (2)
> C5 Untraceable reference (3)
> C6 Unnecessary reliance on grey referencing (2)
> C7 Statement unavailable for review (1)
>
> (between brackets: number of instances found)

Drawing on the information we had got from the interaction with the IPCC scientists involved, we could be much more precise and effectively reduce the deeply problematic category of »inaccurate statement«. The classification did more justice to the work of the authors of the IPCC assessment and was not problematized by journalists or skeptics.

ASSESSMENTS AS A DELIBERATIVE PRACTICE?

The above shows how a deliberative approach, with ample emphasis on the value of engaging different parties in a dialogue of interpretation, helped to combine (1) investigating the quality of the IPCC report with (2) acquiring the legitimacy that this investigation was itself done in a responsible manner.

It reconfirmed my conviction that the authority of science and expertise will have to be acquired in new ways in our mediatized age. The performances in times of crisis and incidents might play an important role in this. First of all, this is the moment at which people are interested in learning something. Hence it is a chance to explain something about what IPCC actually is. By illustration, in a talk radio show in the midst of the festival of errors I spoke for perhaps three minutes and knocked down two percentage points of the number of people that no longer trusted the science. Point is: why assume that people know what IPCC is about in the first place? Perform when it matters.

Secondly, the idea that scientists can judge for themselves what is the case does not speak to the new reality in which there is a larger group of actors contesting scientific claims. To be sure, expert judgements are crucial in deeply complex issues like climate change. By making expert judgements more transparent the reasoning of science can be controlled and questioned.

Thirdly, the very idea of making periodic assessment reports may no longer be the single best way to make sure political debates are fact regarding. At PBL we introduced the practice of what we call »hoovering« the public debate: actively respond to false claims made in public debate so as to avoid they stick around and become more influential than appropriate.

Fourthly, science is to take up a role in public debates. This goes two ways. We allowed the public in, using a public forum to help spot »group think«, and gained credits for our work. On the other hand, we recommended to IPCC to introduce a practice of working with »living documents«. By creating website for errata, you state that science and scientific assessments are not infallible and you show your anticipation of (smaller) errors. You step down one step and you gain a lot of credibility.

Fifthly, there is more to a good performance than a good argument. Over the course of this »case study« we saw many cases in which scientists showed their inability to communicate in a persuasive manner. While it is not at all clear what makes for the most formidable performance (an authentic but perhaps flat performance of a scientist might communicate much better the values of impartiality and commitment to knowledge than scientists that have undergone media training) it is clear that experts were »outflanked« in the mediatized exchanges with other protagonists. Worst performances were those where the scientists from the meteorological institute had been provided with »speaking notes«, which worked as a straightjacket in their exchange with aggressive journalists and bloggers.

Sixthly, there is a politics of science. Like it or not, you engage in boundary work. There is no way to avoid developing story lines yourself, creating meaning, excluding other readings. When it comes to the current climate debate to confine one selves to the facts of whether or not climate change is a reality is a choice in itself. There is a lot of value for an emancipation of good open assessment science. It is focused on trying to mobilize the science needed for public policy responses to urgent challenges. Sticking to pure science is a political choice itself. There is serious evidence that this line of action is promoted precisely for these purposes. Obviously, this domain of boundary work is a risky zone of action. It would be totally irresponsible without a keen eye for the ethical and moral dimensions and a commitment to openness and accountability.

Finally, while I reported on a Dutch investigation that was necessary to rescue a Dutch minister, it provided a case that illustrates how the authority of science can be affected by very local events. Looking back we can safely say it did not aggravate the crisis of credibility and arguably informed the reform agenda for IPCC itself. Had we conducted it differently it could have put IPCC and climate politics in jeopardy. That in itself is a reason to carefully reflect on the sort of pressure field that you have to operate in once you get into a media storm in the global risk society.

References

Beck, Ulrich (1999). *World Risk Society*. Cambridge: Polity Press
Dryzek, John (1990). *Discursive democracy: politics, policy, and political science*. Cambridge: Cambridge University Press
Edwards, Paul N. and Stephen H. Schneider (2001). Self-governance and peer review in science-for-policy: the case of the IPCC second assessment report. In Clark Miller and Paul N. Edwards (eds.). *Changing the atmosphere: expert knowledge and environmental governance*. Cambridge: MIT Press: 219–246
Friedman, Richard (1990). On the concept of authority in political philosophy. In: Joseph Raz (ed.), *Authority*. New York: New York University Press, 56–91
Friedrich, Carl J. (1958). *Authority*. Cambridge: Harvard University Press
Friedrich, Carl J. (1972). *Tradition and authority*. London: Pall Mall
Fung, Archon; Mary Graham and David Weil (2007). *Full Disclosure: The Perils and Promise of Transparency*. Cambridge: Cambridge University Press
Hajer, Maarten A. (2009). *Authoritative Governance: Policy Making in an Age of Mediatization*. Oxford: Oxford University Press
Hajer, Maarten A. and Hendrik Wagenaar (2006). *Deliberative Policy Analysis*. Cambridge University Press
Herbst, Susan (2003). Political authority in a mediated age. In: *Theory and Society*, 32(4): 481–503
Jasanoff, Sheila (1990). *The fifth branch: science advisers and policy makers*. Cambridge, Mass.: Harvard University Press
Morgan, Mary S. (2010). Traveling Facts. In: Peter Howlett and Mary S. Morgan (eds.). *How well do facts travel?* Cambridge: Cambridge University Press
Parry, Martin L.; Osvaldo F. Canziani, Jean P. Palutikof, Paul J. van der Linden and Clair E. Hanson (eds.) (2007). *Climate Change 2007: Impacts, Adaptation and Vulnerability*. Working Group II Contribution to the Fourth Assessment Report of the Intergovernmental Panel on Climate Change, Figure 1.8. Cambridge: Cambridge University Press
PBL Netherlands Environmental Assessment Agency (2010a). *Wetenschapper versus Skepticus*. Den Haag, Bilthoven: PBL
PBL Netherlands Environmental Assessment Agency (2010b). *Assessing an IPCC Assessment – An Analysis of Statements on Projected Regional Impacts in the 2007 Report*. Den Haag, Bilthoven: PBL
Pielke jr, Roger (2007). *The Honest Broker*. Cambridge: Cambridge University Press.
Rein, Martin and Donald Schön (1993 [1986]). Frame-reflective policy discourse. In: Frank Fischer and John Forester (eds.). *The Argumentative Turn in Policy and Planning*. Durham: Duke University Press
Schrope, Mark (2001). Consensus science, or consensus politics? In: *Nature*, 412(6843): 112–114

Warren, Mark (1996). Deliberative democracy and authority. In: *American Political Science Review*, 90(1): 46–60

Warren, Mark (ed.) (1999). *Democracy and Trust*. Cambridge: Cambridge University Press

Weber, Max (1978). *The theory of economic and social organization*. Berkeley: University of California Press

The Political Contradictions
of Second Modernity

TED NORDHAUS AND MICHAEL SHELLENBERGER

In the fall of 2008, in the shadow of the collapse of global financial markets, the German sociologist Ulrich Beck gave a speech at Harvard University that was, in roughly equal measure, a scathing indictment of global capitalism and a hopeful exploration of the possibilities that a new transnational political and economic order might arise from the wreckage of the global financial crisis and the increasing contradictions of a hegemonic neo-liberal economic paradigm that was creating new global risks faster than it could manage them.

Alongside the global financial crisis, Beck posited climate change as the quintessential global risk that would undermine modernist institutions, most especially the nation state and the market economy, as those institutions became increasingly incapable of managing new global risks that were themselves created by the rising complexity, inequality, and resource intensity of modern economies. While Beck is far from the first observer to have compared the global financial meltdown with looming climate catastrophe, his argument deserves serious consideration because, in contrast to the sometimes hysterical conflation of the financial crisis and global warming as twin expressions of the »unsustainability« of modern life by folks like the New York Times columnist Thomas Friedman, Beck offers a framework for thinking about risk, society, and modernity that is well conceived, broad, and comprehensive.

Beck has long argued that modern societies constantly create new risks and contradictions that undermine the foundations of modern social, political, and economic institutions and suggests that we have entered a new phase of human development wherein the »first modern« project of emancipating ourselves from nature, tribalism, peonage, and poverty has been subsumed by the »second modern« project of managing the unintended consequences of modernity itself. But Beck does not view these new second modern risks as singularly disruptive, for he also observes the ways in which the management of new risks expands the power of the state and of those who already possess wealth and power.

Second modern risks simultaneously instantiate existing institutions and power relationships and disrupt them.

Nonetheless, Beck's Harvard speech focused almost exclusively upon the ways in which global risk might disrupt both the nation state as the institutional seat of state power and neo-liberal economic theory and policies as the organizing principles of the global economy and offered little consideration of the ways in which the response to these new crises might actually extend the neo-liberal state and economy. Beck argues that new ›global risks empower states and civil society movements‹ to ›disempower globalized capital‹ (Beck, 2008: 13) and calls for ›clever reflexive regulation (philosophy) on a global scale‹ and ›a new theory of the mixed economy, framed for the global market place of today, as the now defunct Keynesian system was framed for the national post-war economies‹ (Beck 2008: 16).

Beck focuses on catastrophes like Katrina and the financial crisis as what he calls »cosmopolitan moments« that could bring the world together, similar to the way we transcended national boundaries to create things like the Nuremburg principles after World War II, or nuclear disarmament in the 1980s (Beck, 2008: 12). In this, Beck's notion of »world cosmopolitan society« and his notion of »world risk society« are inseparable. The proliferation of unintended consequences of modernity inexorably undermines the nation-state, as new »cosmopolitan risks« increasingly demand institutional arrangements that are trans-national in nature and therefore undermine the nation-state as the central unit of social, political, and economic organization in second modernity. ›The perception of risk [...] creates a public sphere across all boundaries‹ Beck argues, where ›global norms can be created through cosmopolitan moments.‹ (Beck 2008: 13)

Undoubtedly, new globalized risks driven by a new globalized economy are driving the creation of new trans-national institutions that are subsuming and displacing many of the traditional prerogatives of the nation-state. But Beck goes further in his argument, suggesting that these new risks, and the cosmopolitan moments they create might »disempower globalized capital« and ultimately bring about the displacement of »laissez faire« neo-liberal economics with »a new theory of the mixed economy.« And here, Beck's conflation of »laissez faire« economics with neo-liberal economic policy, his identification of neo-liberalism as a »first modern« phenomena that is undermined by second modernity risk, and his positioning of the mixed economy in opposition to neo-liberalism are deserving of closer examination.

Beck's watershed analyses of modernization – of the ways in which second modernity creates problems for older conceptions of modernity and the institutions that underpin it as we become ever more individuated and specialized, as our multiple knowledges start to contradict one another, and as the unintended consequences of modernity, such as climate change and financial crises, multiply – ought to challenge unitary and singular conceptions of the state, the economy, markets, and risk. In the sections that follow, we shall suggest that the rise of neo-liberalism is in fact a second modernity phenomena, closely related to changing notions of the state, the economy, and modernity itself. We shall explore the ways in which the extension of state power and the expansion of markets are consistent features of modernization and not oppositional forces, as often presumed by both Left and Right. And we shall consider the ways in which the manufacture and management of risk in second modernity extends both state power and neo-liberal economic hegemony rather than disrupting them, with a particular focus upon the issue of climate change. Finally, we will consider whether explicit and direct state and collective responses to the crises of second modernity are even possible in a world in which the modern state has become simultaneously ubiquitous, intertwined with virtually every part of modern life, and at the same time virtually invisible to its citizenry.

1.

The importance of Beck's work for understanding what we are here calling the political contradictions of second modernity cannot be overstated. For Beck, »World cosmopolitan society« starts to blur traditional parochial and national boundaries and identities. The nation state is the quintessential first modernity institution and second modernity demands the emergence of transnational institutions that subsume the role and responsibilities reserved for the nation state in first modernity (Beck et al. 2003).

In his Harvard speech, Beck argues that catastrophes like Hurricane Katrina and the 2008 financial crisis represent cosmopolitan moments that perform ›an involuntary and unintended enlightening function [...] Looming catastrophe,‹ he argues, ›is a merciless teacher of all humanity‹ (Beck, 2008: 8).

›[T]he historical power of global risk is beyond all the »saviors« brought forth by history… it is the perceived risks facing humanity, which can neither be denied nor externalized, that are capable of awakening the energies, the consensus, the legitimation necessary for creating a global community of fate, one that will demolish the walls of nation-state borders and egotisms [...]‹ (Beck 2008: 6).

But Beck errs in our view, in his expectation that such reactions would not only galvanize »cosmopolitan« responses but would also undermine hegemonic neoliberalism. Beck's error is that he conflates neo-liberalism with laissez-faire capitalist ideology[1] – an analytical error that results in Beck characterizing con-

---

1 | ›On the rise is state socialism for the rich – the bankers etc. – and at the same time a strict neoliberalism for the poor. Or to put it another way: Is the Chinese form of state-

temporary neo-liberal ideology and policy as a relic of first modernity economic organization in the same way that he sees the nation state as a relic of first modernity political organization. As a result, he looks for transnational institutions to emerge in response to the excesses and contradictions of global capitalism rather than in service of it.

But the great cosmopolitan project of our time capable of »demolishing the walls of nation-state borders and egotisms« – globalization – has always already been a neoliberal project. The geopolitical, juridical, and institutional drive to globalize the world economy has centrally been a project aimed at creating transnational institutions (e.g. WTO) and regulations (e.g. GATT) to privatize public assets, govern and regulate the global economy, and liberalize the national constraints upon trade and the flow of global capital.

Second modernity neoliberalism – created by monetarist economists such as Milton Friedman, and broadly embraced by political left and right in one form or another, from Margaret Thatcher to Ronald Reagan to Bill Clinton to Tony Blair to most of the current heads of G-8 countries, including Barack Obama – purports to repair the unintended consequences of both first modernity capitalism and the first modernity welfare state. In both cases, it a priori proposes regulated markets, combined with market incentives, to correct the market failures of first modernity in place of more direct state interventions to shape the economy and social outcomes. Neoliberals may disagree about what constitutes a market failure and what to do about it. But their acceptance of the same language and economic paradigm demonstrates the power of neoliberal hegemony over intellectuals, civil society actors, and elected officials alike.

Indeed, in second modernity we see the mixed economy replaced by the mixed state. In first modernity, the mixed economy denoted the substantial involvement of the state in the economy, not just in the role of regulator but also provider of economic goods and services that are most efficiently and effectively provided by the state rather than the private economy. The state purchased and regulated agricultural crops, electricity, radios, medicines, microchips, computers and the internet while education, and in most industrialized nations health care, became universal public goods provided directly by the state. In second modernity, by contrast, public goods are increasingly provided by private entities either through public market creation, privatization, or public/private partnerships. Public goods as varied as education, energy, health care, armies, water and other utilities are increasingly provided by private entities, all under the supervision of the state. The result is that private interest and public interest, private goods and public goods, and the state, the economy, and the market become ever more complexly integrated and difficult to disentangle.

---

run private industry now also starting to find its way into the Anglo-Saxon centres of laissez-faire capitalism?‹ (Beck 2008: 1)

Today, the neo-liberal concept of correcting market failures has become virtually synonymous with the provision of public goods, and this conflation should tell us something for they are not the same thing. The concept of market failure suggests that the market might be repaired or perfected in such a manner as to correct the failure in question. The concept of public goods, by contrast, implies that there are goods or services in any society, be they drinking water or education or development of new clean energy technologies, that markets either cannot or should not provide. The Ayn Randian laissez-faire ideology of first modernity rejected the notion of public goods, imagining that with the state entirely out of the way, »the Market« would bring the most efficient and equitable distribution of resources. By contrast, neo-liberal ideology of second modernity substitutes the parlance of »market failures« for »public goods« and imagines that carefully and technocratically managed markets, whether for credit or carbon, will provide the most efficient and equitable outcomes.

Though Beck elides the difference between laissez-faire and neoliberalism, he implicitly recognizes neoliberalism as a second modernity ideology when he says that in second modernity the ›expectation of unexpected consequences‹ comes to dominate decision-making. The result is that ›in the language of economics, externalities have been internalized‹ (Beck et al. 2003: 21). This »language of economics« is, in fact, the neoliberal language of market failure, and the drive to internalize those impacts is the effort to correct, or perfect, the market. Externalities are market failures and once we have replaced the idea of bounding markets with fixing them, a whole new set of unintended consequences are unleashed. First among them is that the neoliberal logic of internalizing economic externalities extends markets into every realm of human behavior, human society and the entire universe of non-human natures. To internalize economic externalities is to give the externality a price. To price an externality, be it carbon emissions or tropical rain forests or human suffering, is to extend the market, and the logic of markets, to that particular domain. The neoliberal desire to correct the market has the consequence of extending its influence to previously unimagined domains.

It is in this sense that we argue that the ideological positioning by both Left and Right of markets and state intervention in the economy as oppositional to one another is erroneous. The long arc of modernization, in both first modernity and even more so in second modernity, has been to expand the power of the state and extend the reach of markets simultaneously. The extension of markets into new social, economic, and geographic domains brings the state with it, and vice versa. Providing public goods and correcting market failures become indistinguishable concepts. You cannot create new markets without creating demand for the state to intervene in or regulate those markets. And you cannot marshal the state to address new crises or provide new services without bringing market forces along for the ride. Little wonder then that despite thirty years of anti-government, pro-market rhetoric and ideology from both political parties, American government has continued to expand and extend its reach, even as we have financialized much of the American economy, deregulated telecommunications, airlines, and other economic sectors, and privatized many formerly public services and amenities.

How did such a progression come about? The mixed economy that Beck suggests could come back into fashion in the wake of crises like Katrina and the 2008 financial crisis was a prominent feature of first modernity economies. The trajectory of political economy in first modernity was generally toward greater state involvement in the economy, not less. The state took increasing responsibility to build infrastructure, educate and provide health care, regulate firms, and even guarantee an income for its citizens. The rise of neoliberalism in second modernity should be understood as an evolutionary development, not a retrenchment. It is the result not of the failure of the first modernity state but rather its spectacular success. The economic security that the modern welfare state makes possible results in rising individuation, narcissism, and self-referentiality. In second modernity, the context for our prosperity, our security, our opportunity, and our accomplishments become invisible. The second modern imagines that her accomplishments and security are her own doing, having become so inured to the modern infrastructure, legal system, social norms, and economic activity all around her that she imagines they are the normal state of the world.

Little wonder then that in second modernity, the state only becomes visible or relevant when something goes wrong. Markets and market actors (e.g., consumers, investors), not the state and national actors (e.g., voters, public servants), becomes the subjects of History. All developments, good and bad, come to be seen as unconnected to the state or the exercise of democracy. When outcomes are good the market – that is, the imaginary, theological, naturalized »Market« – is deemed to have »worked.« When they are bad the Market is deemed to have »failed« and needs to be »fixed.« This leads to neo-liberal »market fixing« not mixed economies in the old first modernity sense.

The result is that whereas in first modernity the driving impetus of state action was to build the physical, legal, political, and economic infrastructures of modernity, in second modernity the basis for the continued existence and function of the state is, literally and figuratively, entitlement. The state is only visible when it fails to provide the services and infrastructure to which its citizens have become accustomed. Neither second modern neoliberals nor second modern environmentalists can see the developmental conditions for their existence or their worldview. Environmentalists do not recognize the foundational role modern prosperity played in providing them with the security, comfort and education that allows them to be concerned about global warming. Neoliberals do not recognize the foundational role the modern state played creating the industries and technologies that made AT&T, Google and Merck possible (Nordhaus and Shellenberger 2007). Both are blinded by second modernity's self-referential reflexivity. In place of grand visions of progress, of building a great society or even just a new clean energy economy, second modernity brings us entitlement, incrementalism, and fear of unintended consequences.

2.

It is through this prism that we might then return to the question of climate risk. If the manufacturing of knowledge and the production and management of second modernity risk in world risk society serve to instantiate and extend existing power relationships not just undermine modernist institutions, as Beck posits, then we ought to ask what power the manufacture and production of climate risk science serves. Al Gore and others say the climate debate is a battle between an underdog »Science« and a fossil fuels Goliath. But the acceptance of what we have described as a »pollution paradigm« among scientists, policy-makers, and other cosmopolitan elites is almost total (Nordhaus and Shellenberger 2007).

Through their highly complicated and obtuse models, climate scientists have performed a remarkable alchemy, transforming the enormous uncertainty inherent to questions of climate sensitivity to atmospheric greenhouse gases and the climate impacts of higher global mean temperatures into a »scientific« consensus that proposes to establish in politics not only the universal acceptance that anthropogenic climate change is occurring, a very reasonable proposition, but also the further and more specific certainty that we must keep global mean temperature increase below 2 degrees Celsius and therefore stabilize atmospheric carbon concentrations below 450 ppm to avoid »catastrophic« and »irreversible« climate change. These are not random conclusions negotiated through the IPCC and other science/policy institutions. These temperature and atmospheric targets only make sense in the context of a particular framework. The purpose of all this risk science is to provide a »scientific« basis for policies to cap global carbon emissions and mandate their reduction.

Once the climate scientists have done their work, the economists take over, dumping the results of the climate models, which have manufactured »climate science« certainty out of enormous scientific (atmospheric, biological, chemical, and geological) uncertainty, into economic models, which perform their own alchemy, transforming enormous uncertainty about future economic growth, fossil fuel availability and cost, technological innovation, and endogenous decarbonization (or recarbonization) into highly certain and specific conclusions about the costs and benefits of various rates and mechanisms (e.g. caps vs. carbon tax, rapid and early action vs. more incremental and gradual paths) to reduce emissions. Both the environmental and economic models are introduced with earnest cautions about the many uncertainties and assumptions inherent to them. But no sooner are those caveats completed than the models functionally become simulacra of the future.

While the many economic models differ in their conclusions, partisans to the resulting battles debate them as if they were competing realities. In two recent debates between neoclassical economists – the first involving British Treasury Secretary Nicholas Stern over how much we should discount the future and the second involving Harvard economics professor Martin Weitzman who questioned whether we could discount the future given the low probability of high-impact climate catastrophe – we can see how little is in question. Climate change is always formally approached as a pollution problem – as a »market failure.« We debate how much is too much and how much we ought to pay to correct it. But we virtually never question whether climate change might be better understood as a different kind of problem, one resulting from our lack of investment in new public goods, namely clean energy sources capable of powering our economy while reducing the risk of catastrophic climate change.

And here we ought to ask: why is this? Why is it that all of that uncertainty and complexity gets reduced to one particular problem/solution set? This is particularly striking given the utter failure of solutions (Kyoto, emissions trading, carbon taxes) constructed from this problem definition to have any impact whatsoever on the problem in question, and given the extraordinary set of obstacles to the solution defined, which have been apparent from the very beginning.

To understand why this is we need to return to our original observation, which is that the rise of neoliberalism is not a first modernity phenomena that has been problematized by the new risks and contradictions of second modernity but rather is a second modernity phenomena that is, in many instances, empowered, instantiated, and expanded by those risks. Nowhere is this more apparent than in the response to climate change, for with the first great transnational project of second modernity – the establishment, codification, and institutionalization of globalization – well under way, we now embark upon the second great neoliberal transnational project: the establishment of a global carbon market.

Beck's call for a »clever reflexive regulation (philosophy) on a global scale« merges with the pollution paradigm, which in its managed and technocratic vision, seeks to expand the neoliberal market economy into previously unimagined domains. Reducing emissions is declared, a priori, a challenge best taken up by the market. The role of governments is to correct the market failure that is global warming and create a market for »emissions reductions« – represented by state pollution allowances and regulated carbon offsets – products that will become the largest commodities market in the world, larger than both oil and gas combined.

The forthcoming global carbon market will manufacture new assets and new markets not from production, however, but from »un-production.« We now create a multi-trillion dollar carbon market whose value is entirely based on, and dependent upon, »clever reflexive regulation« by transnational institutions – one in which rich nations will outsource their emissions reductions in the same way they outsource manufacturing, and almost everything else.

That such a market of carbon unproduction will ultimately have virtually no impact upon the trajectory of global carbon emissions is almost beside the point. Clever reflexive regulation, along with clever reflexive accounting, may profitably trade in the unproduction of carbon for decades until such time as the low carbon technologies emerge that will obviate the unintended consequences of meeting our primary energy needs by burning fossil fuels, at which point the carbon market bubble, like the recent housing bubble will burst – or until there is a second modernity ideology robust enough to challenge neoliberalism – whichever comes first. Either way, the final alchemical miracle is now complete. The modeling of risk, and the costs and benefits associated with managing those risks, transforms worthless homes built on spec in the swamps of Florida, as well as carbon emissions reductions measured against projections of alternate carbon realities, into property and wealth.

The epigraph to this particular alchemical miracle is the neoliberal capture of green ideology – the most well developed ideological challenge to first modernity capitalism. Just as the slave ideology of Christianity becomes the ideology of decadent Roman noblemen, the first modernity anti-modern ideology of environmentalism becomes the ideology of the new neoliberal elites in second modernity, with Obama, EU leaders, and captains of industry now offering carbon markets as recipes for growth.

3.

There is little reason to hope that actual catastrophe, be it Katrina or climate change or financial collapse, will undermine the manufacturing of these new risks. No sooner does catastrophe occur than the models and modelers are back at work. Stress tests conducted by the Obama Treasury Department tell us the banks are fine. Modelers working for the European Environment Agency construct alternate realities (business-as-usual baselines) to show that carbon trading is reducing emissions compared to what would have happened had no carbon caps been established.

We might even ask ourselves if these models might be more than mere con games played by the ruling elite – if the realities we model will become reality. Will stress tests designed so that banks can pass them assure not only that banks will not fail but also that economic activity will return to something like normal? If we can construct models showing that emissions are less than they otherwise would have been without cap and trade, is it not the case that our cap and trade program reduced emissions?

And while neo-liberal ideology and rhetoric continue to hold sway in the halls of power, the business of expanding the second modern state continues apace. While policy-makers, columnists, and captains of industry prattled on about the dangers of moral hazard, the inflationary impact of federal stimulus spending, and the wisdom and efficacy of the TARP, the Federal Reserve forestalled imminent financial collapse by pumping trillions of dollars into the financial sector through a variety of mechanisms and authorities that were invented virtually on the spot. While the cost to the public treasury is still to be reckoned, we should note that while politicians of both parties averred that they still believed in limiting state control over the domestic economy, the Federal Reserve was massively expanding its involvement in and ability to control the U.S. economy. Similarly, while efforts to establish a domestic cap and trade program drag on noisily and endlessly, Congress and the President agreed in a matter of weeks last winter to invest billions of dollars in clean energy technology and infrastructure through the stimulus, investments that by most analysis will have a profoundly greater impact on U.S. clean energy deployment and carbon emissions than the 1200 page cap and trade behemoth currently wending its way through Congress.

If the era of big government is over, what has ended is not big government itself but the willingness of most national politicians to acknowledge or defend it. The expansion of the state proceeds apace, we just prefer not to talk about it and the result of that is that we have lost our ability to critically consider what roles we want the state to play and how the state might most effectively provide the amenities which we desire of it. This outcome may not be an inevitable result of second modernity. But until some coherent and competing second modernity theory of the economy and the state emerges, neoliberal visions of the state and the economy will in fact predominate.

The greatest challenge at present to neoliberalism, as Beck somewhat elliptically notes at the beginning of his talk, is China. Undemocratic though it is, China continues to demonstrate the efficacy of direct state involvement in the economy. To date, China appears to be weathering the Great Recession better than any other economy. And it now has moved to establish a dominant position in the development and deployment of clean energy technologies.

But we should recognize that since its traditional monetarist measures stopped working last fall, China has taken Keynesian approach to the crisis that is consistent with first modernity economies and nations which is consistent with China's present development. China is today engaged in the largest and most rapid first modernity project in history, building the infrastructure of a modern state and educating a population of over a billion people in the span of a generation. So it is not clear that China is much help for second modernity societies.

Perhaps a better model is the EU's coal and steel partnership, created after World War II to repair Germany and France materially and psychologically, which was heavily funded in the early years by the United States. That prototypical transnational project was based upon the shared provision of a public good – energy. It has become the basis of a multi-decade project of transnational economic and political integration from which emerged second modernity in Europe. And yet, as predicted by Beck, this project is threatened by second modernity dynamics. Entitlement, be it to the welfare state in France or a strong international currency in Germany, has confounded the transnational project because the benefits of the EU, like the benefits of the state, are less visible. Milton Friedman is reported to have said,

›Only a crisis, real or perceived, produces real change. When that crisis occurs, the actions that are taken depend on the ideas that are lying around. That, I believe, is our basic function: to develop alternatives to existing policies, to keep them alive and available until the politically impossible becomes politically inevitable.‹

Friedman succeeded not because the crises that allowed for the emergence of multi-partisan transnational neoliberalism – oil shocks and stagflation – were themselves essentially neoliberal moments, but rather because Friedman, his colleagues and their students diligently constructed a comprehensive theory of the economy and the state, created models and analysis to support it, and then told stories that could narrate catastrophe and risk for the public and policymakers. Dealing with climate change and financial instability will require a role for the state that goes beyond both Keynesian demand creation and neoliberal market corrections and will similarly require theory, analysis, and narrative capable of defining and supporting that role.

Finally, as important as new institutional and economic models is a new ethic, one that replaces entitlement, and the cynicism that comes with it, with gratitude for our second modernity lives and past shared investments in the future. World risk society confounds world cosmopolitan society because, in its obsession with risk – the unintended consequences of modernity – it becomes blind to the remarkable and unprecedented benefits of modern life. When the second modern turns on the lights, she worries about her carbon footprint, her electricity rates, or whether her consumption might be underwriting terrorism in the Middle East, but she cannot see the now commonplace modern miracle that the lights come on at all. Without a deep and abiding appreciation of modernity, of the remarkable journey that the human species has taken, one cannot appreciate or even see the remarkable common investments that our predecessors have made through the institution of the state. And without seeing those state investments and the context that makes modernity possible, one cannot embrace a meaningful role for collective action to shape the future.

REFERENCES

Beck, Ulrich; Wolfgang Bonß and Christoph Lau (2003). The Theory of Reflexive Modernization: Problematic, Hypotheses, and Research Program. In: *Theory Culture and Society*, 20(2): 1–33

Beck, Ulrich (2008). *Risk Society's ›Cosmopolitan Moment‹*. Lecture at Harvard University, November 12, 2008

Nordhaus, Ted and Michael Shellenberger (2007). *Break Through: From the Death of Environmentalism to the Politics of Possibility*. New York: Houghton Mifflin

**Inequality and Governance
in the Global Age**

Global Inequality and Human Rights: A Cosmopolitan Perspective[1]

ULRICH BECK

The political explosiveness of social inequalities has seriously been underestimated both by social sciences and politics. Why is this so? Because politics and social sciences frame (in one way or the other) inequalities in a nation-state perspective. The social sciences up to this date are still prisoners of the nation-state. In order to unravel and understand the political explosiveness of inequalities, we have to consider one of the fundamental beliefs about modern society and its class dynamics that is »methodological nationalism«. I will develop my argument in six steps:

(1) I shall ask: what does methodological nationalism mean?
(2) What is wrong with methodological nationalism?
(3) What does »cosmopolitization« mean?
(4) What are the consequences of the human rights regime for the de-legitimation of global inequalities?
(5) How can human rights be positioned in the current cosmopolitan conjuncture?
(6) How are new cosmopolitan communities of global risk being imagined and realized?

WHAT DOES METHODOLOGICAL NATIONALISM MEAN?

Social inequality can no longer be understood in the nation state frame. The perception of social inequality in everyday life, politics and scholarship is based on a world-view that equates territorial, political, economic, social and cultural borders. In fact, however, the world is becoming ever more networked and inter-

---

[1] | Minerva Lecture, Tel Aviv University, March 2011.

connected. Territorial, state, economic, social and cultural borders still do exist, but they no longer coincide!

In the sociology of inequality everything has been questioned – classes, strata, life-styles, milieus, individualization etc. – but not the territorial reference, not the nation state framing of social inequality. Put in other words that means: the conception of social inequality is based on principles of nationality and statehood, without this so far having been (adequately) addressed in sociology. Most theorists of class, including Bourdieu (1984), who thought so extensively about globalization in his final years, identify class society with the nation state. The same is true of Wallerstein (1974), Goldthorpe (2002), in fact of almost all non-class theory sociologists of inequality, and incidentally also of my initial individualization theses of social inequality (Beck 1983).

In order to illuminate the range of this background assumption, it is useful to distinguish between *first order* and *second order* questions. First order questions refer to the »What questions« of social inequality, second order questions to »*Who* questions«. *First* order questions take as their subject the material distribution of chances and duties, resources and risks, i.e. income, education, property, etc. They presume the answer to the unposed second order questions, that is: *Who* is unequal? What *unit* of reference precedes the social inequalities? What is the appropriate frame within which the first order questions can be raised – and answered – politically as well as sociologically? Even today the congruence of political status (national membership, passport) and socio-economic status (position in the nation state hierarchy of inequality) is a tacit assumption of inequality analysis. Social researchers understand and analyze their object from the standpoint of a national us-sociology. Inequality conflicts assume nation-state norms of equality as much as they do the exclusion of the non-national others (Beck 2007). This paradigm, which unreflectingly equates political with socio-economic status, is what I call ›methodological nationalism‹ (Beck 2006; Beck and Grande 2010; Beck and Sznaider 2006, 2010; Gilroy 1993, 2008; Wimmer and Glick Schiller 2002). It is only the cosmopolitan perspective which reveals that the meta-principles of state, nationality and ethnicity constitute the frame of reference, within which the material distribution of resources is conflictually negotiated. The gaze of social science, under the spell of methodological nationalism, cannot even *see* the externalization of all the kinds of risk which are most important for the social inequality and conflict dynamics of world risk society (Beck 1999; 2009); it cannot even see that the linkage of nationality and territoriality primarily fixes the position of individuals and groups on the world scale – and that is a very important dimension of inequality! Status within a national-territorial frame, which can be *acquired*, is secondary to a *given* status of rank and politics of the *country of origin* within the international system (for example, in accordance with the distinction between centre and periphery).

In other words: methodological nationalism is based on a double assumption of congruence: on the one hand the congruence of territorial, political, economic, social and cultural boundaries; on the other, the congruence of actor perspective and social scientific observer perspective. The premise of the normative-political nationalism of actors becomes unreflectedly the premise of the social scientific observer perspective. These congruence assumptions are mutually reinforcing. The historical trend, however, is running in the opposite direction: territorial, state, economic, social boundaries continue to exist, but they are no longer coterminous!

CRITIQUE OF METHODOLOGICAL NATIONALISM

»National income« has been the main unit of research of social inequalities during the nineteenth and the first half of the twentieth century; that is, how total income was split between large social classes (workers and capitalists). This was the framing to be kept self-evident as the key topic in political economy. Methodological nationalism determines all thinking and all research concerned with inequality in three ways.

The first type of methodological nationalism asks: what determines inequality among individuals *within* a single nation? Social inequality is a dependent variable – that is something that ought to be explained by the conditions *inside* of the nation-state.

The second type of methodological nationalism could actually be called methodological *inter*nationalism, because it deals with inequality in income *among different* nations. Why is this a type of methodological nationalism? Because here again the basic unit of research on inequality is the nation-state. The advantage is the comparative method – comparing inequalities, their conditions and dynamics, between different nations. Looking at these »between-country« is, of course, an important step forward, because this way we learn what happens beyond our own national garden fence.

The third type of methodological nationalism makes »*global* inequality«, or inequality among *all* citizens of the world, to be the unit of research and politics. This inequality is the *sum* of the previous two types of inequalities: that of individuals *within* nations and that *between* nations. But this is a new topic because only with globalization have we become used to contrasting and comparing national conditions with the conditions of individual people around the globe (Milanovic 2011).

Why is this global inequality again a type of methodological nationalism? Isn't it exactly the opposite? The global perspective on inequality is the national perspective *writ large*. The »world« or »globe« becomes the unit of research (of thinking and acting). And this outlook on global inequalities will doubtlessly grow in its importance as the process of globalization enfolds.

The global perspective on inequality tries to transform national data and notions (e.g. class) into global ones. Those transformative procedures and methods have become quite sophisticated. But the more there has been a critical reflection upon their background assumptions, the more there is the conclusion that, first, »global inequality« is (like, for example, climate change) an *abstraction* which is detached from local and regional meanings; secondly, global inequality *neglects* fundamental features of reality at the beginning of the 21st century (Jasanoff 2010).

The ›nation-writ-large principle‹ also holds true for the notions some people use. For example, »the world« does have a »global middle-class« and this »global middle class« is losing status, confidence, etc. But what does »global middle class« mean? This notion is again implicitly defined as a *national* middle-class writ large! Or is it to be the majority of national middle classes? Or the middle class of the most powerful nation?

Why do I define these three ways to do research on inequalities – national, international and global – as different forms of methodological nationalism? Because all three are in fact parts of the *logic of »the national«*. You find them in the dualisms national/international and local/global. They form an »onion-model«: the local is in the core, then comes the national, then the international, then the global. And these distinctions *exclude* even the possibility, the thinkability of an alternative. But the opposite is true: this alternative exists. Reality at the beginning of the century does not fit into these dualisms any longer. These categories have become *zombie categories*. So there are problems in making the globe to be the unit of research on inequalities. But isn't this always the case? Aren't there always problems? Yes, but there is more to it.

WE DO NOT LIVE IN AN AGE OF COSMOPOLITANISM BUT IN AN AGE OF COSMOPOLITIZATION

The global perspective on inequality does *not* capture the new, irreversible, interconnectedness of the world at the beginning of the twenty-first century.

This calls for an *idea of »cosmopolitization« as »enmeshment« with the cultural Other* (Beck 2006; Delanty 2009), rather than simply being dependant with something that is on the outside. Cosmopolitization therefore is not cosmopolitanism, not globalization, not only diversity or transnationalism, since neither diversity itself or transnationalism or globality guarantee the *existential encounter with »the Other«*. This notion »cosmopolitization« is normally misunderstood, because even if I put all my emphasis on the gulf between the normative philosophical notion of »cosmopolitanisms« and the social scientific notion of »cosmopolitization«, people don't take this essential difference seriously. So there is an urgent need to clarify the empirical-analytical meaning of »cosmopolitization« by giving some examples:

- Fresh kidneys;
- Football clubs;
- World families;
- Transnational competition between »workers«;
- World religions;
- Climate change.

Fresh kidneys

The victory of medical transplantation (and not its crisis!) has swept away its own ethical foundations[2] and opened the floodgates to an occult shadow economy supplying the world market with »fresh« organs. In the radically unequal world there is obviously no shortage of desperate individuals willing to sell a kidney, a portion of their liver, a lung, an eye, or even a testicle for a pittance. The fates of desperate patients waiting for organs have become obscurely embroiled with the fates of no less desperate poor people, as each group struggles to find a solution to basic problems of survival. This is what the ›Age of And‹ (Beck 1997) creates: a cosmopolitanism of deprivation.

In a fascinating case-study the anthropologist Nancy Scheper-Hughes (2005) has shown how the excluded of the world, the economically and politically dispossessed – refugees, the homeless, street children, undocumented workers, prisoners, ageing prostitutes, cigarette smugglers, and petty thieves – are lured into selling their organs and this way becoming physically, morally, and economically »embodied« in mortally thick bodies and in persons who are rich enough to buy and »incorporate« the organs of the poor global others.

In the name of the neo-liberal ideology of the free market and a basic democratic right to unlimited choice, the fundamental values of modernity – the sovereignty of the body, the human being and the meaning of life and death – are being eliminated without anyone noticing, let alone recognizing this for what it is: a process that symbolizes our age.

We live in the Age of Both/And but think in categories of Either/Or. The notion of »Both/And« is *not intended to convey* the shallow political message that »we are all connected«; *nor* does it refer to the »*inclusive*« or »*synthesizing*« that normalizes imperialism and existing power relations by pointing to the lifesaving »spare« organs of »the global others«. The notion of the discontinuous,

---

2 | This is the basic idea of reflexive modernization (see: Beck 1994; Beck and Lau 2005).

contradictory Both/And I have in mind stands for »*impure*« cosmopolitanism *and* commerce, consent *and* coercion, gifts *and* theft, science *and* sorcery, care *and* human sacrifice. This impure, banal, coercive, dirty, bloody cosmopolitization of »living kidneys‹ has »bridged« the Either/Or between North and South, core and periphery, haves and have-nots, unbounded freedom and commodity fetishism.

In the individualized bodyscapes of Both/And, continents, races, classes, nations and religions all become fused. Muslim kidneys purify Christian blood. White racists breathe with the aid of one or more black lungs. The blonde manager gazes out at the world through the eye of an African street urchin. A secular millionaire survives thanks to the liver carved from a Protestant prostitute living in a Brazilian favela. The bodies of the wealthy are transformed into patchwork rugs. Poor people, in contrast, have been mutilated into actually or potentially one-eyed, one-kidneyed spare-parts depots, and this has occurred »by their own free will«, and »for their own good«, as the affluent sick constantly reassure themselves. The piecemeal sale of their organs is their life insurance. At the other end of the process, the bio-political »citizen of the world« emerges – a white, male body, fit or fat, with the addition of an Indian kidney or a Muslim eye, etc. In general, the circulation of living kidneys follows the established routes of capital from South to North, from poor to more affluent bodies, from black and brown bodies to white ones, and from females to males, or from poor males to more affluent ones. Women are rarely the beneficiaries of purchased organs anywhere in the world. From this it follows that the Age of And is divided and recombined into organ-selling nations versus organ buying ones.

Football clubs

The cosmopolitization of football clubs is a product of »pure« global capitalism (Milanovic 2011). The richest club is able to buy the best players of the world and will thereby be likely to dominate domestic and European championships. »Cosmopolitization« means clubs lose the national and local character but acquire, in terms of players and capital as well as supporters, a cosmopolitan flavor because the »global Other« plays in our midst.

For example London's Arsenal or Milan's Inter often do not have a single player on the field (or on the bench) who is respectively English or Italian. Their coaches are foreigners, too. Bayern München, Real Madrid, Manchester United etc. are only marginally different: they may have eight or nine foreigners out of eleven players.

This cosmopolitization, this enmeshment with the Other, has become so common that practically no one notices this anymore. From this follows: cosmopolitanized situations can be *naturalized* – in the same way as national identities.

The same is true with the »cosmopolitanized« fans. The European football clubs do have a huge fan-base in Asia, the Middle-East and a somewhat smaller one in North America. Cosmopolitization, that is the divorce between interest in and support of a club and its geographically proximity to the fans is now persuasive.

A »cosmopolitan inequality« which comes out of this is, finally, very evident too. Inequality in wealth between clubs has led to the concentration of the best players and clubs in the richest countries. Thus four nations – England, Spain, Italy and Germany – have become so thoroughly dominant in the European club football scene that this rule applies: the richest clubs, since they are able to buy the best players, are also the most successful clubs.

World families or global care chains[3]

When we speak of the family, we mostly think of emotions, of love and belonging and desire, of anger and hatred. Sometimes, we romanticize the family as a »haven in a heartless world« (Lasch 1977). Sometimes, we see it as a place filled with secrets and lies. Yet quite some time ago, feminists brought into focus that the family is not only a site of emotions but also a site of work. This work includes a broad range of activities, often summarized by the label the »Three Cs«: caring, cooking, cleaning. And, of course, far into the 20th century these tasks were considered to be women's work, assigned to them by the will of God or by nature.

Then in the 1960s in many Western countries a new role-model for women began to emerge, slowly and accompanied by many contentious debates. No longer should women be confined to the home; instead, they should take part in higher education, hold jobs, and earn their own salaries. Feminists, fiercely criticizing the polarized sexual division of labour, proclaimed a new gender order. Both men and women, so they claimed, should be active in the labour market *and* in the family household. In particular, men should do their share of family work, for instance cleaning floors, sorting rubbish, changing nappies. In recent years, the sexual division of labour has been the subject of many studies. From among the results, two trends stand out.

First: men of the younger generation, when compared to their fathers or grandfathers, take a much more active part in the upbringing of their off-spring, from taking them to kindergarten to supervising sports or playground activities.

Second: with the exception of the Scandinavian countries, the changes are modest in scope. In most countries of the West, women still bear the greatest burden of responsibilities in regard to childrearing. And when it comes to household activities, men's participation is even lower. The result is: the cosmo-

---

3 | For the following case study see Beck and Beck-Gernsheim 2011.

politization of many middle-class households; the outsourcing (or in-sourcing) of family work to women from countries of the so called Second or Third world; or, to put it differently, the rise of a transnational shadow economy.

The family household is a transnational shadow economy. When we speak of migrant domestic workers we speak of women from all parts of the globe: women from Mexico who work in California as nannies; women from the Philippines who care for the elderly in Israel and Italy; women from Poland who clean houses and do the laundry for German families.

Faced with high rates of unemployment in their home countries, these women have decided to look for work in the wealthier regions of the world. Viewed in this light, a perfect fit: supply and demand correspond closely. Yet when we look closer we find that there is a crucial flaw to this solution, a major imbalance of risks and profits for the parties involved. Obviously the migrant workers have to bear most of the risks. They are trapped in a semi-legal shadow economy. They often have no visa, no work permit, and no residence rights; also, often they have no access to public health services, unemployment benefits, or pension rights. They are vulnerable to exploitation. Last but not least, their political rights are severely restricted. Three words characterize those working in the shadow economy: hard-working, cheap, illegal.

Many of the women working abroad have left their families back in their home countries. In the old times it was proof of your love that you would stick together, no matter what. Yet now, in long distant families, for many the opposite holds true: ›For migrant domestic workers all over the globe, love means, first of all: having to go away‹ (Spring 1998: 63). In this way, new patterns of »transnational motherhood« are being created. They result in »global care chains«. While these care chains extend in many directions, crossing borders, mountains, oceans, how they do so is by no means accidental. On the contrary, they follow a distinct pattern, rooted in global inequality. ›Mothering is passed down the race/class/nation hierarchy‹ (Hochschild 2000: 137). The age of globalization creates a new global hierarchy of delegation. The work implied by the three Cs – caring, cleaning, cooking – is outsourced along the lines of nation, colour and ethnicity.

When we look at the family from a nation-state perspective, for instance with regard to the changes in national family law in the West, we find that a move toward more equality has taken place. But the picture takes on a different colour once reflexive cosmopolitization comes into view:

There is a new enmeshment with the global Other occurring right in the centre of homogenous, normal, national middle-class families and households in the US, in Europe, in Israel, in South Korea, in Canada, etc. This »fusion of horizons« is not a condition of external agency but an *internal* condition of households that develops out of the interplay of Self, Other and World relations behind the façades of one-passport, one-language face-to-face families.

This way the world's antagonisms are becoming internal to the family and at the same time transcend the national walls of national families. Suddenly and involuntarily the unequal world is personally present behind the locked doors of family live. From this encounter with the excluded global poor within Western households moral and political evaluations arise. What happens to the children of these migrant-mothers, born in Israel, who only speak Hebrew and without any accent but are still being excluded, who have no chance of gaining the legal status and rights of an Israeli citizen?

On both sides of the global divide, among rich and among poor nations, families are being fundamentally transformed. While in some ways they are drawn together, become mutually dependent, at the same time they are growing further apart, moving in opposite directions. The former gain in vital resources and the latter lose. New hierarchies are taking shape, both within middle-class families of the old Centre and within families without mothers in the poor nations.

There is a need to distinguish between two types of cosmopolitization – *with* and *without* the dialogic moment.[4] Cosmopolitization *without* dialogue and interaction, for example, occurs in outsourcing capitalism between those groups of workers whose jobs are being outsourced to different countries or continents. This creates the negative cosmopolitization of competition without dialogue or interaction – »negative« because from this arise nationalistic, *anti*-cosmopolitan sentiments and movements. In the case of global care chains a hierarchical mixture might exist. In the perspective of the Western family this is often cosmopolitization without dialogue, while the transnational mother has to wrestle with contradictory expectations, being at the same time a mother »here« and »there«. And in both cases cosmopolitization exists even or because »the Other« in the midst of our households is still excluded from civil, political and social rights.

Of course, you can neither analyse nor understand – nor even »see«! – these global transformations internal to love and family life from a national point of view.

Gainful employment: jobs are migrating to the poor regions

The increasing power of capital is prompting a sweeping transformation of the labour market, and this is occurring without public ballots or democratic decision-making processes, without consultation and without those affected having any say in the process. The labour market is being rocked by tectonic shifts and upheavals – from North to South and from West to East – which threaten the existence of millions of human beings. The latter are confronted with a new historical experience: employees in the affluent countries are becoming replace-

---

4 | This distinction has to be added to Delanty's Critical Theory of Cosmopolitanism (Delanty 2009; Delanty and He 2008).

able; they can be laid off and replaced by employees in the poor, low-wage countries.

In the era of the (First) Modernity, when the nation-states were still strong and sovereign, national borders prevented international competition among workforces. Today, by contrast, in the phase of the Second Modernity, a capitalism specialised in outsourcing breeds an increasingly virulent competition between domestic and foreign labour, pitting Korean factory workers against Japanese factory workers, Polish tradesmen against British tradesmen, etc. Here existential interdependence means that the unknown other in another country, or even in a different global region, is becoming the internal economic enemy for the inhabitants of the affluent countries because he is threatening their jobs, their wages and their prosperity. The result is that hostility towards foreigners is spreading, reaching epidemic proportions?

A coercive process of cosmopolitization is taking place above the heads of those affected, without their say, and without dialogue or communicative interaction. National borders are not presenting any obstacles to this enforced cosmopolitization, which is bypassing the claim to power and sovereignty of the nation-states. The political consequences are profound. As global competition between employees becomes a reality, resentment against the »other« in the affluent regions is on the increase. Hostility towards foreigners is spreading.

The fact that lifeworlds are no longer small-scale, isolated and provincial, but are increasingly being drawn into the turmoil of global events, by no means entails that people's horizons are becoming broader and that they are turning into urbane cosmopolitans. The cosmopolitization of living conditions and lifeworlds does not necessarily engender cosmopolitanism as consciousness and mentality. In other words, world-shock does not always entail world-openness.

The competition over truth among the world religions

For centuries, the universalistic claim of the three major monotheistic religions was tamed and civilised by the governing principle of »*cuius regio, eius religio*« – in other words, it was contained by drawing territorial boundaries. For centuries, most human beings lived in the shadow of the three monotheistic cults, each of which is founded on the claim to universalism of its »one and only God'. As the flows of migration are accelerating, as populations are becoming more multicoloured and intermingled and as the new communications media are feeding the streams of information, the different religions are coming into more direct contact. Muslims, Jews and Christians are praying in the same places. With the many millions of believers scattered throughout foreign lands, their one true gods have also spread across the globe. They, the lords of the world who brook no rivals, must now learn to live with one another in a confined space. The explosive force of this simultaneity of geographical proximity and social distance is only now becoming tangible when all of their attempts to isolate themselves from each other are already futile.

What we are experiencing here is the intermeshing and antagonism of the world religions, a multi-monotheistic entanglement (Beck 2010a). The one and exclusive God of the religious other is no longer elsewhere but is here alongside us, in our midst. The universalistic claims to validity of the different groups clash directly, leading to conflict and potentially to violence.

Climate change as an existential predicament of humankind

On the traditional understanding, climate and local weather were one and the same. Climate and weather were examples of *nature in itself*, a separate category independent of society and culture. Different regions and countries had their own specific climate: in Italy, lemon trees blossom; in England, it rains; at the North Pole, it is freezing cold; and in Germany, there is the succession of seasons and of climatic conditions: spring, summer, autumn and winter.

At the beginning of the twenty-first century, we are witnessing the »end of nature«, we are entering the post-weather era: nature and society are connected in climate change (Beck 2010c; Hulme 2010). At the same time, weather is now no longer synonymous with climate. Weather is local or regional, climate is global – or, to be more precise, cosmopolitan. The destiny of human beings in far-off regions is linked with our own, and our destiny with theirs. Climate change is calculated using global climate models because it does not stop at the borders of nation-states. Our own lives and the lives of others are directly interconnected: a person who uses an electric toothbrush in Germany bears joint responsibility or is complicit when a catastrophic thunderstorm breaks out at the other end of the earth, in Japan or Australia.

What are the consequences of these very different case studies of cosmopolitization? My answer to this question is: the word »cosmopolitan« becomes indispensable for describing a situation in which »humanity« and »world« are not only thinkable, but unavoidable moral categories for humans the world over. It is also a situation in which explicit appeal to cosmopolitan ideals is, for an elite minority, no longer merely an abstract gesture, but ostensibly a very literal possibility for the first time in human history. But at the same time we have to see the Janus face of cosmopolitization. It is clear that this consciousness comes with the unsettling recognition that the very processes that have brought the cosmopolitan possibility of human cooperation and transnational coordination so close to hand have simultaneously aggravated existing differences and, in many cases, inspired anti-cosmopolitan cleavages to emerge. Sociologically speaking, then, cosmopolitization has gained plausibility and immediacy more as a widespread elucidation of humanity's collective dilemmas at the start of the third millennium than as any specific ethical or political programme for their solution:

›Rather, we are witness to the opening of a new chapter full of strife and controversy over the very meaning not of the »good society« but of the *good world* and, significantly, who gets to define it‹ (Yates 2009: 8).

HUMAN RIGHTS OR THE DELEGITIMATION OF COSMOPOLITAN INEQUALITIES

Let me once again come back to the question: what are the basic problems of methodological nationalism? Firstly, analytically it excludes the fundamental realities of our time: the cosmopolitization of inequalities. Why? Because secondly it affirms the dualisms of local/global and national/international, which are being dissolved. Thirdly, methodological nationalism (in its different forms) *fails* to capture the problems of delegitimation of inequalities and its political explosiveness.

These fundamental weaknesses can clearly be seen in John Rawls' *Theory of Justice* (1971), but also in his later work, *The Law of Peoples* (1999; see Cheah 2006). Rawls as a philosopher is very explicit about being a methodological nationalist. How to achieve fairness within a nation was the topic of his first book; in the latter one Rawls went further and addressed the issues of global governance and global justice. But even then he only adapts an international perspective by arguing: it is a duty of liberal, »well-ordered« peoples to help »burdened« societies. Once »burdened« societies are transformed into »well-ordered« societies, differences in income levels between the nations are no longer of any relevance.

He argues: ›once […] all peoples have a working liberal or decent government, there is…no reason to narrow the gap between average wealth of different peoples‹ (Rawls 1999: 114). Those differences in Rawls' perspective are the outcome of differences justified by the (collective) performance principle and national preferences.

This nationally bounded and biased perspective on justice totally misses the question which is so important in order to understand the political dynamics and transformations of inequalities; that is, why, and under what conditions, do social inequalities (no matter if they rise or fall objectively) *lose their legitimation* (Beck 2010c). There are two conditions which are of obvious importance:

- first the *creation of equal norms*,
- second the *comparability of inequalities*.

The first condition is met by the distribution, advocation and institutionalization of human rights; the second is met by cosmopolitization of inequalities.

Both conditions interact, making inequalities (no matter if they increase or decrease) politically highly explosive.

The ongoing transformation of the Arab world demonstrates how the belief in equal norms – human rights – makes inequalities comparable and thereby politically highly explosive. And it is exactly the transnational cosmopolitical dynamics which is so obvious and surprising at the same time. A networked and jobless Arab generation is overturning the Middle East's old order of totalitarian Arab regimes. The uprising erupts across a region long resistant to change. Islamists were part of these revolts but not the instigators. They have been driven by secular youth hoping for freedom. This young »global generation« is individualized and at the same time cosmopolitanized by the internet and facebook, etc. This generation is comparing – encouraged by taking human rights seriously. Although the young Arab does not express it as loudly, his or her rebellion should be seen as a revolt not only against the aging rulers of the Middle East, but also against the political elites of their own countries who have often fallen prey to co-option tactics by regimes adept at manipulation of their opposition.

And again mainstream sociology which thinks in categories of reproduction of order, authority and systems *fails* to capture the historical moment.

POSITIONING HUMAN RIGHTS IN THE CURRENT COSMOPOLITAN CONJUNCTURE

The practical discourse of human rights claims the burden of safeguarding the most fundamental features in conditions of our humanity. In so far as this universalistic vocation can conflict with the state's governance of its citizens, human rights discourse is the other way of giving a human face to cosmopolitization as Natan Sznaider and Daniel Levy (2010) argue in their work. Thus in this perspective there is a moral and political *contradiction* between processes of cosmopolitization and human rights.

It is not difficult to illustrate this in relation to the case studies I mentioned: cosmopolitization means the global Other is no longer out there, not only near us but »*in*« us; in the case of »fresh kidneys« this »in us« does have a »bodily« meaning. At the same time »inclusion« does not exclude »exclusion«: a »Southern kidney« purifies »Northern blood«. This »inclusion« does *not* mean that the »one-kidneyed« Southern person will be included in the West; the opposite is true, he or she stays excluded. And it is exactly because he or she stays excluded that her or his »fresh kidney« is cheap and therefore becomes included into the body of, for example, a rich Western bishop or cardinal (this doesn't matter). Thus the material processes that I call cosmopolitization, touch the core and heart of what it means to be human.

On the one hand, cosmopolitization enforces an enmeshment with the global Other, which opens up spaces and perspectives for the implementation of human rights regimes. Not only transnational media and telecommunications networks but also global risks (like climate change, financial crises, and to some extent even the terrorist threat) create global publics and promise to unite us into a common humanity. This kind of »reflexive cosmopolitization« refers to the multiplicity of ways in which the social world is constructed through the articulation of a ›third culture‹ (Delanty 2009). Rather than see cosmopolitization as a particular or singular condition that either exists or does not, a state or a goal to be realized, it should instead be seen as an ethical political medium of societal transformation that is based on the principle of world openness; and this principle of world openness is associated the notion of *global publics*. Today global publics are playing a critical role in such processes of transformation. There is an emphasis on cosmopolitan moments of world openness created out of the encounter of globally mediated global risks. Viewed in these terms, reflexive cosmopolitization is a form of world disclosure and arises out of the immanent possibilities of the social world for transformation (Beck 2006; Delanty 2009).

On the other hand, in so far as these processes are related to global risks (and imperatives of capital accumulation), they also raise the deepest concerns about the continuing preservation of our humanity. This understanding of cosmopolitization as a set of processes that can have *inhuman* consequences if they are not regulated by humane influences are, of course, not new (Cheah 2006). It repeats a time analytic schema whereby the entropy characterizing human interaction and social endeavor requires a higher normative force to hold it in check, for instance, moral sentiments (Adam Smith), socialized labour (Marx), or critical reason (The Frankfurt School from Adorno to Habermas). The intensified debates about human rights in recent years are driven by this logic. As a normative system for ordering the totality of interactions between collective actors such as state and groups organized around particular interests, and between collective actors and individuals, as well as relations between individuals, a universal human rights regime confers a human face on our cosmopolitanized world. It enables us to figure the cosmopolitan condition as the human condition.

I want to distinguish here two ways of linking globalization to the actualization of humanity – human rights – in order to clarify my own position against this background: first the *liberal* account, the *transnational* account[5] and the *cosmopolitan* account.

(1) In the *liberal account* liberalization of world trade and the globalization of production in the post-Cold-War era are conductive to the worldwide institutionalization of universal human rights because the global spread of market mechanisms is necessarily accompanied by the spread of the rule of law and

---

5 | In the liberal and transnational account I follow Cheah 2006.

democratic culture, and the introduction of a »modern« mode of production erodes traditional *Gemeinschaft*-type social structures in which the rights of the rational individual are sacrificed to collective duty. Interesting enough in the current academic climate, where nationalism is often dismissed as a right-wing patriarchal ideology, this is a widely accepted account of globalization: globalization is good and national parochialism is bad for human rights in general and women's rights in particular. This narrative can be found in academic cultural studies, for example, in Arjun Appadurai's argument for post-national global order. It is also present in social policy, for example, in the entrepreneurial, corporatist internationalism informing large sections of the international organization (UN, World Trade Organization etc.).

(2) The *transnational account* acknowledges the unequal character of globalization, but still considers it as contributing to the actualization of universal humanity. It is argued that although globalization leads to increased inequality, it is nevertheless the crucible for the formation of new geographical spaces in which transnational political institutions and human rights regimes can flourish and lay the ground work for global citizenship. Saskia Sassen's (2001, 2010) influential work on global cities is the best example of this second position. Another example of this position is Michael Hardt and Antonio Negri's book, *Empire* (2000). Hardt and Negri argue that the multitude of migrant labour constitutes »a new human geography«.

(3) In the cosmopolitan account – in my understanding – the axiomatic link between transnational migration and the actualization of humanity has to be challenged by confronting this link with the »Janus-faced« processes of cosmopolitization. In order to illustrate this, I shall now challenge one of the current problems of humankind, namely the interfaces/interferences between climate change and cosmopolitanism. Climate change alters society in fundamental ways, by entailing new forms of power, inequality and insecurity – as well as new forms of corporation and solidarity – on local and global scales. There could be a hidden juncture between human rights and global risks, which needs exploration. Therefore my question is:

HOW ARE NEW »COSMOPOLITAN COMMUNITIES OF RISK« BEING IMAGINED AND REALIZED?

The key concept of cosmopolitan risk communities is extended from the work of Benedict Anderson (1983) on the rise of nation-states as »imagined communities«. As Anderson showed, nationalism is formed not through the face-to-face encounters as much as the conscious awareness that one is living through and affected by similar experiences and events with distant others. Anderson coined the term »imagined communities« to refer to how national identity is constructed. My ambition is to extend this concept and address the following question: how can we turn the concept of »imagined cosmopolitan risk communities« (Beck 2011) into a strong explanatory tool for the entangled social, economic and political consequences of climate change? To unpack this question, four points must be made:

(1) *The dynamics of climate change are Janus-faced:* with climate change, the very notion of »community« is no longer solely based on shared values. Rather, new global interconnections are established via causal interpretations of threats and responsibilities, which create a space for pragmatic accountabilities. This new cosmopolitan space, which transforms rather than replaces local and national communities, depends heavily on the power of causal definitions; and it is open to negotiation. »Climate skepticism« illustrates a degree of ambivalence within the natural sciences. Even when a working consensus on the anthropogenic nature of climate change has attained world-wide credibility (Oreskes 2004), a total agreement is unlikely across social and geographical distances. Dynamics of cooperation and conflict continue to intermingle.

(2) *Remapping political power and social inequality of changing climates:* climate change transforms short and long term social inequalities and political antagonisms at local, national, regional and global levels. The emergence of new cosmopolitan communities of risk are essentially shaped by power and resource distribution, social and natural vulnerabilities, and rich and poor regions' perceptions of injustice.

(3) *Cosmopolitization is not a fully voluntary choice:* the general social theory of cosmopolitization – as this applies to issues of finance, terrorism, migration, mass media, and environmental risks – differs starkly from normative theories of cosmopolitanism, ranging from the Stoics to Immanuel Kant (Beck 2006). Cosmopolitization is not a conscious, top-down task. Rather, it unfolds the unwanted, unseen tensions underlying existing national jurisdictions. Although nation-states remain important, there is a growing antagonism between national closure and cosmopolitan opening to the world. Yet how the cosmopolitization of climate change leads to new cosmopolitan communities of risk and how it will initiate or promote movements of re-nationalization remains an open question.

(4) *Intensified international cooperation becomes the stark realism of a cosmopolitan imperative:* this, finally, raises the question: how can global risks be successfully dealt with under the conditions of multiple competing modernities with their different normative models, material interests and political power constellations? The key to answering this question is provided by the concept of *cosmopolitical realpolitik*. In order to understand and develop this concept it has to be distinguished in particular from normative-philosophical *cosmopolitanism* on the one hand, and idealistic utopian cosmopolitanism (Held 2004; Archibugi 2008) on the other. Cosmopolitical realpolitik does not appeal (at least not pri-

marily) to shared ideas and identities, but to power and interests to be brought into play. If we adopt such a »realist« perspective, the crucial question is how the hegemonic »meta-power games« of global domestic politics (Beck 2005; 2010b) can be shaped and interests pursued in such a way that they serve the realization of common cosmopolitan goals? In short (following Mandeville 1989 [1714]), how can private vices be transformed into public, cosmopolitan virtues?

The concept of cosmopolitical realpolitik, which aims at answering this question, is based on the following assumptions. The new historical reality of world risk society is that no nation can master its problems alone. And those who play the national card will inevitably lose. Cosmopolitanism thus understood calls for neither the sacrifice of one's own interests, nor an exclusive bias towards higher ideas and ideals. On the contrary, it accepts that for the most part political action is interest-based. But it insists on an approach to the pursuit of one's own interests that is compatible with those of a larger community. Thus cosmopolitical realism basically means the recognition of the legitimate interests of others and their inclusion in the calculation of one's own interests. In this process, interests become »reflexive national interests« through repeated joint strategies of self-limitation; more precisely, empowerment arises from self-limitation. Ideally, individual and collective goals, both national and global, can be achieved simultaneously. In reality, however, there are often limits and dilemmas of cosmopolitan realpolitik (Beck and Grande 2007: chapter 8). It is no panacea for all the world's problems and it by no means always works. In particular, whether a problem has a cosmopolitan solution depends on the normative and institutional framework, in which decisions have to be taken. Nevertheless, the basic message of cosmopolitan realpolitik is this: the future is open. It depends on decisions we make.

Arguably for the first time in history, cosmopolitan commitments exert real world significance not only in responding to world risk society. A *»Hegelian« scenario* promises the emergence of a *collaborative cosmopolitan imperative: cooperate or fail*! Human rights or human catastrophe!

However, the radically unequal distribution of climate change impacts, separating the »rich producers« (the »global North«) from the »poor receivers« (the »global South«) of climatic risks, suggests a possible sinister alternative, or the *»Carl Schmitt« scenario*: »normalizing the state of emergency« (Holzinger et al. 2010). Yet, little is known about how these two opposite tendencies intermingle and their social and political consequences.

References

Anderson, Benedict (1983). *Imagined Communities: Reflections on the Origin and Spread of Nationalism.* London/New York: Verso

Appadurai, Arjun (1996). *Modernity at Large: Cultural Dimensions of Globalization*. Minneapolis: University of Minnesota Press

Archibugi, Daniele (2008). *The Global Commonwealth of Citizens: Toward Cosmopolitan Democracy*. Princeton, Woodstock: Princeton University Press

Beck, Ulrich (1983). Jenseits von Klasse und Stand? Soziale Ungleichheit, gesellschaftliche Individualisierungsprozesse und die Entstehung neuer sozialer Formationen und Identitäten. In: Reinhard Kreckel (ed.) *Soziale Ungleichheiten* (Soziale Welt – Sonderband 2). Göttingen: Verlag Otto Schwartz

Beck, Ulrich (1994). The Reinvention of Politics: Towards a Theory of Reflexive Modernization. In: Ulrich Beck, Anthony Giddens and Scott Lash (eds.). *Reflexive Modernization: Politics, Traditions and Aesthetics in the Modern Social Order*. Cambridge: Polity Press/Blackwell Publishers

Beck, Ulrich (1997). *The Reinvention of Politics: Rethinking Modernity in the Global Social Order*. Cambridge: Polity Press/Blackwell Publishers

Beck, Ulrich (1999). *World Risk Society*. Cambridge, Malden: Polity Press/Blackwell Publishers

Beck, Ulrich (2005). *Power in the Global Age: A New Global Political Economy*. Cambridge, Malden: Polity Press

Beck, Ulrich (2006). *The Cosmopolitan Vision*. Cambridge, Malden: Polity Press

Beck, Ulrich (2007). Beyond Class and Nation: Reframing Social Inequalities in a Globalizing World. In: *British Journal of Sociology*, 58(4): 679–705

Beck, Ulrich (2009). *World at Risk*. Cambridge, Malden: Polity Press

Beck, Ulrich (2010a). *A God of One's Own: Religion's Capacity for Peace and Potential for Violence.* Cambridge, Malden: Polity Press

Beck, Ulrich (2010b). *Nachrichten aus der Weltinnenpolitik*. Berlin: Suhrkamp

Beck, Ulrich (2010c). Remapping Social Inequalities in an Age of Climate Change: For a Cosmopolitan Renewal of Sociology. In: *Global Networks*, 10(2): 165–181

Beck, Ulrich (2011). Cosmopolitanism as Imagined Communities of Global Risk. In: Edward A. Tiryakian (guest editor). »Imagined Communities« in the 21st Century. Special issue of the *American Behavioral Scientist*, 55(10): 1346–1361

Beck, Ulrich and Elisabeth Beck-Gernsheim (2011). *Fernliebe. Lebensformen im globalen Zeitalter*. Berlin: Suhrkamp

Beck, Ulrich and Edgar Grande (2007). *Cosmopolitan Europe*. Cambridge, Malden: Polity Press

Beck, Ulrich and Edgar Grande (2010). Varieties of Second Modernity: The Cosmopolitan Turn in Social and Political Theory and Research. In: *British Journal of Sociology*, 61(3): 409–443

Beck, Ulrich and Christoph Lau (2005). Second Modernity as a Research Agenda: Theoretical and Empirical Explorations in the ›Meta-Change‹ of Modern Society. In: *British Journal of Sociology*, 56(4): 525–557

Beck, Ulrich and Natan Sznaider (2006). Unpacking Cosmopolitanism for the Social Sciences: A Research Agenda. In: *British Journal of Sociology*, 57(1): 1–23

Beck, Ulrich and Natan Sznaider (2010). New Cosmopolitanism in the Social Sciences. In: Bryan S. Turner (ed.). *The Routledge International Handbook of Globalization Studies*. Abingdon, New York: Routledge

Bourdieu, Pierre (1984). *Distinction: A Social Critique of the Judgement of Taste*. Cambridge: Harvard University Press

Cheah, Pheng (2006). *Inhuman Conditions: On Cosmopolitanism and Human Rights*. Cambridge, London: Harvard University Press

Delanty, Gerard (2009). *The Cosmopolitan Imagination: The Renewal of Critical Social Theory*. Cambridge: Cambridge University Press

Delanty, Gerard and Baogang He (2008). Cosmopolitan Perspectives on European and Asian Transnationalism. In: *International Sociology*, 23(3): 323–344

Gilroy, Paul (1993). *The Black Atlantic: Modernity and Double-Consciousness*. Cambridge: Harvard University Press

Gilroy, Paul (2008). The Black Atlantic as a Counterculture of Modernity. In: Sanjeev Khagram and Peggy Levitt (eds.). *The Transnational Studies Reader: Intersections and Innovations*. London, New York: Routledge

Goldthorpe, John H. (2002). Globalisation and Social Class. In: *West European Politics*, 25(3): 1–28

Hardt, Michael and Antonio Negri (2000). *Empire*. Cambridge: Harvard University Press

Held, David (2004). *Global Covenant: The Social Democratic Alternative to the Washington Consensus*. Cambridge, Malden: Polity Press

Hochschild, Arlie Russell (2000). Global Care Chains and Emotional Surplus Value. In: Will Hutton and Anthony Giddens (eds.). *On the Edge: Living with Global Capitalism*. London: Jonathan Cape

Holzinger, Markus; Stefan May and Wiebke Pohler (2010). *Weltrisikogesellschaft als Ausnahmezustand*. Weilerswist: Velbrück Wissenschaft

Hulme, Mike (2010). Cosmopolitan Climates: Hybridity, Foresight and Meaning. In: *Theory, Culture & Society*, 27(2/3): 267–276

Jasanoff, Sheila (2010). A New Climate for Society. In: *Theory, Culture & Society*, 27(2/3): 233–253

Lasch, Christopher (1977). *Haven in a Heartless World: The Family Besieged*. New York: Basic Books

Levy, Daniel and Natan Sznaider (2010). *Human Rights and Memory*. University Park; PA: Penn State University Press

Mandeville, Bernard (1989 [1714]). *The Fable of the Bees: or, Private Vices, Publick Benefits*. London, New York: Penguin Books

Milanovic, Branko (2011). *The Haves and the Have-Nots: A Brief and Idiosyncratic History of Global Inequality*. New York: Basic Books

Oreskes, Naomi (2004). The Scientific Consensus on Climate Change. In: *Science*, 306(5702): 1686

Rawls, John (1971). *A Theory of Justice*. Cambridge: Belknap Press Harvard University Press

Rawls, John (1999). *The Law of Peoples: with »The Idea of Public Reason Revisited«*. Cambridge: Harvard University Press

Sassen, Saskia (2001). *The Global City: New York, London, Tokyo*. Princeton, Woodstock: Princeton University Press

Sassen, Saskia (2010). Cities are at the Center of our Environmental Future. In: *SAPIENS*, 2(3): 1–8

Scheper-Hughes, Nancy (2005). The Last Commodity: Post-Human Ethics and the Global Traffic in ›Fresh‹ Organs. In: Aihwa Ong und Stephen J. Collier (eds.). *Global Assemblages: Technology, Politics and Ethics as Anthropological Problems*. Malden, Oxford, Carlton: Blackwell Publishing

Spring, Michelle (1998). *Running for Shelter*. Orion: London

Wallerstein, Immanuel (1974/1980/1989). *The Modern World-System, Vol. I–III*. New York, London, San Diego: Academic Press

Wimmer, Andreas and Nina Glick Schiller (2002). Methodological Nationalism and Beyond: Nation-State Building, Migration and the Social Sciences. In: *Global Networks*, 2(4): 301–334

Yates, Joshua J. (2009). Mapping the Good World: The New Cosmopolitans and Our Changing World Picture. In: *The Hedgehog Review*, 11(3): 7–27

The Politicization of Europe
A Cosmopolitan Project

EDGAR GRANDE

1. THE EUROPEAN PROJECT AND THE CONCEPT OF POLITICIZATION

In my contribution I would like to address a problem that until recently played a subordinate role in research on Europe but that nevertheless appears central to me in connection with the future of the »European project,« namely, the politicization of the European integration process. My *thesis*, on which I would like to elaborate, is that the political foundations of the process of European integration and the conditions governing how the political system of the EU functions have undergone a fundamental transformation, and this has occurred in a completely different way from that hoped for until now by the proponents of the »European project.« As a result, the political conditions for the further development of a cosmopolitan Europe have changed fundamentally – and in a paradoxical way.

The concept of *politicization* serves as the starting point for my analysis. In recent years, it has acquired steadily increasing importance in studies in political science on the European integration process, though also in studies analyzing international organizations (e.g. Bartolini 2006, 2009; Hix 2006, 2008; Hooghe and Marks 2009; Magnette and Papadopoulos 2008; Zürn 2006; for a summary, see de Wilde 2011). This concept marks a striking shift in emphasis in the research dealing with Europe. The center of attention has now shifted to the *politics* dimension of the European integration process and away from institutional (*polity*) and *policy*-oriented issues. I conjecture that the concept of »politicization« will play a similarly pivotal role in research on Europe in the coming years to the concepts of »multi-level governance« and of »Europeanization,« which have decisively shaped research on Europe over the past 10 to 15 years – and this for good reasons.

This impending new orientation in research on Europe reflects real problems and crises of the European integration process, problems that were already apparent before the current »euro crisis« (Szczerbiak and Taggart 2008). The increasing »Euroskepticism« of the populations of numerous member states of the EU, the successes of parties critical of Europe in national and European elections, the failure of the European Constitutional Treaty in the constitutional referenda in France and the Netherlands in 2005 and the rejection of the Lisbon Treaty in the Irish referendum in 2008 – all of these point to the fact that the approach to integration pursued until now ran up against its *political* limits during the 2000s. The integration of Europe by economic and political elites to the virtual exclusion of the population and the neglect of collective political opinion-formation and consensus-building, together with the resulting »deformations« of the European project, are provoking growing dissent and opposition on the part of the citizens.

What is meant by politicization in this context? Although a uniform use of the concept has not yet crystallized out in the recent literature, »politicization« can be defined, drawing on Schattschneider (1960: 16), essentially as ›expansion of the scope of (political) conflict.‹ Politicization in this sense can extend to three aspects of the political process in particular: first, the intensification of political conflicts, second, the extension of the objects of conflict, and, third, the broadening of the circle of those involved in conflicts. This conceptualization is deliberately broader than the concept of politicization in political economy, which is primarily geared to the relation between the state and the (capitalist) economy and designates an expansion or intensification of interventions by the state in the economy, and hence is focused on the second of the three dimensions of politicization (see, among others, Ronge 1980).

We can distinguish two variants of the concept of politicization in recent research on Europe, namely, a normative and an empirical variant. In the *normative* variant, politicization is treated as a *solution* to the legitimation problems of the EU (see Beck and Grande 2007; Habermas 2001; Hix 2006, 2008; Chopin 2009). »Rise up, Europeans« (Beck 2011) is the slogan of Europe's cosmopolitan friends. Extending possibilities of political participation and objects of conflict is supposed to spark the interest and mobilize the support of the citizens of the EU for the process of European integration. In this way, the democratic legitimation of the EU is supposed to be enhanced. Here research in political science is especially interested in those institutional reforms and political mechanisms through which a politicization that is regarded, all things considered, as positive and desirable can be strengthened. Relevant examples would be Europe-wide referenda, the election of the president of the Commission by the European Parliament, or the direct election of the president of the EU Council by the citizens of Europe.

In the *empirical-analytical* variant, by contrast, politicization is conceived as a *consequence* of the existing democratic and legitimation deficits of the EU – as part of the problem and not as part of the solution. In this context empirical research on politicization asserts that the stages of integration and phases of enlargement over the past twenty years have fundamentally changed the political basis of the process of integration itself. According to Lisbet Hooghe and Gary

Marks (2009), who have offered the most systematic elaboration of the concept to date, European politics has undergone a transformation from »elite politics« to »mass politics« (*politicization thesis*). According to them, not only has the level of conflict in the European politics increased as a result of this politicization, but at the same time support for the European project has also dwindled. Overstating somewhat, the citizens are rising up – but *against* Europe. Hence, politicization is proving to be a major hindrance to the further process of integration (»constraining dissensus«).

In what follows, I would like to deal in particular with this second, empirical variant of the politicization thesis. The findings of my own research projects conducted in collaboration with Hanspeter Kriesi (Kriesi et al. 2006, 2008, 2012) support the conclusion that, since the 1990s, there has in fact been a significant politicization of the process of European integration and that this politicization is has structural causes – and that its consequences involve a considerable frustration potential for normative concepts of politicization. I would now like to explain this systematically in three steps.

2. Why is the Politicization of Europe occurring?

Why did a politicization of Europe occur in the first place? The customary, and obvious, answer is that this is an immediate reaction to the recent increases in integration and rounds of enlargement of the EU, in particular to the Maastricht Agreement and the completion of the economic and monetary union. That is not completely wrong, but it does not go far enough. If one wants to understand the politicization of the European integration process, then, according to *starting hypothesis*, one must analyze it as part of a fundamental transformation of political conflicts in Europe (Kriesi et al. 2006, 2008, 2012). The weakness of large parts of research on Europe in this context resides in the fact that it is too EU-centric.

The process of social ›denationalization‹ (Zürn 1998) over the past thirty years, which includes not just European integration but all ›global transformations‹ (Held et al. 1999), has given rise to new social disparities, new antagonisms, and new forms of competition. These conflicts cut across the existing political structures of conflict at least in part and have led to a wide-ranging restructuring of political conflicts in Western Europe. At least three different types of social conflicts can be distinguished in detail:

(1) *economic conflicts* owing to the greater economic competitive pressure exercised by a globalized market;
(2) cultural conflicts owing to greater cultural diversity within national societies; and

(3) political conflicts owing to the loss of national sovereignty rights and national political identities, conflicts which are especially intense in Europe because of the integration process.

These conflicts are giving rise to new groups of (real and potential) »winners« and »losers«, through which a *new political fault line*, a new »cleavage« in the sense of Lipset and Rokkan (1967), has arisen in the Western European countries. This conflict between winners and losers of denationalization can be described in general terms as a conflict between *integration* and *demarcation* or between *cosmopolitanism* and *nationalism*. This new antagonism has both economic and cultural dimensions and in each of these two dimensions one can distinguish an outward-looking, or global market-oriented, integrationist (»cosmopolitan«) position from a defensive, protectionist (»national«) one. In its normative variant, ›cosmopolitan Europe‹ (Beck and Grande 2007; cf. Delanty and Rumford 2005) makes a plea for such an integration-friendly intensification of the European project in a global context.

In this way, the concrete significance of the cultural dimension of conflict in the Western European countries (Germany, France, Great Britain, the Netherlands, Austria, and Switzerland) has changed fundamentally over the past two decades. In the meantime, the cultural line of conflict in these countries is constituted by those themes that are shaped by the globalization conflicts outlined above. These are, on the one hand, cultural conflicts over the integration of foreigners: The old religious conflicts are being replaced in all Western European countries by new kinds of culturally conditioned conflicts over the social and cultural integration of societies marked in particular by attitudes towards foreigners, immigrants, and foreign cultures (»Islam«). On the other hand, it is the theme of Europe that is providing the emblematic articulation of problems of political globalization. In all countries, the importance of attitudes to political globalization (in particular to European integration) for the formation of political identities has increased (by comparison with older liberal values). The planned EU accession of Turkey derives its political explosiveness from the fact that here two conflict issues (»Islam« and the EU) come together that until now were constitutive for the new cosmopolitanism-nationalism cleavage.

Comparing the relative importance of the two dimensions of conflict shows, in addition, that the importance of the cultural conflict dimension has increased in most of the countries we have studied. In four of the six countries it now represents the dominant dimension of conflict and it is especially pronounced in Great Britain and the Netherlands. The two exceptions over the past decade were Germany and Switzerland.

3. WHAT ARE THE IMPLICATIONS OF THIS RESTRUCTURING OF POLITICAL CONFLICTS FOR THE EU AND THE PROCESS OF EUROPEAN INTEGRATION?

The question becomes whether and in what way this new political potential is organized and articulated. The main factor in this context is which of these conflicts is emphasized and how they are related to each other. We can distinguish between two *different logics of political conflict* in this regard, an economic and a cultural logic. Both logics articulate structural conflicts of globalization and of the European integration process, but they do so in completely different ways. A cultural conflict logic not only stresses the negative consequences of political integration and growing cultural diversity but also interprets economic conflicts in cultural categories. In contrast, an economic conflict logic accords central importance to the negative consequences of economic integration and transforms cultural and political conflicts in such a way that they exacerbate the economic confrontation. One can conjecture in this regard each of that the two political logics is utilized by different political actors. As our analyses of the political consequences of globalization have shown, the cultural conflict logic is utilized above all by the new right-wing or right-wing populist parties, whereas left-wing populist parties and social movements thematize the conflicts of the European integration process primarily in economic categories.

The decisive point is that, in both conflict logics, the EU is perceived as part of the problem – and not as part of the solution. If one follows the economic conflict logic, then the EU with its single market program does not appear to the »losers« of globalization to represent a counterweight to a »neoliberal« form of globalization, but instead its acceleration and intensification. From this perspective, it is difficult, if not impossible, to distinguish between the advantages of a single European market and the drawbacks of a global economic integration, assuming that such a distinction even makes sense. In the cultural conflict logic, the EU is regarded as an immediate threat to national identities, national institutions, and national democratic practices; and an enlargement process without clearly defined limits and goals is perceived as a threat to the (supposedly existing) cultural homogeneity of »old« Europe. At best, the process of European integration seems to confront the European citizenry with a highly risky choice: they are supposed to forgo their national sovereignty and identity in exchange for a new economic and political power that is difficult to understand and control. And they are supposed to respond to crises of the European project with »more Europe« and not less. Against this background it is hardly surprising that the EU has become a decidedly soft target for all possible forms of – right- and left-wing – populist protest.

4. Manifestations of the Politicization of Europe

What effects does this have on the politicization of the European integration process? First, I have to concede by way of qualification that, although empirical evidence can indeed be cited in support of the politicization thesis, it nevertheless still stands on shaky feet. In particular, there is a lack of analyses that study the politicization of the integration process over a long period of time and for all relevant political levels and arenas. This is the subject of a research project currently being conducted under my and Hanspeter Kriesi's direction. Analyses of *national* politics are especially important in this connection, however paradoxical this may sound. Based on our findings to date, one can identify a quite specific *politicization profile* for the European integration process that exhibits three characteristic features in particular:

(1) The politicization of Europe is taking place in the electoral arena in particular, whereas »Europe« hardly occurred in the protest arena at all. Our analysis of protests events in six Western European countries from the mid-1970s to 2009 shows that the number of protests on the topic of Europe is vanishingly small (Hutter 2010; Kriesi et al. 2012). Overall, less than one percent of all protest events are correlated with this topic. Only during the 1990s can one discern a slight increase in importance of the European theme in the protest arena, though it disappears again during the 2000s. This is not to imply that the new cultural conflicts as a whole do not play any role in the protest arena. But, in contrast to the electoral arena, here it is exclusively the theme of foreigners and immigration that provides the occasion for mobilizations. Europe as a political project has yet to »move« people. This picture is confirmed by the constellation of actors featuring in public debates on the theme of Europe in recent years. These debates are dominated by the political elites, in particular by government or public figures from national or European politics (see also Koopmans 2007). Civil society actors, including unions, scarcely feature in these debates.

(2) Europe has now advanced to a salient theme in *national elections* in all of the countries studied. Aside from the theme of foreigners and immigration and classical themes of cultural liberalism, it defines the cultural dimension of the political space. In the electoral arena, the political potentials of globalization are mobilized especially by right-wing populist parties, though in the meantime also by new left-wing populist parties (such as the Socialist Party in the Netherlands). Both groups advocate national protectionist and interventionist programs, and both groups mobilize against the EU in its current form. The success of the right-wing populist parties is due to the fact that they articulate conflict issues that are situated in the cultural dimension of the new cleavage (Mudde 2007). Aside from a critique of the political establishment – that is, the established major parties and interest groups – two themes in particular feature centrally in the right-wing populist mobilization strategy: the rejection of further integration

and of a liberal integration and asylum policy, on the one hand, and the defense of national sovereignty over against the European Union and the rejection of Turkey's accession to the EU, on the other. These two themes constitute the »demarcation« or »nationalism« pole of the new cleavage – and it is here, in particular, that the politicization through the new right-wing populist parties takes place. The current crisis of the euro is also interpreted by the radical right in cultural terms in a variation on »affluence chauvinist« positions. Emblematic of this position is the Austrian FPÖ, which, under the slogan »Our money for our people,« mobilized in summer 2011 against the »euro rescue parachute« and financial transfers to countries such as Greece.

(3) The last two European elections, finally, have given rise to a new type of populist party that sets itself apart exclusively through its rejection of the EU. These anti-EU parties, in contrast to right-wing populist parties, are single issue parties that mobilize support exclusively through their criticism of the EU and do not share the hostility toward foreigners of the right-wing populist parties in the same way. The UK Independence Party, which campaigns for the withdrawal of Great Britain from the EU, describes itself expressly as »libertarian« and »non-racist,« even though it broadened its ideological profile in recent years by adopting restrictive positions in immigration and integration policy. In the 2004 and 2009 European elections, the UKIP won 16.8 and 16.5 percent of the votes, respectively, and thereby became the second-strongest British party (ahead of the Liberal Democrats and Labour). A second example is Hans-Peter Martin's List in Austria, which in the 2004 European election won 14 percent and in the 2009 European election almost 18 percent of the popular vote. It is significant that to date both parties have remained irrelevant in national elections. This need not necessarily remains so. The success of the »True Finns« in the Finnish general election shows that, in the wake of the euro crisis, right-wing populist parties can also be extremely successful at the national level with strictly anti-European positions.

5. THE PARADOX OF THE POLITICIZATION OF EUROPE

These empirical findings can be summarized in three theses:

- The *first thesis* is that the European integration process has led to the emergence of new structural antagonisms that form the basis of an increasing and enduring politicization of the European political process.
- The *second thesis* is that the politicization of Europe is occurring to a large extent on the national level. Since the 1990s, Europe has become a salient theme in national elections and an object of »mass politics.«
- The *third thesis* states that the politicization of Europe is not taking place – as

Simon Hix (2006, 2008), for example, assumes – along the traditional left-right axis but instead on a newly defined cultural line of conflict, especially through new right-wing populist parties (and in European elections also through new anti-EU parties).

Therefore, the politicization of Europe, until now at least, was not brought about by the advocates of the EU who in recent years have called for such a politicization, and it did not take place in the way they proposed either. In the mobilization of European citizens on themes of European integration, the greatest successes were achieved by the critics of the EU and the defenders of national identity and sovereignty. And the »euro crisis« has had the effect of increasing skepticism toward the EU and its institutions among the citizens rather than of fostering their willingness to act in solidarity in a European »community of fate.« From a normative perspective, therefore, the politicization of Europe appears at first sight to be a highly ambivalent process.

This is hardly surprising since openness and structural ambivalence are basic hallmarks of the process of reflexive modernization in which the denationalization of society is embedded (see Grande 2008). The transformation of modern contemporary societies currently taking place is an open process that can proceed in fundamentally different directions. The theory of reflexive modernization chiefly developed by Ulrich Beck is neither fixated on a specific result nor does it claim to predict such a result (see Beck et al. 1994). It can at most specify the conditions that make one particular, normatively preferred course of development more probable than another. The direction that the process of reflexive modernization actually pursues and its social effects depend crucially on social and political constellations of forces, options and strategies for coalitions, institutional opportunity structures, and public possibilities for thematization, among other factors (Beck 2002).

This also holds for the process of European integration. The politicization of the European integration process by civil society actors and movements is a key presupposition for advancing Europe as a cosmopolitan project (Beck and Grande 2007: Ch. 5). Where this politicization is missing or the civil society actors are too weak, the European project is unavoidably deformed. This presupposes, however, that these actors also in fact constitute the cosmopolitan pole of the new cleavage. Empirically speaking, however, this is not at present the case, as is shown by our analysis of the European policy debates between 2004 and 2006. In these debates, in which the decisive issues of the Constitutional Treaty and the enlargement of the EU (including Turkey's EU accession) were discussed, the cosmopolitan pole of the new cleavage was occupied only by a small »cosmopolitan coalition« in which primarily the Greens, and in Germany and Switzerland also in addition the social democratic parties, featured (see Kriesi et al. 2012: Ch. 10). Civil society actors (unions, social movements,

NGOs) form a different »economic-interventionist coalition.« This coalition sets itself apart primarily in the economic dimension from the »neoliberal consensus« in Western European politics. The different players comprising this coalition are united by the demand for interventionist and protectionist policies in the domain of the economy and of the social security systems. In the cultural dimension, hence on themes such as immigration and Europe, the profile of the individual groups tends to be diffuse, heterogeneous, and in part critical of Europe and globalization.

Nevertheless, the alternative to a politicization of Europe by the new populist right cannot reside in a rejection of politicization, much less in a de-politicization of the process of integration. Such a rejection would not strengthen Europe in the face of its (populist) critics, but on the contrary would weaken it. For the already serious (technocratic, national, and economic) deformations of the European project would thereby inevitably increase – and as a result provide further grist to the mill of the populist critique.

If renouncing politicization does not offer a way out of the political crisis in which the European project has been plunged by its politicization, then the politicization of Europe leads to a paradox. The only remaining answer to the mounting criticism by right-wing and left-wing populists of the European project and its further politicization is: *more politicization*. However, such a counter-politicization must not simply allow itself to be drawn into the discourse and the political logics of the Eurosceptic populists. Instead it must itself change the conditions of the discourse. However, its success, and not least the prospects of a cosmopolitization of Europe, must not depend crucially on whether it manages to unite the hitherto separate »coalitions,« which provide a home for such pro-European political parties and civil society actors, into a »cosmopolitan coalition.« The radical right has shown in recent years that a politicization of Europe is a very real possibility. Through its mobilization of the citizens, Europe changed into a theme of »mass politics« instead of the subject of »elite politics.« Whether this »uprising« of the citizens can also be harnessed *in support of* its further cosmopolitization – that is currently not just an open political question but also an open question for research.

References

Bartolini, Stefano (2006). Should the Union be ›Politicised‹? Prospects and Risks. In: *Notre Europe Etudes & Recherches,* Policy Paper No 19: 28–50

Bartolini, Stefano (2009). The Nature of the EU Legitimacy Crisis and Institutional Constraints: Defining the Conditions for Politicisation and Partisanship. In: Olaf Cramme (ed.). *Rescuing the European Project: EU Legitimacy, Governance and Security.* London: Policy Network

Beck, Ulrich (2005). *Power in the Global Age.* Cambridge: Polity Press
Beck, Ulrich (2011). Empört euch, Europäer. In: *Der SPIEGEL,* 34: 128–129
Beck, Ulrich; Anthony Giddens and Scott Lash (1994). *Reflexive Modernization.* Cambridge: Polity Press
Beck, Ulrich and Edgar Grande (2007). *Cosmopolitan Europe.* Cambridge: Polity Press
Chopin, Thierry (2009). The Limits of the Functionalist Method: Politicisation as an Indispensable Means to Settle the EU's Legitimacy Crisis. In: Olaf Cramme (ed.). *Rescuing the European Project: EU Legitimacy, Governance and Security.* London: Policy Network
Delanty, Gerard and Chris Rumford (2005). *Rethinking Europe: Social Theory and the Implications of Europeanization.* London: Routledge
De Wilde, Pieter (2011). No Polity for Old Politics? A Framework for Analyzing the Politicization of European. In: *Journal of European Integration* 33(5): 559–575
Grande, Edgar (2008). Reflexive Modernisierung des Staates. In: *der moderne staat* 1(1): 7–27
Habermas, Jürgen (2001). *The Postnational Constellation.* Cambridge: Polity Press
Held, David; Anthony McGrew, David Goldblatt, and Jonathan Perraton (1999). *Global Transformations: Politics, Economics and Culture.* Cambridge: Polity Press
Hix, Simon (2006). Why the EU Needs (Left-Right) Politics? Policy Reform and Accountability are Impossible Without It. In: *Notre Europe Policy Etudes & Recheres,* Policy Paper No 19: 1–27
Hix, Simon (2008). *What's Wrong with the European Union and How to Fix It.* Cambridge: Polity Press
Hooghe, Liesbeth and Gary Marks (2009). A Postfunctionalist Theory of European Integration: From Permissive Consensus to Constraining Dissensus. In: *British Journal of Politic Science,* 39(1): 1–23
Hutter, Swen (2010). *Protest Politics and the Right Populist Turn: A Comparative Study of Six West European Countries, 1975–2005.* Ph.D. Thesis: Munich University
Koopmans, Ruud (2007). Who Inhabits the European Public Sphere? Winners and Losers, Supporters and Opponents in Europeanised Political Debates. In: *European Journal of Political Research* 46(1): 183–210
Kriesi, Hanspeter; Edgar Grande, Romain Lachat, Martin Dolezal, Simon Bornschier and Timotheus Frey (2006). Globalization and the Transformation of the National Political Space: Six European Countries Compared. In: *European Journal of Political Research* 45(6): 921–956

Kriesi, Hanspeter; Edgar Grande, Romain Lachat, Martin Dolezal, Simon Bornschier and Timotheus Frey (2008). *West European Politics in the Age of Globalization.* Cambridge: Cambridge University Press

Kriesi, Hanspeter; Edgar Grande, Martin Dolezal, Marc Helbling, Dominic Höglinger, Swen Hutter and Bruno Wüest (2012). *Restructuring Political Conflict in Western Europe.* Cambridge: Cambridge University Press

Lipset, Seymour M. and Stein Rokkan (1967). Cleavage Structures, Party Systems, and Voter Alignments: An Introduction. In: Seymour M. Lipset and Stein Rokkan (eds.). *Party Systems and Voter Alignments: Cross-National Perspectives.* New York: Free Press

Magnette, Paul and Yannis Papadopoulos (2008). On the Politicization of the European Consociation: A Middle Way Between Hix and Bartolini. In: *European Governance Papers (EUROGOV)* No. C–08–01, [http://www.connex-network.org/eurogov/pdf/egp-connex-C-08-01.pdf]

Mudde, Cas (2007). *Populist Radical Right Parties in Europe.* Cambridge: Cambridge University Press.

Ronge, Volker (ed.) (1980). *Am Staat vorbei: Politik der Selbstregulierung von Kapital und Arbeit.* Frankfurt/M., New York: Campus

Schattschneider, Elmer E. (1960). *The Semi-Sovereign People: A Realist's View of Democracy in America.* New York: Holt, Rinehart and Winston

Szczerbiak, Aleks and Paul Taggart (eds.) (2008). *Opposing Europe? The Comparative Party Politics of Euroscepticism.* 2 Vols. Oxford: Oxford University Press

Zürn, Michael (1998). *Regieren jenseits des Nationalstaates: Globalisierung und Denationalisierung als Chance.* Frankfurt/M.: Suhrkamp

Zürn, Michael (2006). Zur Politisierung der Europäischen Union. In: *Politische Vierteljahresschrift,* 47(2): 242–251

The Future of Global Inequality

ANJA WEISS

Like how to deal with beggars. They seemed to be everywhere, a gallery of ills – men, women, children, in tattered clothing matted with dirt, some without arms, others without feet, victims of scurvy or polio or leprosy walking on their hands or rolling down the crowded sidewalks in jerry-built carts, their legs twisted behind them like contortionists'. At first, I watched my mother give over her money to anyone who stopped at our door or stretched out an arm as we passed on the streets. Later, when it became clear that the tide of pain was endless, she gave more selectively, learning to calibrate the levels of misery. Lolo thought her moral calculations endearing but silly, and whenever he caught me following her example with the few coins in my possession, he would raise his eyebrows and take me aside.
»How much money do you have?« he would ask.
I'd empty my pocket. »Thirty rupiah.«
»How many beggars are there on the street?«
I tried to imagine the number that had come by the house in the last week. »You see?« he said, once it was clear I'd lost count. »Better to save your money and make sure you don't end up on the street yourself.« [...]
»Your mother has a soft heart,« Lolo would tell me one day after my mother tried to take the blame for knocking a radio off the dresser. »That's a good thing in a woman. But you will be a man someday, and a man needs to have more sense.«
It had nothing to do with good or bad, he explained, like or dislike. It was a matter of taking life on its own terms.
Barack Obama, »Dreams from my Father«, p. 38-9

Barack Obama spent part of his childhood in an Indonesian middle class neighbourhood and he wrote about it in his autobiography 1995. The story quoted above is a focal metaphor for the problem of global inequality.[1] It points at the atrocity of abject poverty and the overwhelming numbers of the absolute poor. Then it offers two solutions: Obama's American mother tries to give as much

---

1 | I would like to thank Karen Shire and Manuela Boatcă for their helpful comments.

as she can. Faced with a disproportion between her means and the degree of misery she attempts »moral calculations endearing but silly«. His Indonesian middle class father[2] Lolo, on the other hand, advises the young Barack to save his sparse means and to focus on himself not becoming poor. Whereas Barack is inclined to see inequality as a moral question Lolo sees acting upon self-interest as a fact of life. Finally it is interesting that the story exists at all. It is unusual – to say the least – that a future US president has actually encountered abject poverty and that he chooses to write about it. Many stories in Obama's autobiography are open ended as he lets other persons offer solutions. Still, this one seems to offer particularly little perspective.

This could also be said about the sociology of global inequalities. Most of sociology does not look beyond the OECD world and if sociologists do take a glimpse they are mostly occupied with a cartography of inequalities performed in a methodologically nationalist perspective (for a critique see Beck 2007a; Weiß 2005). Comparison focuses on the interior of nation states and then goes on to compare indicators averaged for an entire nation-state. It therefore is easier to compare an unemployed person in Essen with an industrialists' wife living at Lake Constant than to compare a Chinese seamstress with the customers wearing the products of her labour. Citizenship may be an important foundation of social rights in strong states able to impact on the welfare of their citizens. For a person situated in Sierra Leone her citizenship is a very good empirical indicator of her life chances, but analyses using the national frame as an explanatory concept create the wrong impression that weak states are agents in the structuration of inequality rather than for example: the bio-political development of the HIV crisis, the agendas of large donor agencies and large corporations, and worldwide struggles over the continued significance of race (Weiß 2006).

Sociology has not invested much thought in the nature of global inequalities. Consequently the major conceptual contributions to the theory of social inequality have recently come from economists (Milanovic 2005; Sen 1985, 1999b) and philosophers (Fraser 2007; Nussbaum 2007). Sen has for example suggested that capabilities develop in the interplay between personal characteristics and life goals on the one hand and social and physical environments on the other (Sen 1999a: 70ff). The capability approach has been operationalized in a somewhat simplistic manner in the World Bank's Human Development Index. Still it moves beyond a mere distribution approach. Newer economic approaches try to place individuals or households both in a national and a global frame (Milanovic 2008). And the philosopher Fraser asks the important question how justice can be framed beyond the nation state.

---

2 | I am trying to avoid the term »step father« here as it is derogatory, but I am aware of the fact that Lolo is a father in social and not in genealogical terms.

›Although it went unnoticed at the time, the Keynesian-Westphalian frame gave a distinctive shape to arguments about social justice. Taking for granted the modern territorial state as the appropriate unit, and its citizens as the pertinent subjects, such arguments turned on what precisely those citizens owed one another. [...] Engrossed in disputing the ›what‹ of justice, the contestants apparently felt no necessity to dispute the ›who‹. With the Keynesian-Westphalian frame securely in place, it went without saying that the ›who‹ was the national citizenry‹ (Fraser 2007: 253).

According to Fraser (2008) debates about political (mis-)representation constitute a meta-discourse about the preconditions of struggles about justice.

Given the current constraints of sociological thought on the matter we must use economic and philosophical foundations as a starting point and then aspire to a more sociological perspective understanding the institutional structures underlying the genesis and perpetuation of global inequality. In a nutshell Obama's story contains the most relevant strands in social thought on the matter. There is a »rational« and realist perspective focusing on the capitalist world-economy contained by national welfare states at least in the core. It can explain the »hoarding and ignoring« approach proposed by Lolo. Its moral stance is more aspiring than that of Lolo, but, given the expiration of revolutionary dreams, it offers little hope of overcoming the »facts of life«. A much less prominent strand of theory has dealt with non-capitalist economies or »non-economic« economies of gifts reproducing social life such as soft hearted women with moral standards. ›Global care chains‹ (Hochschild 2000; for a discussion of care see Nussbaum 2007: 164 ff.) are characterized by »irrational« emotional connections both based on and overcoming extremes of inequality. Finally sociology also has something to say about the fact of an American president facing up to the problem of global poverty. Is this a chance event or a telling episode? The three perspectives discussed in this contribution start from diverging assumptions and they offer disparate ideas about the future of global inequalities. But they emphasize the main points: It is in the spheres of the economy, of the exploitation of »other« resources and in changed perceptions of the world that the future of global inequality unfolds.

HOARDING AND IGNORING. THE »FACTS OF LIFE« APPROACH

Political theory has it that the segmentation of the world into nation-states is a necessary precondition for the sovereignty of the people (Habermas 1998). Especially liberal states depending on general suffrage have to decide who belongs to their citizenry and whose welfare should be guarded by their institutions (Brubaker 1992; Marshall 1950). In this perspective, the fact that some states are not treating their citizens well and that these citizens may then drown in the

Mediterranean, is viewed as an unavoidable side-effect of a nation-state system which is still the best of many bad alternatives.

From the perspective of world-systems theory the state serves a largely different purpose. Wallerstein has argued that margins for profit would be so low in truly non-regulated markets that capitalist enterprising would not be worth the effort (Wallerstein 2004: 26). Therefore, for the functioning of a capitalist world-system protectionism is a must. States are needed in order to protect monopolies in the core and thereby increase rates of profit (Wallerstein 1979: 223, 291). This is not to say that monopolies remain stable. For example textile production was a monopoly guaranteeing Britain's position in the world throughout early industrialization. By now it has moved to low-wage countries and patent offices make sure that core states profit from the biodiversity still found in the periphery (Randeria 2003). Monopolies need not be complete and they can change in content, but they must be guaranteed by core states in order to institutionalize the unequal terms of trade ensuring profits for core state industries.

Viewed in this perspective, the position of »workers« in core states becomes an ambivalent one (Korzeniewicz and Moran 2009: 104). On the one hand, they struggle against capital. Therefore, institutions such as labour relations and the welfare state can be interpreted as results of anti-bourgeois struggle as they mediate the impact of capitalism. On the other hand, the funding of these institutions depends on unequal exchange in the capitalist world-system. In economic terms, Wallerstein argues, workers in core states are de facto bourgeois because they live off the surplus value generated by core state protectionism (Wallerstein 1979: 291).

This should be a problem for critical and especially leftist perspectives on global inequalities. In core states it is common practise to commiserate the fate of the lower middle classes and the negative impact of »globalization« on job security. These discourses conveniently forget that their object of solidarity may be poor, at risk etc. and at the same time drives cars at the price of a village elsewhere. Analyses of industrial relations, social policy, and the labour market have to face up to the fact that even some of their most innovative and radical suggestions such as the idea that every citizen of Germany (or Europe respectively) is entitled to a »guaranteed basic income« (Beck 2000: 144, 2007b) can be seen as based on national protectionism and unfair terms of trade.[3]

In contrast to arguments prevailing in political theory Wallerstein is pessimistic about the ability of peripheral states to guard their citizens' interests (Wallerstein 1979: 61). Under conditions of unequal exchange peripheral states do not and cannot have the financial means to gain independence from the eco-

---

3 | Beck (2007b: 215) actually notes that transnational social movements are dependent on capitalism, but he focuses on the cultural impact of capitalism, not on economic exploitation.

nomic sphere.[4] We have found this view supported by newer research on world society: John Meyer and his group show that norms about the tasks of states do indeed spread, but practice is a wholly different matter. Instead zones of limited statehood (Beisheim and Schuppert 2007) are characterized by facade offices simulating the ›proper‹ workings of a state.

Lolo's idea of ›keeping your pocket money to yourself‹ is institutionalized in a system of states in which core states protect their capital's and workers' interests from free competition and in which peripheral zones of limited statehood and their populations have little chance of prosperity. This system of states makes sure that economic gains in the core states – including the ›pocket money‹ for the poorer parts of the population – amount to a lot more than the economic resources in the periphery.

This picture, of course, is too simplistic. Wallerstein himself has emphasized that semi-peripheries are vital for the capitalist world-system as they serve as buffers between core states and peripheral regions. However, in a »realist« perspective some movement in the middle does not contradict the main point. Also, Wallerstein's empirical analyses have been refined and debated (Abu-Lughod 1989; Gilroy 1993). Countries have been known to rise in world hierarchies[5] and newer theories of modernization and globalization point to the importance of path-dependencies, the cultural and historical sphere (Boatcă and Spohn 2010; Eisenstadt 2000).

Also, the mobility of people has not been a main interest in Wallersteinian analyses, but was taken up as an issue by newer analysts of the capitalist world-system (Boatcă 2009; Korzeniewicz and Moran 2009: 107 ff.). In a different version of systems theory Hoffmann-Nowotny (1970) has argued that migration may buffer some of the structural tensions in the world system. However migration is not unconstrained, but globalization has resulted in ›globalization for some, localization for some others‹ (Bauman 1998). The state system is causal for significant inequalities (Weiß 2005), not only because peripheral states are treating their citizens badly, but also because core states regulate non-citizens' mobility in a highly exclusive manner (Pécoud and De Guchteneire 2007; Shamir 2005) neglecting even very basic human rights.

A realist picture of the future of global inequality is stark. If things remain as they are there is little incentive nor chance for change. Global inequality is woven into a system of nation-states; political theory assumes contra-factually that all states are or will be able to contribute to their citizens' well-being and it is legiti-

---

4 | Lockwood (1964) has argued aptly that system differentiation depended on the development of an efficient system of taxation in Europe, too.

5 | Korzeniewicz and Moran (2009: 106) argue that the rise of individual countries has not changed the general structure, but they also think that the rise of China and India due to their largeness *may* result in structural impact.

mized by a sociology of social inequality which focuses on the interior of wealthy states.

ENDEARING BUT SILLY:
THE »OTHER« SIDE OF CAPITALIST PRODUCTION

Take a second and consider with whom you are sympathizing in Obama's story, Lolo or his mother? And: how would you advise your child?

Marginal but pervasive perspectives in realist theories have developed arguments about the »non-economic« bases of capitalism. Rosa Luxemburg for example thought that primary accumulation feeds on non-capitalist forms of economic exchange:

›The general result of the struggle between capitalism and simple commodity production is this: after substituting commodity economy for natural economy, capital takes the place of simple commodity economy. Non-capitalist organisations provide a fertile soil for capitalism; more strictly: capital feeds on the ruins of such organisations‹ (Luxemburg 1951 [1913]: 416).

Bourdieu and other authors in the tradition of social anthropology show an interest in economies of symbolic goods and their interaction with capitalist market economies in the process of increasing asymmetric incorporation (Bourdieu 1998; Rehbein 2006). Feminist scholars follow a similar line of reasoning by saying that subsistence economies grant a living for large parts of the world's population which enables capitalist economies to use only the young and healthy for work in industrial production (Bennholdt-Thomsen and Mies 1997; Evers 1987; Ong 1987; Potts 1988). Generally any division of reproductive labor between men and women means that capitalism profits from the lesser remuneration of women's family work. Even in the core, where capitalists had to start paying family wages, women remain responsible for the physical production and social reproduction of capitalist workers in addition to them being employed as workers (Becker-Schmidt et al. 1984) – a combination which Beck-Gernsheim and Beck have characterized as partial modernization of women's lives or, put differently, as a continuance of feudal status in the lives of women (Beck-Gernsheim 1980; Beck and Beck-Gernsheim 1994).

All the arguments in this line of reasoning are characterized by an ambiguity. On the one hand they show how capitalist markets exploit and destroy non-capitalist modes of (re-) production. On the other hand, one wonders how capitalism could sustain itself without feeding on other logics. The invisible hand of the market (Smith) may be vital for capitalist market economies, but the support of the invisible hands of persons like Obama's mother bound by personal loyalty, acting in the shades of informal economies, and considering symbolic goods to be more important than material advantage may be as important.

Women who are able to care for others are however becoming a scarce resource fast. The commodification of care work in the core is growing, and the importation of care workers from abroad has resumed in core states. Migrant domestics are themselves importing care workers from abroad who in turn depend on family members accepting additional care work at home and so on (Hochschild 2000; Lutz 2008; Morokvasic-Müller et al. 2003; Parreñas 2000). We know little about the other end of these global chains of care. Considering that more and more persons in the world are directly included in market economies, we may suspect that the »other« ends of chains of care may not be happily enfolded in a well functioning extended family.

Research on employment in the private sphere nevertheless shows a similar ambiguity as that discussed above. Irrespective of their exploitative relationship both employers and employees in private households emphasize that they are friends or that they respect each other (Cyrus and Weiß 2005). If we compare forms of unequal exchange which are mediated by abstract institutions in the world economy with unequal exchange taking place in chains of care where employers might actually meet or see pictures of the children whose mother is working as a nanny for their own children, might there be a difference? Employers in care markets struggle with the difference because on the one hand they are not offering fair working conditions but on the other hand the specific woman whom they employ now has a job which supports her family. Also very often they themselves are under significant pressure to both work and take care of their families. So it is both unfair to employ an informal worker and not to employ her and this is exactly the situation in which Obama's mother finds herself: She is unable to rectify the evils of her world, but she tries to and shows compassion.

In the realist strand, sociology has treated emotional connections in exploitative labor relations as »ideology« glossing over the contradictions of unfair exchange. If we assume that »non-economic« forms of reproduction continue to exist and even offer sustenance to capitalism, this could result in a different kind of evaluation. By describing their (unfair) employment relation as a friendship employers and employees create a moral economy which offers some sustenance in the face of moral dilemmas.

So far the sociology of social inequalities has focused on the distribution of material resources and mostly left debates about moral economies, recognition and hegemony to other disciplines. Justice however comprises two interwoven aspects: a fair distribution of resources and a chance for recognition (Fraser and Honneth 2003). The sociology of global inequality should develop a stronger interest in informal, moral and »other« economies and their interaction with formal institutions. With respect to global inequality the representation and recognition of »others« as humans endowed with human rights (Butler 2009; Nussbaum 2007) may be as important as and closely interconnected with struggles for a more justifiable resource distribution.

MORAL ECONOMIES TRANSCENDING NATIONAL CONTAINER STATES

Changes in moral economies and discourse are an interesting topic in itself, but they are even more relevant, if we interpret them as signs of institutional change. The theory of reflexive modernization argues that modern institutions may develop in a manner which undermines the bases on which they are implicitly built (Beck et al. 2001). If for example women were included in a highly competitive labor market under similar conditions like men and no migrants were in sight who could fill the gap, this would undermine the social and physical reproduction of labour in the »modern« nuclear family – a process well under way, if we take the low birth rates in core states at face value.

Viewed in this perspective it is somewhat significant, that a future US President did not only spend part of his youth in an Indonesian middle class neighbourhood, but that he also chooses to write about the experience in his autobiography. Firstly, we can interpret this as sign of a factual change in the degree of mobility and interconnectedness across national borders. In terms of migratory patterns Obama's family does not fit the standard-description of emigrants who want to *settle* in another country. Instead his African father studied abroad temporarily, his mother – though coming from a traditional mid western family – was able and inclined to marry and later divorce an African student. She then married an Indonesian and lived with him in Indonesia, but also decided to place her son in the US American nation state frame – and an elite high school in particular. This kind of migration trajectory is not one of permanent emigration nor is it free floating. It is situated in pluri-local social networks and social spaces which transcend national container states (Levitt and Glick Schiller 2004; Pries 2008b). Connectivities of this kind are often characterized by relations of profound inequality; still it becomes possible for a future US president to develop a personal idea of what abject poverty might mean.

Secondly, we may assume that increased interconnectedness in the world may also result in changed perceptions of global inequality. With respect to migration these perceptions will probably remain strictly regionalized, i.e. migrants from poorer regions may or may not remain connected to their country of origin, but even if they continue to take an interest their moral economies will remain diasporic, that is centred around a specific region and generally marginal (Pries 2008a: 156ff.).

Ulrich Beck has identified another kind of institutional change as more likely to impact on moral economies: In his view a global moral economy does not only develop as a result of social connectivity but – in a more materialist vain – in response to an objectively increasing connectivity of risks (Beck 1999, 2007a; Beck and Grande 2010: 422ff). The risks of industrial production impact on the general population and even if core states try with some success to externalize risk they can never be sure that these risks will not backfire. Take recent »global« catastrophes as an example: 9/11, the oil spill in the gulf of Mexico, Fukushima. Publics in the »West« sympathized because they felt that it could have happened to them, too: Al-Qaeda might as well have attacked the cities of London and Frankfurt. Given the prestige of Japanese »discipline« and technology, Germans were impressed by the idea that Fukushima could have happened close to Munich, too. If risks are transcending national boundaries, it becomes »materially« more difficult to restrict political perspectives to the interior of nation states. If risks go global, if they can back-fire across national borders the world is growing together not only socially and normatively but also in the form of institutionalized interdependence.

Arguments about »economies of risks« connect the realist strand with concerns about capitalism's tendency to exploit non-economic resources. Much like the social and moral economies on which capitalist production feeds natural resources used to appear as boundless. It is in the moment in which the exploitation of »given« resources creates material problems that institutions change. »Aging« societies with few children have to think about opening their borders. And states who have seen nuclear clouds move across Europe justly start to wonder about national-sovereignty if expressed by neighbor states toying around with nuclear power.

THE FUTURE OF INEQUALITY IN THE WORLD

What can sociology say about the future of global inequalities? Currently, the strength of sociological analyses is not in the conceptual debate about global justice or in empirical analyses on a world scale. Sociology's institutional analyses could offer a meaningful contribution, but only if more sociologists followed the rare example of those who explicitly theorize institutions which go beyond the nation state (Beck 1999; Heintz et al. 2005; Leisering 2009; Leisering and Tao 2010; Meyer et al. 1992).

Institutional analyses usually take a look back and try to understand how institutions historically emerged or were created. This is a good precondition for an assessment of potential future developments. However, if we accept diagnoses like those of Bauman's »interregnum« (in this book) or Beck's »reflexive modernization« we should not assume that institutions continue on, but also consider potential and radical change.

So what can the perspectives discussed in this contribution say about the future of global inequalities? In a realist perspective it is likely that inequalities continue and that the nation state system continues to legitimize them. Some states may move to the top, some people may migrate, but bottom-line things will remain the same. Perspectives emphasizing the necessity and boundedness of »non-economic« reproduction do not really change the picture. »Non-economic' resources are endangered and exploited by capitalist economizing, but insignificant in their impact on capitalism as long as they continue to function or can be replaced. It is in the realm of the moral that some change is most likely to happen. Continued migration, increasing interconnection via social media which can stimulate political mobilization, the interconnection of risks together with the development of global care chains could result in a degree of interconnectedness which encourages a moral discourse which goes beyond national borders even if it still remains particular and bound to specific (global) regions.[6] Whether and where globalizing global circuits will develop and stabilize is profoundly unclear. We may expect the interconnections to increase through shared risks and the reality of global (grass-roots) communication. But political efforts to curtail and regulate mobilities are also on the rise. And as a result of higher energy costs and the need to curb carbon output opportunities to physically travel the globe will likely be much reduced.

So far the future of global inequalities is debated by economists and philosophers; public discourse follows the myth of neoliberal deregulation. Sociology's contribution is in the identification of institutions governing global inequalities, in understanding the ways in which these institutions change and the paths which »new« institutions may take.

References

Abu-Lughod, Janet (1989). *Before European Hegemony. The World System A.D. 1250–1350*. Oxford: Oxford University Press

Bauman, Zygmunt (1998). On Glocalization or Globalization for Some, Localization for Some Others. In: *Thesis Eleven*, 54(Aug.): 37–49

Beck-Gernsheim, Elisabeth (1980). *Das halbierte Leben. Männerwelt Beruf, Frauenwelt Familie*. Frankfurt/M.: Fischer

Beck, Ulrich (1999). *World Risk Society*. Cambridge: Polity

Beck, Ulrich (2000). *The Brave New World of Work*. Cambridge: Polity

---

6 | This vision is taken up by the still evolving discourse on normative and sociological cosmopolitanism (Beck 2004; Beck and Grande 2010; Nowicka and Rovisco 2009).

Beck, Ulrich (2004). Cosmopolitan Realism: On the Distinction Between Cosmopolitanism in Philosophy and the Social Sciences. In: *Global Networks*, 4(2):131–156
Beck, Ulrich (2007a). Beyond Class and Nation: Reframing Social Inequalities in a Globalizing World. In: *British Journal of Sociology*, 58(4):679–706
Beck, Ulrich (2007b). *Schöne neue Arbeitswelt*. Aktualisierte Neuauflage. Frankfurt/M.: Suhrkamp
Beck, Ulrich and Elisabeth Beck-Gernsheim (1994). *Riskante Freiheiten. Individualisierung in modernen Gesellschaften*. Frankfurt/M.: Suhrkamp
Beck, Ulrich; Wolfgang Bonß and Christoph Lau (2001). Theorie reflexiver Modernisierung. Fragestellungen, Hypothesen, Forschungsprogramme. In: Ulrich Beck and Wolfgang Bonß (eds.). *Die Modernisierung der Moderne*. Frankfurt/M.: Suhrkamp
Beck, Ulrich and Edgar Grande (2010). Varieties of Second Modernity: The Cosmopolitan Turn in Social and Political Theory and Research. In: *British Journal of Sociology*, 61(3):409–443
Becker-Schmidt, Regina; Gudrun-Axeli Knapp and Beate Schmidt (1984). *Eines ist zu wenig – beides ist zu viel. Erfahrungen von Arbeiterfrauen zwischen Familie und Fabrik*. Bonn: Verlag Neue Gesellschaft
Beisheim, Marianne and Gunnar Folke Schuppert (eds.) (2007). *Staatszerfall und Governance*. Baden-Baden: Nomos
Bennholdt-Thomsen, Veronika and Maria Mies (1997). *Eine Kuh für Hillary. Die Subsistenzperspektive*. München: Frauenoffensive
Boatcă, Manuela (2009). Class vs. Other as Analytic Categories. The Selective Incorporation of Migrants into Theory. In: Terry Ann Jones and Eric Mielants (eds.). *Mass Migration in the World-System. Past, Present, and Future*. Boulder, London: Paradigm Publishers
Boatcă, Manuela and Willfried Spohn (eds.) (2010). *Globale, multiple und postkoloniale Modernen*. München, Mering: Rainer Hampp Verlag
Bourdieu, Pierre (1998). The Economy of Symbolic Goods. In: Pierre Bourdieu (ed.). *Practical Reason. On the Theory of Action*. Stanford: Stanford University Press, 92–123
Brubaker, Rogers (1992). *Citizenship and Nationhood in France and Germany*. Cambridge: Harvard University Press
Butler, Judith (2009). *Frames of War: When Is Life Grievable?* London: Verso
Cyrus, Norbert and Anja Weiß (2005). »Ich bin eine Firma! Ich bin meine Sekretärin, mein Direktor, mein Arbeitsstellensucher« In: Franz Schultheis and Kristina Schulz (eds.). *Gesellschaft mit beschränkter Haftung. Zumutungen und Leiden im deutschen Alltag*. Konstanz: UVK,
Eisenstadt, Shmuel N. (2000). Multiple Modernities. In: *Daedalus*, 129(1): 1–29
Evers, Hans-Dieter (1987). Subsistenzproduktion, Markt und Staat. In: *Geographische Rundschau*, 39: 136–140

Fraser, Nancy (2007). Reframing Justice in a Globalizing World. In: David Held and Ayse Kaya (eds.). *Global Inequality*. Cambridge: Polity Press

Fraser, Nancy (2008). Abnormale Gerechtigkeit. In: Helmut König, Emanuel Richter and Sabine Schielke (eds.). *Gerechtigkeit in Europa. Transnationale Dimensionen einer normativen Grundfrage*. Bielefeld: transcript

Fraser, Nancy and Axel Honneth (2003). *Umverteilung oder Anerkennung? Eine politisch-philosophische Kontroverse*. Frankfurt/M.: Suhrkamp

Gilroy, Paul (1993). *The Black Atlantic: Modernity and Double-Consciousness*. Cambridge: Harvard University Press

Habermas, Jürgen (1998). *The Inclusion of the Other: Studies in Political Theory* (Studies in Contemporary German Social Thought). Cambridge: MIT Press

Heintz, Bettina; Richard Münch and Hartmann Tyrell (2005) (eds). *Weltgesellschaft. Theoretische Zugänge und empirische Problemlagen* [Sonderheft der Zeitschrift für Soziologie]. Stuttgart: Lucius & Lucius

Hochschild, Arlie Russell (2000). Global Care Chains and Emotional Surplus Value. In: Will Hutton and Anthony Giddens (eds.). *On the Edge. Living with Global Capitalism*. London: Jonathan Cape

Hoffmann-Nowotny, Hans-Joachim (1970). *Migration. Ein Beitrag zu einer soziologischen Erklärung*. Stuttgart: Ferdinand Enke

Korzeniewicz, Roberto Patricio and Timothy Patrick Moran (2009). *Unveiling Inequality. A World-Historical Perspective*. New York: Russel Sage Foundation Publications

Leisering, Lutz (2009). Extending Social Security to the Excluded. Are Social Cash Transfers to the Poor an Appropriate Way of Fighting Poverty in Developing Countries? In: *Global Social Policy*, 9(2): 246–272

Leisering, Lutz and Liu Tao (2010). Globale Wissensdiffusion in der Sozialpolitik. Die Einführung einer Arbeitsunfallversicherung in der Volksrepublik China. In: *Zeitschrift für Sozialreform*, 56(2): 173–205

Levitt, Peggy and Nina Glick Schiller (2004). Conceptualizing Simultaneity: A Transnational Social Field Perspective on Society. In: *International Migration Review*, 38(3): 1002–1039

Lockwood, David (1964). Social Integration and System Integration. In: George K. Zollschan and Walter Hirsch (eds.). *Social Change: Explorations, Diagnoses, and Conjectures*. New York, London, Sidney, Toronto: John Wiley & Sons

Lutz, Helma (ed.) (2008). *Migration and Domestic Work. A European Perspective on a Global Theme*. Aldershot: Ashgate

Luxemburg, Rosa (1951 [1913]). *The Accumulation of Capital*. [http://www.marxists.org/archive/luxemburg/1913/accumulation-capital/accumulation.pdf]. London: Routledge and Kegan Paul

Marshall, Thomas H. (1950). *Citizenship and Social Class and Other Essays*. Cambridge: Cambridge University Press

Meyer, John W.; Francisco O. Ramirez and Yasemin Nuhoglu Soysal (1992). World Expansion of Mass Education, 1870–1980. In: *Sociology of Education*, 65(2): 128–149

Milanovic, Branko (2005). *Worlds Apart: Measuring International and Global Inequality.* Princeton: Princeton University Press

Milanovic, Branko (2008). *Where in the World Are You? Assessing the Importance of Circumstance and Effort in a World of Different Mean Country Incomes and (almost) No Migration.* World Bank Policy Research Working Paper 4493, Washington D.C.: World Bank

Morokvasic-Müller, Mirjana; Umut Erel and Kyoko Shinozaki (eds.) (2003). *Crossing Borders and Shifting Boundaries. Vol. I: Gender on the Move.* Opladen: Leske + Budrich

Nowicka, Magdalena and Maria Rovisco (eds.) (2009). *Cosmopolitanism in Practice.* Aldershot: Ashgate

Nussbaum, Martha (2007). *Frontiers of Justice. Disability, Nationality, Species Membership.* Cambridge: Harvard University Press

Ong, Aihwa (1987). *Spirits of Resistance and Capitalist Discipline: Factory Women in Malaysia.* Albany: State University of New York Press

Parreñas, Rhacel Salazar (2000). Migrant Filipina Domestic Workers and the International Division of Reproductive Labor. In: *Gender and Society*, 14(4): 560–580

Pécoud, Antoine and Paul De Guchteneire (eds.) (2007). *Migration without Borders: Essays on the Free Movement of People.* Paris, New York, Oxford: UNESCO Publishing and Berghahn

Potts, Lydia (1988). *Weltmarkt für Arbeitskraft. Von der Kolonisation Amerikas bis zu den Migrationen der Gegenwart.* Hamburg: Junius

Pries, Ludger (2008a). *Die Transnationalisierung der sozialen Welt. Sozialräume jenseits von Nationalgesellschaften.* Frankfurt/M.: Suhrkamp

Pries, Ludger (ed.) (2008b). *Rethinking Transnationalism. The Meso-Link of Organisations.* London: Routledge

Randeria, Shalini (2003). Cunning States and Unaccountable International Institutions: Legal Plurality, Social Movements and Rights of Local Communities to Common Property Resources. In: *European Journal of Sociology*, 44(1): 1–27

Rehbein, Boike (2006). Sozialstruktur und Arbeitsteilung. Eine historische Skizze am Beispiel Festlandsüdostasiens. In: *Asien*, 101(Okt.): 23–45

Sen, Amartya (1985). *Commodities and Capabilities.* Amsterdam, New York, Oxford: North-Holland

Sen, Amartya (1999a). *Development as Freedom.* New York: Alfred A. Knopf

Sen, Amartya (1999b). Global Justice. Beyond International Equity. In: Inge Kaul, Isabelle Grundberg and Marc A. Stern (eds.). *Global Public Goods. In-*

ternational Cooperation in the 21ˢᵗ Century. New York, Oxford: Oxford University Press
Shamir, Ronen (2005). Without Borders? Notes on Globalization as a Mobility Regime. In: *Sociological Theory*, 23(2): 197–217
Wallerstein, Immanuel (1979). *The Capitalist World-Economy*. Cambridge: Cambridge University Press
Wallerstein, Immanuel (2004). *World-Systems Analysis: An Introduction*. Durham: Duke University Press
Weiß, Anja (2005). The Transnationalization of Social Inequality. Conceptualizing Social Positions on a World Scale. In: *Current Sociology*, 53(4): 707–728
Weiß, Anja (2006). The Racism of Globalization. In: Donaldo Macedo and Panayota Gounari (eds.). *The Globalization of Racism*. Boulder, London: Paradigm Publishers

A Good Job Well Done: Richard Sennett and the Politics of Creative Labour

ANGELA MCROBBIE

> ›An eagle-eyed reader will notice that the word creativity appears in this book as little as possible‹ (Sennett 2008: 290)

> ›[...] flexible forms of underemployment meet increasing interest among (young) men and women, in fact are virtually demanded of them in order to balance wage labour and family work, work and life more equitably‹ (Beck 1996: 143)

INTRODUCTION

In this chapter it is my aim to show how the writing of Richard Sennett can be helpful in re-positioning the current debates on working lives in the new creative sector. This entails a downgrading of the exceptional status of this kind of work, so that it overlaps more visibly with the more ordinary jobs and occupations which have recently been transformed, or being destandardized, (as Beck puts it) so as to concur with the requirements of the new regime of flexible labour. In so doing I also hope to show how this offers a more integrated and egalitarian methodology for urban research which is primarily concerned with the increasing numbers of young people who are connected with the growth of the culture industries and who congregate in city spaces more typically inhabited by poor and disadvantaged social groups including ethnic minorities, migrants and an indigenous working class. They move into such neighbourhoods for reasons of relative cheapness, space and because there is some nebulous sense of potential, opportunity, or »buzz«. Such a move on my part here, to bring these dynamics together, rectifies a tendency to de-contextualise creative labour and to disconnect it from locality and neighbourhood. Or alternatively when neighbourhood is factored in, in many recent research studies, it appears that only the creatives really matter, and the others, young and old, living and working in the same shared spaces, are faded out into invisibility (Lloyd 2009). Sennett provides a strong counter-current to the now infamous writing of Richard Florida. He talks to old and disenchanted workers from many occupations, he investigates the everyday life of cities, he is drawn to unremarkable people, and he is a sociologist with a strong sense of history and continuity, as well as change. (Like Florida he is listened to by governments, not because he offers a kind of magic formula for building creative sectors in rundown urban districts but on the basis of deeper and more sustained ethical concerns such as why the giving of respect to disadvantaged people is both important and complicated.) Sennett also enquires into what happens to people when their jobs become projects, and when their workmates become team members? When rosters bring in different groups of people who don't talk to each other and who simply come in and leave, who are employed on different kinds of contracts, and who, with the impact of new technology become operatives rather than people with distinct skills[1]? Creative work often seems quite far removed from the kinds of activities Sennett is interested in, indeed the old jobs disappear as the new ones emerge. But there is a middle-ground, where new technology and new media impact across the lives of young and old alike, where flexible working means different working rhythms, where more people seem to be at home during times in the day when in the past, residential areas would only be busy with mothers and children, or with the retired and the unemployed. It is my intention here to draw these strands together, in a bid to think in new ways about the creative industries. I will assess how far Sennett's concept of craft helps us to develop a less inflated and overblown vocabulary for thinking about the rise of the creative sector. Can it provide the basis for a kind of everyday ethics of work, and a counter to the prevailing individualism of the so-called talent-led economy? How well does it function in fields of activity which are socially necessary but unpaid or under-paid such as domestic work, child-care and care of the elderly? If, following Beck we need to be looking at investing in areas of hitherto unpaid labour, e.g. »family work«, which could, in the light of underemployment, become a source of value and enrichment, how does craft replenish the kind of jobs which have always carried connotations of drudgery or of monotony (Beck 1996, Beck 2000)? There is a sense in which craft seems to have the power to make all work rewarding and interesting as long as the craftsman has patience, concentration and a desire to see a good job well done. Sennett makes his case, convincingly, against the writing of Hannah Arendt on this subject. For sure by downgrading the spectacular aspirations of creative work, craft provides a

---

1 | The remarkable film by German film director Nikolaus Geyrhalter (2005) *Our Daily Bread* shows the isolation of the operative in a chicken rearing factory who now works alone all day, and even has her tea breaks alone, because advanced technology has depleted the need for other workers.

kind of calmness and a steadfastness in the relation between the worker and his often recalcitrant object. Sennett is of course alert to gender problematics and his use of the word craftsman is carefully rehearsed and gender neutral. Still I am left wondering about the recalcitrant child and the tired mother, who may also be trying to keep her freelance work and flexible job in the creative sector viable, while also having a clean and tidy house, or at the other end of the spectrum, the stressed out young woman who is also a freelance, let us say a web-designer and who cannot consider taking time out to have a baby for fear of losing her network and who becomes depressed and drinks too much?[2] Sennett's comments on parenting as craft may well disguise a feminist deficit, which points to a political weakness in his analysis. Likewise he overlooks the toll which new creative labour takes on the young, so that it is not only the old and seemingly displaced or redundant for whom there is loss and displacement. Does Sennett's idea of »corrosion of character« imply that young creatives who have grown up with the new entrepreneurial ethos and been trained in it and so know nothing else, are in effect tainted in advance by this process of corrosion? Does this mean that it is next to impossible to envisage a turning away from the apolitical individualism endemic in creative circles, or might this process be reversed and a new spirit of co-operation emerge? Sennett for sure provides a challenge to the frenetic speeded-up and then burn-out mentality currently experienced by »young creatives«. He does not claim for his writing an explicit political agenda, nevertheless, the question has to be raised, does craft have purchase, as an ethics of work, to be of assistance by way of offering an alternative to those caught up in the anxieties of multi-tasking and a future of short term multiple job holding? Sennett for sure does provide a potential vocabulary for a new radicalism from within the spaces of the »flexible city« and this will be expanded upon at the end of this chapter, but in regard to craft, while the benefits of patient labour are palpable, the ability to implement such practices seem increasingly distant and this may call for a more substantial overhauling of the politics of work, in the light of the rise of both creative labour but more generally of destandardized work.[3]

---

2 | See the film *Eine flexible Frau* (Turanskyj 2010).
3 | This article was completed before some recent developments came to my attention regarding the interest on the part of groups of urban young creatives in establishing a »revival of crafts«. What can be seen here is a new focus in traditional production methods for textiles and woollen clothing with small-scale fashion designers learning old crafts and bringing high-quality goods to new consumers, see for example the Albam menswear shops in London. This interest also combines with an ethical interest in fabric production and with a slower process which gratifies producers and consumers alike, akin to if not close up to Sennett's model.

CREATIVE UNDER-EMPLOYMENT?

Across the world and in the global cities where artists and creative people gather, it is hard to make a good and secure living in the field of the arts and creative practice. The pathway of the artist has always entailed uncertainty of income and an unreliable career. Nevertheless many academics[4] have been struck by the tenacity with which the young people, the thousands we have taught in London in recent years, cling to the expectation that a rewarding, indeed exciting job in this sector, from practising as an artist, to working in the wider creative and arena, will be theirs sooner rather than later. These are not wealthy young people drawn from an international global elite, who can afford to hang around working as interns, many (though not all) are indeed international, and they come from middle-class and lower middle-class backgrounds, (from Brazil to Italy, from Poland to Trinidad, from Slovakia to Canada, to name just a few), and there is a good deal of faith and enthusiasm from their parents in regard to these youngsters pursuing studies which will greatly improve their chances in what is in effect a geographically wide but ›thin-growth‹ sector of work, the culture or creative industry.[5] Without this conviction, underpinned by savings, and some

---

4 | I draw here on countless conversations, some in formal committee settings, others informal taking place in the corridor or snatched over a coffee, giving rise to a kind of unstated professional academic viewpoint on this phenomenon.

5 | Of the 80 MA (2010-11) students I asked at the end of a class on the subject of creative economy, all but four said they were being helped financially by their parents. 70% said on top of this they were doing paid work while also studying. Adam Arvidsson suggests this parental support is a kind of *Buddenbrooks* effect, as a younger generation of the middle classes fulfils frustrated yearnings for self-expressive work. (Adam Arvidsson, Conference Milan on April 14th 2011). Pierre Bourdieu offers the most sustained sociological analysis of an anti-economy ethos within the intergenerational landscape of middle class families (Bourdieu 1993). I would add to these comments, the compounding significance of young women, now enthusiastically enrolled in higher education and wishing to pursue a career, as bearers of a new romanticism in this respect. The way in which work has become the space of heightened affect and the investment of passion is explored in various papers by McRobbie 2002a, McRobbie 2011, Gill and Pratt 2008, Arvidsson and Malossi 2011. We might also want to factor in the point Foucault makes rather cryptically about how, within neo-liberal rhetoric, for families the child is an investment, an »abilities machine«, this is something difference from traditional patterns of inherited privilege, nor is it just a matter of a larger middle-class able to support offspring into early middle-age (Foucault 2006). We need to investigate in more detail these global processes, a cosmopolitanisation of work as Beck would put it, (with the universities playing a distributive function), which intersects with the spread of under-employment and its attendant anxieties, alongside new dynamics of family de-

parental help, my own university would not be able to run so many courses at Masters level which are designed to train this kind of young person for the duration of one intense year of study in areas which reflect critically on the informal, even impromptu, or undesignated fields of work which have sprung up in so many major cities in the last two decades. Even just a few years ago this kind of work had clearer parameters and tight job descriptions such as arts administration, or curatorial practice, but now, in the last five years or so, there is a much more inter-disciplinary and cross-cutting range of activities which means that courses offered by universities begin to reflect this in their titles eg MA in Culture Industries or MA Cultural and Creative Entrepreneurship. These hybrid jobs correspond with the emergence of sustained underemployment, as described by Beck (1996, 2000). A term such as this is rarely deployed in discussing creative labour, the reality is disguised through a much more cheerful rhetoric of projects, multi-tasking, and most importantly, entrepreneurialism. It is incumbent on the university to provide structure, rationale, in the form of a syllabus and a curriculum which gives disciplinary coherence to a sprawling and often informal set of creative processes which can encompass activities from the production of art work itself, to online publishing, events management and fashion public relations. Here the word entrepreneurialism is pivotal for its ability to encompass all the activities that are unpaid in the process of »starting up«. Curriculum planning and pedagogy in this regard entail a significant ethical as well as intellectual responsibility. The university more so than before provides a direct bridge into the domain of precarious creative work, and we as academics and teachers intersect on a daily basis with this constituency, we provide assessment criteria, and marking grids for coursework and the gaining of qualifications. We offer validation alongside critique, the two are interwoven.[6] We are also ourselves inscribed within traditionally bureaucratic structures which elsewhere are becoming anachronistic. Such proximity to the world of work and responsibility in regard to training marks something relatively new for the arts and humanities. We find ourselves inside this creative machine, and called upon to endorse working practices which sometimes run counter to the values established through a century of labour struggles. In a subtle and inexorable way the

---

pendencies as an older generation of possibly more secure workers reach to retirement, and share the rewards of their lifetime of labour downwards, prior to the norms of simple inheritance. Thus there are profound shifts in both work and family life.

6 | There are exceptions to the traditional autonomy of arts and humanities teaching from the incursion of future labour markets. Fashion colleges and design schools have always been expected to work closely with industry in order to justify their existence within the art school system (McRobbie 1998). In the new areas of creative enterprise informed by social science and by cultural theory, this role is now the subject of more intense scrutiny and critique.

core of social democratic practices which underpinned the history of educational provision in the UK are being eroded. The rise of the Masters course in these creative areas brings the university sector much closer to the labour market than has been the case in previous times, indeed the two mutually encroach upon one another through internships and work experience programmes embedded formally or informally into the academic provision. We require a better theoretical vocabulary for addressing this situation and the dilemmas it poses. Of course another source of rationalisation, systematisation and validation for the creative economy is the field of cultural and creative policy-making. With the exception of EU-led programmes these remain largely locked within the nation-state, and then are regionally devolved, often to the level of urban-regeneration schemes. In contrast the global university finds itself positioned as a transnational milieu, creating academic zones of cosmopolitan populations participating in studies which draw on internationally produced research and teaching materials.[7]

Here is an anomaly. In the sphere of academic research which has grown up around the new creative sector, the nature of working lives are of great interest for researchers, but rarely are these jobs considered alongside other unexceptional occupations also undergoing changes. Creative work is lifted out of and disconnected from what used to be called the sociology of work, and before that, industrial sociology.[8] The field of normal jobs is conspicuously absent from debate. In this way, the focus of academic research parallels the ideas of exceptional or extraordinary creative work, and critical intervention is directed towards dissecting and then challenging a vocabulary of personal success, or its opposite personal despondency, or burn out. Many of us, myself included have contributed to this separating out of creative work through attention to its youthfulness, and to the way in which these permanently transitional jobs, have given rise to new structural divides and exclusions (McRobbie 2002a; 2002b, Lloyd 2009). This has been at the expense of looking at the longer term and with where these people move onto once they can no longer consider themselves to be young. In this chapter I aim to see how we can address the new creative work, not by isolating it and lifting it out from the routines of everyday working lives, and thus making it exceptional, but quite the opposite. I seek to re-embed creative work, so that it can be viewed alongside other kinds of jobs which are not associated with the aura of inspiration, and which do not require this magic ingredient of creativity. I also want to re-embed it spatially so that we can consider these kinds of working lives within the context of the everyday life of the city. I want to find a

---

7 | The limits of this teaching-machine are reached when national governments translate the logic of global recruitment into fears about migration, and the issuing of foreign visas for students.

8 | See the journal of the British Sociological Association, *Work, Employment and Society*.

way of countering the romance and emphasising more the ordinary rewards in the sense of a »good job well done«. Richard Sennett helps me to move in this direction (Sennett 1993,1998, 2003, 2006, 2008). Instead of the existing models of success and failure, of euphoria or of burn out and new psychopathologies of anxiety, depression, panic and worthlessness, as fleetingly examined by Berardi, there is another possibility which is connected to a radical critique of the existing prevailing ethos (Berardi 2009). For Sennett this lies in the possibilities of craft. He also provides a counter to the assumptions of youthfulness, by insisting on a longer view. Sennett's own research traces occupational dynamics over the long term. He re-visits and interviews again people who were the subjects of his research into work and organisations thirty years ago. He also integrates discussion of new kinds of flexible working within a wider remit which means that his focus spans jobs which are far removed from those connected narrowly with the new creative economy. He considers the working practices of bakers, and computer programmers, of bar-owners and of musicians. Sennett is best-known for his research on cities, architecture and urban space, and this too permits a widening of the current perspectives on urban creative economy for reasons that will be examined later in this chapter.

Two further observations may be helpful. The search for exciting jobs, or those which promise rewards connected with the aura of creativity, invariably means that other jobs which lack these possibilities are cast aside as, at best, something to fall back on if all else fails. I am thinking here of jobs which are within the realm of possibility for arts and humanities graduates, eg librarian, benefits office manager, publishing assistant, social worker or youth worker etc. Even when such jobs promise regular pay, promotion and benefits and entitlements, they are discounted. Why is this the case? Today we live in a world of collapsing boundaries and with the intensification of the working day, working lives nowadays merge with leisure time and with non-work activities, so these kinds of creative careers are especially desirable because they promise a social life as part of the job. This is one of their key attractions. One is killing two birds with one stone. A final year student who had gained high passes in all of her assessed work and who considered herself politically radical explained to me why she was hoping to turn her ongoing part-time job in the night-time economy into a more promoted full-time career in party and social network management. During her degree she had worked as a hostess for an events management company which was dedicated to bringing young single professionals together not for dating but for exchange, intelligent conversation, for company and an enjoyable night out. My student's job was to be an ice-breaker and keep the flow of conversation and sociability flowing. The company had opened branches outside London and she was hoping to run one in Bournemouth where she already lived. When I commented on the shallowness of party management work she agreed that a socially valuable job with, let us say, disadvantaged youngsters, would be something to consider, but not for the present.

The second observation is one which Ulrich Beck has also made which is that there is less regular and full-time employment available (Beck 1996). I gestured to this above. For the affluent countries of the West stable work has been shrinking over the last two decades. Many young people now work within the shadow of threatened unemployment. Indeed Beck's analysis of under-employment is absolutely central to a fuller understanding of creative work, because it is inextricably bound up with the anxious and frenetic pace of multi-tasking. Institutionalised long term under-employment can be seen as a way of managing and holding at bay, the impact of actual unemployment. It also serves to suspend the periods of »rest«, or the time between projects, as true unemployment. Instead these periods have to be planned for and covered financially by the ongoing projects, so that they become short holidays, or time to devote to domestic obligations, or else time for pitching for new work. Projects are symbolically central to the rise of under-employment and downtime, they are often under-funded or barely funded which means that while they signal to the outside world a confident buzz of endless activity, they are significantly under-renumerated and so frequently hardly count as paid work at all. But still, busy under-employment bears no stigma, and the constant stream of projects serves a kind of social face-saving function. At the exact same time working under the shadow of unemployment brings the seemingly-privileged new creatives closer to other social groups experiencing the hard consequences of de-industrialisation, the de-standardisation of work, and the disappearance of traditional jobs (Beck 1996). The slimming down of the gigantic bureaucratic structures which, as Sennett reminds us created inflated layers of work, means that old jobs are lost (Sennett 2006). The growth of new communications technologies, where machines and computers replace people, limits the opportunities for lifetime work for many people across the world, and in poor and slowly developing countries unemployment levels regularly encompass the majority of the population. In the former communist states of east Europe there is high unemployment which leads to the exodus of young people to the more prosperous cities of the west, often in search of work in the field of social care. In third world countries the flow of people out of the country of origin, creates whole new social strata of migrant labour seeking work in the service sectors of the developed world and sending money or remittances back home to support family and kin who are unable to become mobile in the same way.

These forces of change can mean that in the context of the large urban environments there is a collision of new cosmopolitan populations in and across many of the sites of work. This is especially noticeable in London in flexible labour markets appealing to young people. One female student tells me her part-time job, held onto through all the years of study, is in a well-known chain of coffee shops. Here she works alongside what we might call the truly precarious who are often young migrant men and women (from Algeria, Brazil, Egypt) trying to earn a basic subsistence income. The coffee chain know that this young women is a student and they offer her an additional role writing press releases and working on brand development, while also serving from behind the counter. The coffee chain might even offer to keep the student on in a more formal role after she graduates but her sights are set on her career as a freelance writer and journalist, and member of a band, so it is unlikely she will take up this option. Instead she will carry on with her shifts and hope that her real career takes off. City department stores also provide work opportunities for equally diverse groups of young people, since in retail there has also been a marked reduction in traditional full-time jobs which would have recruited relatively low qualified working-class young people and offered some of them longer term prospects and a way of moving into retail management. Here too there is a new mix, smaller numbers of full-time school leavers are taken on, and much larger numbers of young people, some of whom are spending time in a big city like London having come from east Europe and hoping they can eventually find a way of gaining more of a foothold in the labour market, while others are working part- time while engaged either in study, or in pursuing another more prestigious career.[9] In effect the retailers can only benefit from this shift to employing flexible and better- educated and less invested personnel, for whom they will not be fully responsible as employees. For a start they lower their costs for training. Today many young people working behind the counter in stores like *Cos,* or *Gap,* or *Agnes b,* have other aspirations, in much the same way as waiters and waitresses in upmarket restaurants are typically understood to be actors or models who are working between jobs. Sennett might propose we investigate what the outcome of this transformation of retail is for those for whom such work remains an end in itself, rather than a temporary way of paying the rent. These days it seems few such personnel still exist.[10] For the moment I want to stress that different layers of the workforce and different kinds of workers are responding to similar macro-social processes. Greater emphasis is now put on self- reliance and on inventiveness in creating jobs for oneself. An underlying argument is that the arts and the creative sector embody an economic space for novel forms of job creation, or for creating a piecemeal

---

9 | Goldsmiths University of London BA student, Heike Muller described in her BA Dissertation the employment culture in a major west end retailer, where she herself also had a part-time job. She reported divisions between the small number of full-timers, who were more subjected to traditional labour discipline and managerial control, in contrast to the part- timers who worked shifts and had no interest in a longer term career.

10 | I know of no current research which examines the extensiveness of casual jobs in comparison to secure full time work in urban fashion retail.

livelihood, from a range of ever-changing projects, which have become a defining feature of the lives of well-qualified young people across the west and the affluent world. (What this means overall is that in the affluent countries of the west, the younger middle-classes are being re-stratified and forced to become less reliant on the infrastructure of welfare and the institutions of the public sector which were defining features of the social democratic post-war state. I return to this point later.) The energetic meanings attributed to such jobs, that they are exciting and desirable, occurs within a biopolitical landscape overseen at government and employer-level, in the light of the diminishing opportunities for work.[11] The key instrument is entrepreneurialism. This functions to solve the problems thrown up by the decline of the employment society for an aspirational sector of the workforce. We could say these young well-qualified graduates are also being proletarianised at the same time as they are being heralded as at the forefront of the new economy. The proletarianisation thesis is widely referred to in the discussions of immaterial labour, so that, contrary to the era of industrial labour, entrepreneurialisation and proletarianisation now can go hand in hand (Lazzarato 1999). While the prevailing value system celebrates the growth of the creative economy and the rise of talent, the talented themselves are working long hours under the shadow of unemployment in a domain of intensive under-employment, and self-activated work. But does proletarianisation really capture the meaning of this process or is social re-stratification and the creation of new hierarchies more appropriate? Maybe Sennett's writings on urban life and work can furnish us with another way of analysing these movements? Beck has talked about »Brazilianisation« to refer to the way the informal or popular economies of the street,[12] are now extended to include middle-class self employment practices in the West (Beck 2000). He is right in one crucial respect, but is at risk here of comparing the patchwork of emergent work cultures in western affluent countries which are nevertheless underpinned by a residue of welfarism, with cities suffering from extremities of violence and destitution and characterised by massive populations living in abject poverty. More apposite is his analysis of work destandardization as a ›risk-fraught system of flexible, pluralized, decentralised underemployment,

---

11 | We need only refer to the many reports from the Department of Culture, Media and Sport between 1997 and 2007 for evidence of the centrality of culture to questions of population management. See also NESTA.

12 | Perhaps such activities appear more unusual to Beck for the reason that their existence in German cities is more hidden. There are greater restrictions on opening up 24 hour local shops and convenience stores, and small internet shops doubling up as cafes and late night groceries are only to be found in neighbourhoods with high migrant or Turkish populations such as Kreuzberg and Neukölln in Berlin.

which however, will possibly no longer raise the problem of unemployment in the sense of being completely without a paid job‹ (Beck 1996: 143).

BEHIND THE COUNTER

What Sennett's *Conscience of the Eye* contributes to my attempt to bring creative labour down to a ground level so that it can be analysed alongside and in the context of more mundane activities, is this, and here I choose selectively. Attention is paid to the cityscape and the neighbourhoods where people are going about their business, Sennett remarks on unremarkable economic activities such as the Indian and Pakistani shopkeepers. ›The shop owners stand in their doorways in summer, making jokes or comments‹ (Sennett 1993: 128). The rhythms of the neighbourhood and its architecture point to the intersection of working and non-working lives, in unspectacular ways, and his walks up and down the grids of New York undertaken in the spirit of Baudelaire's *flaneur*, allow him to make an argument about impersonality and the subjective life of the city. Sennett aims to develop a visual anthropological method for urban analysis, a »conscience of the eye« in regard to the complexity of power and powerlessness in the city spaces. He wishes to retrieve sympathy and self-expressiveness in the city across diverse social groups, and to encourage exposure through ›mobilizing [...] artistic energies in everyday life‹ (ibid: 149). This is a proposal for artists to become more outward-looking and more energetic in their civic life. Sennett looks at shops and small shopkeepers on 14th Street in New York, which is run down, but where there is a kind of solidarity in the various attempts to hold the mafia with their demands for protection money, at bay. The weak borders and porous boundaries of working-class neighbourhoods offer scope, he claims, for more than just impersonal co-existence. The jarring discontinuities, the differences and the disorientations, could become the basis for binding people together in new more politicised ways. Sennett brings into the current discussion of urban creative economies the idea of locale, of neighbourhood, of the diverse people living and working there, alongside each other. He urges us to consider what the shops and pubs look like inside and who the people are who are working behind the bar.

What then if we were to consider the artists and creatives who seek out spaces for living and for showing and selling their work, or for setting up a bar or a café as a mini-business to support the art, in rundown or under-resourced areas, where they also act as local shop-keepers? They open small shops, they present their objects and collections for sale to a passing as well as to an invited public. They play their part in the expressive life of the street, alongside the other small entrepreneurs. The shop acts as a critical interface between the creative activity behind the scenes and its public exposure. The public front, the space of creative display, the craft shop, the design outlet, the shop that doubles up as a bar or café or place for launch parties, these are all highly valued spaces for those working in the creative economy (Lange 2010). With the exception of Doreen Jakob and Sharon Zukin this shop-keeping function has not been closely considered in most accounts of the growth of this sector (Jakob 2009; Zukin 2010). Jakob considers the city-funded initiatives which allow young creatives to set up shop in rundown parts of the city of Berlin. But she only fleetingly considers the relations between the artists and the locals. Doubtless this is because of the loftier aspirations typically associated with the world of the arts, which would separate out the newly opened gallery from the internet café next door. Nevertheless the reality for so many creative economy people is that they are also doubling up as shop-keepers of sorts and in some of my own other writing the reader will find various references to young people who are simultaneously running a bar or a café or who have started off with a space which is also a local café and a gallery at the same time.[13] So we could propose that this is one way of re-embedding artistic economies into the normal everyday life of the city. It is a weakness of existing accounts that ordinary people in these urban milieus are faded into the background, only visible as local colour.

URBAN AUTOBIOGRAPHY

Across most of Sennett's recent work, there is a strongly autobiographical current. This is most vivid in *Respect* where he reflects more directly on neighbourhood and social class, and where he describes his own early years in one of Chicago's housing projects, the Cabrini estate where he lived with his mother who went on to train as a social worker (Sennett 2003). Through these personal reflections Sennett provides a way of thinking about creative work itself, or art working, in a less grandiose way, which is a counter to the highly individualistic notions of inspiration, genius, talent and competition. He gets to this by describing his own training as a child in classical music and how he was thwarted in his intended career through an accident which meant that his left hand was no longer able to play his instrument at the level that would have been required for a highly successful career. He was forced to give up his dreams and re-consider his options. This personal tragedy permits a changed relationship to art and to playing music where the qualities of craft, rather than the brilliance of individual performance come to the forefront. It is a matter of reconciling oneself to a life among the ranks of the chorus or the *corps de ballet*.[14] What is important here is that the work itself continues, the musician has to practice for many hours

---

13 | See interview with Richard Hedges of The Hales Gallery (McRobbie 2004).
14 | See the documentary by Frederick Wiseman *La Danse* (2009).

each day, irregardless of what position he or she occupies in the orchestra, as does the dancer. It is what is needed to ensure a good job well done. And this in turn becomes the focal point for satisfaction and reward. Such close attention to the craft of playing an instrument well, as a »good job well done« also permits a different relation to career and to working life, one which is less competitive and no longer defined in terms of great success or abject failure. A craft approach means being able to work all the time with failure, with material and instruments that will not easily do what the craftsman hopes or wishes they will do. There is constant struggle, there is patience and slowness, rather than the glamour of speed, there is a kind of quietness and concentration. Sennett also sees this idea of craft as something within the reach of most people. It is both an accessible and an abstract concept, a template for working across the range of activities which gives dignity and self-value to the person engaged in this way. Craft lifts the individual out of the »space-time compression« of contemporary capitalism and its over-charged rhythms, restoring a sense of tranquillity and quiet, but not as some backward looking nostalgic idyll. It is more about the ability to work in a way which is not flashy, not spectacular or flamboyant but which entails attention to detail, and to the value of trial and error. This ethos can be seen as a counter to the dependency on seemingly innate talent. There is something much more rewarding about constant practice and then seeing improvement or finding a solution to a problem. Here is a more modest and down-to-earth idea of a working life in the creative sector.

»NO LONG TERM«

Sennett makes us think about the temporality of the flexible city, where the patterns of working life no longer focus round the office, but are less fixed, often based round meetings which can take place in cafes or bars. Streets in these neighbourhoods become busier places when the people are no longer hidden away in their office blocks. This idea of placeless work has been associated thanks to the influence of Richard Florida with intense gentrification, with young people working on their laptops from coffee shops in newly fashionable areas of town. The many articles and journalistic commentaries focus entirely on the young people in front of their laptops in *Starbucks,* attention is never paid to the wider environment. Few urban creative economy writers focus on mothers and children, on grandmothers and older women, on play parks or on local amenities such as swimming pools or public libraries. Old people seem to fade out of view as do aggressive youths or young teenage mums pushing prams. Even the critics of gentrification duplicate this selective vision, and few urban sociologists or commentators on the new creative economy stop to talk with the ordinary people going about their business. Rarely is there a focus on the people in these neighbourhoods whose daily movements are indicative of their irregular work. In areas of long term working-class unemployment, the daytime streets are often crowded with men, perhaps more men than women for the reason that their female counterparts are more likely to have jobs e.g. Neukölln and Wedding in Berlin, Partick in Glasgow, Brixton and Finsbury Park in London. These men are also increasingly joined by the under-employed creatives who are also out and about. Sociologists tend to focus on how the arrival of the middle classes results in old spaces being re-claimed for more upmarket uses, with the original inhabitants being at best screened out by various filtering processes and at worst being evicted. This often has the ring of deadly inevitability. But if the policy language of the new creative economy had not been cast in such deeply individualistic terms and had instead been concerned with questions of how artists and creative people could work in ways which would be valuable to others, and with how they could engage in pressing social and urban issues, the current self-conscious hipness and the distance from the normal life of the working class or migrant city would not have been so prevalent.[15] Working class culture and its institutions would have been better protected, anti-racist community politics would have impacted on opportunities for youth in the area, and so on. In effect there would have been plenty for the new creative workers to do in their downtime, some unpaid, some potentially rewarded on the longer term. Sennett does not spell this out, but some traces of earlier waves of urban activism along these lines in New York echo in his writing.

It is hard to slot Sennett into current trends in social or cultural theory. His sociological training combines conventional American social psychology and psychoanalysis with (pre-Marxist) organisational sociology. He is influenced by Hannah Arendt and familiar with all the Marxist traditions. He spurns current interest in Deleuze, and instead espouses the US tradition of pragmatism. One wonders if it is this which limits the political imagination in his recent work. It is hard to see exactly how craft might be taken up as a force for change in the world of work. Those already working as artists or designers may welcome the attention Sennett gives to the sheer difficulty of working with materials and objects and the endless processes of trial and error. But the patient labour of craft is likely to remain a distant ideal for freelancers working on a piece-rate system and having to cut corners.[16] In *The Corrosion of Character* Sennett isn't going for so many walks, but he does provide, in an elegiac tone, a series of accounts or

---

15 | See, for example, the profile in *Vogue Italia* on Dalston, East London, ›Benvenuti a Dalston‹ by Chiara Zampetti May 2009 (also see footnote 3).

16 | I find myself cutting corners as an academic, with 80 MA students taking an option, there is no longer the possibility of an »office hour« to help students to prepare the 6000 word assessed essay, since even 30 minutes per student would entail an extra weeks work.

sketches of the dramatic changes in the working lives of a handful of respondents with whom he built up lasting friendships. In a sense he is talking about much more than these specific individuals, he is talking about America itself. It is hard not to think of great American dramatists like Arthur Miller and David Mamet who like Sennett allow their characters, ordinary men and women, to ruminate about work, the organisation, and personal life. Sennett writes movingly about Rose, a bar-owner who gives up her job in mid-life to try her hand in advertising, only to return to her »Trout Bar« some years later chastened. In this new America there is a sundering of ties, »no long term«. Flexible capitalism gives rise to fleeting and impermanent relations. In the past when men could gather in the pub after work, even though the work itself might have been routine, they could tell their stories of their jobs and colleagues often over a lifetime. This narrative capacity is depleted with team work, and with the requirement to display a kind of shallow friendliness at all times. As Sennett says ›teamwork is the group practice of demeaning superficiality‹ (Sennett 1998: 99). Discussing how new technology appeared to create efficiency he writes ›Computerised baking had profoundly changed the balletic physical activities of the shop floor. Now the bakers make no physical contact with the materials or the loaves of bread‹, this produces ›weak work identity‹ and a ›lack of attachment‹ which is also ›coupled with confusion‹. Looking back at the age of the bigger institutions and the legacy of bureaucracy Sennett suggests that one of the great strengths here for ordinary people was ›the gift of organised time‹ (Sennett 2006: 36).

ARTISTS, CRAFTSMEN, MOTHERS, CITY-DWELLERS

Sennett proposes the revival of the idea of craftsmanship as a counter to the prevailing ethos of creative work and the wider environment of speeded-up flexible labour. This is also a much expanded notion of craft.

› (I)it cuts a far wider swath than skilled manual labour, it serves the computer programmer, the doctor and the artist.; parenting improves when it is practised as a skilled craft, as does citizenship‹ (Sennett 2008: 9).

It is not simply a matter of extending craft values to professional activities however. Sennett is emphasising the value of jobs which could be seen as monotonous or mundane, and here he challenges Arendt's idea of transcending the drudgery of sheer repetitive work undertaken to fulfil basic human needs, in contrast to the more stimulating work when men use their brains and imaginations, something that can only be done when the drudgery of mundane work is completed or carried out by someone else. In an egalitarian spirit, Sennett refutes this division. The two are frequently bound and are mutually dependent on each other, requiring deep concentration and producing pleasures and satisfactions from getting it right. In a kind of post-feminist move Sennett's writing serves to re-valorise housework, cooking and childcare and on several occasions he refers to the craft of parenting. And yet, although nowadays often carried out by both mothers and fathers, both housework and childcare, remain disproportionately women's work. It is hard to read Sennett's work as a feminist and not think about the work of the domestic sphere. Its temporality lies outside the time relations of capitalism, (as 1970s feminists argued, if such work was subjected to market forces and had to be paid for, the cost of nanny-time would be exorbitant) its space is often the home or the local public facilities of park, swimming pool, library, football pitch. The idea of a good job well done, takes the form of emotional satisfaction, and the deep but often overlooked pleasures of motherhood. In the late 1970s Julia Kristeva discussed ›women's time‹ (Kristeva 1981). Despite numerous and often cited objections, notably from Gayatri Spivak, it retains value for its notion of a different temporality imposed on women's lives through their primary responsibility for looking after children and the home (Spivak 1981). But can women's work looking after children be really incorporated into the idea of craft? This modality of labour remains too closely tied to the image of the solitary male worker, engrossed in the task at hand, which entails an object. And the frustrations he may experience when things go wrong are quite far removed from the frustrations and tiredness of doing the same thing day in day out with pre- school age children. Some of what Sennett finds important in the idea of craft can also be seen to exist in the bringing up of children. Both exist outside the time relations of speeded up capitalism, both bring body and mind together, one must handle a child with the same care as the craftsman, and with a constant eye and relentless concentration. Here too is improvisation, and there is also the entrenched inter-generational passing on of knowledge and advice between mothers, and indeed between women. So where does this lead to? Does Sennett's concept of craft subsume the rewards of mothering and of parenting? As mothers, women have always been flexible workers. Close to home and community, both under-employed and over-employed with wildly irregular hours, they have also relied on female friendships and support networks which refute the mentality of the »no long term« ethos. Their narratives just like those of the older male workers to whom Sennett listens in great details, also give sustenance and maintain social bonds. But housework in itself is not part of paid labour, so it cannot be considered alongside the traditional jobs now being eclipsed or left to die. There may be an increasing demand for jobs associated with motherhood such as cleaning and care work, which are now part of the new service sector. These are frequently low paid jobs performed by migrants who are desperate to get a foothold in the labour market. Caring for the elderly may well bring some rewards but repetitive cleaning and caring are more often associated with monotony and exhaustion. This marks the egalitarian limits of craft. Where it may be fruitful to downgrade the dizzy expectations of artists and creative people so that they can sit alongside others, and benefit from the time-slow pace of a mode of working which gratifies on the basis of the job being done for its own sake, it proves more difficult to upgrade some stubbornly unrewarding jobs such as domestic cleaning.

What Sennett calls the »new culture of capitalism« has the opposite effect of reducing social ills. In regard to the new creative economy it resurrects social hierarchies and disconnects the young people habiting the spaces of the urban cultural economy, from their neighbours and from the other people making a living in these same spaces. Often these are poor and disadvantaged communities dominated by informal or irregular economies (fruit and vegetable shops, cab companies, internet shops, small cafes, cheap clothing outlets etc). The artists and creative people are also led to believe their work is exceptional and unique through the prevailing vocabularies of coolness and hipness which pervade the various forms of media that monitor and promote the rise of the talent economy. Hence this creative work is understood to have nothing in common with more ordinary people trying to make a living in difficult circumstances. This disaggregating ethos also serves to further de-politicise creative work, lifting it out of any obvious connection with other more mundane work and separating out people by means of complex »dividing practices« which allow for the creation of new, more competitive social hierarchies. Likewise in the often rundown and hence relatively cheaper areas of the cities in which such young people often live, there too they are isolated from others and dependent instead on their own party network and club scenes. Such a scenario, although immediately recognisable, is not inevitable. It is a sign of the success of the strategy embarked upon by New Labour under its *Cool Britannia* agenda that we now think of graduates of art schools as largely apolitical and individualist with little concern about the urban environment other than as a »site specific« showcase for their own talents. There has been a very determined strategy to sever the connections between the creative economy and the social democratic and radical values which have historically underpinned the provision of education and training for this sector through the post-war years. We could see this as an attempt, through the insertion of neo-liberal vocabularies, to disconnect a sector of the middle classes who in the past, through their cultural and creative training and expertise, would often have aligned themselves with radical political perspectives such as anti-racism, multi-culturalism, feminism, anti-poverty issues etc. The new generation of city dwellers are also disconnected from, or seemingly disinterested in, the histories of urban activism of past generations. The question is, can this be reversed? Is it possible that by re-visiting the history of how feminists, anti-racists, artists and creative people have, in the not so distant past, involved themselves productively in many forms of urban and neighbourhood politics, the hype around creativity as network sociality, and on the artist as manager of his or her own brand, may be eclipsed?[17] In this chapter and following Sennett I have argued that there is scope for developing a more critical perspective so that the Florida-led euphoria could be interrupted with an insistence on a vocabulary which refuses hyperbole, glamour and excitement and which brings into play topics such as under-employment, craft, dedication, public-mindedness, social care and the retrieval of time and space from the speeded-up creativity-machine. To sum up, we could say that contemporary neo-liberal values seek to extol the importance of entrepreneurial activities in the cultural and creative sector as a means of re-stratifying sectors of the educated middle-classes so that this group are weaned off reliance on the public sector which used to provide a »job for life« while also seeing their seeming privileges maintained through the idea of pleasurable or self-expressive work, even when this entails a shift to dependency on over-stretched family economies as part of the new rhetoric of human capital. This is effected through the injecting of positive and exciting meanings into a terrain of work which is precarious and insecure and often poorly paid. Because the arts and culture have long enjoyed high status and prestige, this further enhancement through glamour and the encouragement of talent is particularly appealing and has become a mode of self-government, a disciplining of the self through the extraction of creativity from some inner sources of the soul, the psyche or the heart. The value of Sennett's work is to demote creativity and to emphasise craft. In short finding some occupational niche nowadays within the fields of art and culture serves as a valid passport into the ranks of the middle classes, as the old careers are transformed or in decline. The value of Sennett's work however, is to demote creativity and emphasise craft. This permits a more egalitarian ethos to prevail. Likewise his writing on the urban landscape permits a potential for new radicalism within and beyond the dictates of the flexible city.

References

Arvidsson, Adam and Giannino Malossi (2011). Customer Co-production from Social Factory to Brand: Learning from Italian Fashion. In: Detlev Zwick and Julien Cayla (eds.). *Inside Marketing*. Oxford: Oxford University Press
Beck, Ulrich (1996). *The Risk Society: Towards a New Modernity*. London: Sage

---

17 | The artist Isaac Julien's life history, as a young black boy growing up in east London in the late 1970s and early '80s, and also many aspects of his art works, tell one version of this alternative story. Further back to the mid 1970s every city in the UK had artists, musicians, film-makers and writers who were deeply invested in the urban culture around them and committed to defending disadvantaged people in these areas from social injustice, aggressive policing and from various forms of mistreatment on the basis of poverty and powerlessness.

Beck, Ulrich (2000). *The Brave New World of Work*. Cambridge: Polity Press
Berardi, Franco (2009). *The Soul At Work: From Alienation to Autonomy*. Boston: MIT Press
Bourdieu, Pierre (1993). *The Field of Cultural Production*. Cambridge: Polity Press
Foucault, Michel (2006). *The Birth of Biopolitics: Lectures at the College de France 1978–79*. Basingstoke: Palgrave
Geyrhalter, Nikolaus (director) (2005). *Our Daily Bread*. Austria
Gill, Rosalind and Andy Pratt (2008). In the Social Factory? Immaterial Labour, Precariousness and Cultural Work. In: *Theory, Culture & Society*, 25(7-8): 1–30
Jakob, Doreen (2009). *Beyond Creative Production Networks: The Development of Intra-Metropolitan Creative Industry Clusters in Berlin and New York*. Berlin: Rhombos
Kristeva, Julia (1981). Women's Time. In: *Signs*, 7(1): 13–35
Lange, Bastian et al. (2008). Berlin's creative Industries: Governing Creativity. In: *Industry and Innovation*, 15 (Summer): 531–548
Lazzarato, Maurizio (1999). *Immaterial Labour*. [www.generation-online.org]
Lloyd, Richard (2009). *Neo-Bohemia: Art and Commerce in the Postindustrial City*. Chicago: University of Chicago Press
McRobbie, Angela (1998). *British Fashion Design: Rag Trade or Image Industry?* London: Routledge
McRobbie, Angela (2002a). From Holloway to Hollywood: Happiness at Work in the New Cultural Economy. In: Paul du Gay and Michael Pryke (eds.). *Cultural Economy*. London: Sage
McRobbie, Angela (2002b). Club to Company: Notes on the Decline of Political Culture in Speeded Up Creative Worlds. In: *Cultural Studies*, 16 (4): 518–531
McRobbie, Angela (2004). Making a Living in London's Small-Scale Creative Sector. In: Allen J. Scott and Dominic Power (eds.). *Cultural Industries and the Production of Culture*. London: Routledge
McRobbie, Angela (2011). *Der Himmel ist nicht so blau*. [www.angelamcrobbie.com]
Sennett, Richard (1993). *The Conscience of the Eye: The Design and Social Life of Cities*. New York, London: W.W. Norton
Sennett, Richard (1998). *The Corrosion of Character: the Personal Consequences of Work in the New Capitalism*. New York, London: W.W. Norton
Sennett, Richard (2001). *The Flexible City*. [www.richardsennett.com]
Sennett, Richard (2003). *Respect: The Formation of Character in an Age of Inequality*. London: Penguin
Sennett, Richard (2006). *The Culture of the New Capitalism*. New Haven, London: Yale University Press
Sennett, Richard (2008). *The Craftsman*. London: Penguin

Spivak, Gayatri Chakravorty (1981). French Feminism in an International Frame. In: *Yale French Studies*, 62: 154–184
Turanskyj, Tatjana (director) (2010). *Eine flexible Frau*. Germany
Wiseman, Frederick (director) (2009). *La Danse*. France/USA
Zukin, Sharon (2010) *Naked City: The Death and Life of Authentic Urban Places*. Oxford: Oxford University Press

Individualization Cosmopolitanized

Of the Individual and Individualization: The Striving Individual in China and the Theoretical Implications[1]

YUNXIANG YAN

The individualization thesis, one of the three theorems in Ulrich Beck's theory of reflexive modernization, or second modernity (Beck and Beck-Gernsheim 2010: xiv), has become increasingly influential in the English-speaking world, as evidenced by both its wide application in empirical research (Hansen and Svarverud 2010; Howard 2007; Yan 2009) and the theoretical debate about its key notions and methodology (Atkinson 2007; Beck 2007; Roberts 2010; Woodman 2009).

To better understand the individualization thesis, one must be aware of the differences between individualization and individualism, institutional changes at macro level of society and biographical changes at a micro level of the individual, and finally the objective and subjective dimensions of the individualization process. These distinctions are made primarily to prevent the misunderstanding that individualization is a manifestation of the values of individualism, or simply the rise of the individual; instead, individualization under second modernity often presents itself as the antithesis of individualism (Beck 1992, 2007). In a recent response to his critics, Beck reemphasizes the importance of making these distinctions:

›In other words, *individualization* must be clearly distinguished from *individualism*. Whereas individualism is commonly understood as a personal attitude or preference, individualization refers to a macro-sociological phenomenon, which possibly – but then again perhaps not – results in changes in attitude in individuals. That is the *crux of con-*

---

[1] | I owe special thanks to Ulrich Beck, Elisabeth Gernsheim-Beck, Angelika Poferl and Charles Stafford for valuable comments on an earlier draft as well as the participants in the Symposium ›Futures of Modernity‹ for their questions and comments. I am grateful to John Simon Guggenheim Foundation for the 2010-2011 Guggenheim Fellowship that allowed me to concentrate on the writing of this article.

tingency – how individuals deal with it remains an open question‹ (2007: 681; italics in original).

The intriguing point is that despite Beck's numerous efforts to clarify this basic point, there is still no lack of misunderstandings about individualization as individualism. The most interesting example is Paul de Beer's empirical test of individualization. He begins with a concise summary of the individualization thesis, especially the passivity of the individual in the process, and the distinction between individualization and individualism. He then proceeds to examine how individualized the Dutch have become by testing the extent of detraditionalization, emancipation, and heterogenization, based on the hypotheses that individuals should no longer be influenced by objective standards and should be less predictable and more heterogeneous in choice-making. By doing this, de Beer overlooks the fact that institutionalized individualization in second modernity actually leads to an increased dependence of the individual on institutions (Beck 1992, 2007) and to the paradoxical process of conformity through choices (Bauman 2001). Thus, he ends up falling into the same trap of equating individualization with individualism, concluding that the empirical test does not support the last two of the three indicators and therefore Dutch individuals have not become more individualistic (de Beer 2007: 404 ff.).

Why it is so easy to confuse individualization with individualism or to overlook the three distinctions that Beck has made on a number of occasions? Habitual thinking is one reason because the term »individualization« historically has been entangled with individualism. Another reason, however, may lie in the relationship between the individual and individualization. Although the general pattern of individualization under second modernity shows that the individual is forced to choose and to act upon herself (Bauman 2001; Beck 1992; Rose 1998), in some specific areas of social life the individual seems indeed to act proactively and to be motivated by values of individualism. The quest for gender equality and the feminist movement provide good examples in this regard, and the fact that the politics of gender caused further changes in family law and the family institution shows that, in some cases, individualization can be initiated and pursued by the individual instead of being imposed on the individual, as shown by Beck and Beck-Gernsheim's study of the radical changes in intimate relationship and the family institution in Germany (1995, 2002: 54 ff.).

Moreover, the distinction between the objective and subjective dimensions of individualization may obscure as much as it clarifies and it may risk excluding the individual from studies of individualization. The macro-objective and micro-subjective dimensions of individualization may be conceptually distinguishable (and must be separated for the sake of theoretical clarity), yet they are the two sides of the same coin in the actual process of individualization in everyday life. »A life of one's own,« or »DIY biography,« can hardly become new patterns of social situations unless a sufficient number of individuals actively pursue them as new life ideals, which at the same time is intrinsically subjective. An emphasis on the passivity of the individual helps to support the institutional nature of individualization under second modernity, yet it also carries the risk of excluding the actor – the individual – from the action of individualization and consequently delinks the two sides of the same process of social interaction. It is both timely and important to take a closer look at the *crux of contingency* to which Beck refers in the above quote, that is, how the actual, flesh-and-bone individual deals with individualization in a specific temporal and special context.

This is precisely the aim of this essay. In the following, I will first briefly describe the role of the Chinese individual in the ongoing process of individualization; next I will examine the kind of new individual that the Chinese process of individualization has produced. I conclude by comparing the Chinese case with that of Western Europe, arguing that it is quite important to examine the different roles of the individual in individualization and consequently the different impacts of individualization on the making of the new individual in different social settings.

THE INDIVIDUAL AND THE CHINESE PATH TO INDIVIDUALIZATION

In traditional China, the individual belonged to and remained secondary to the group or collective. The group (be it the family or the state) did not exist to support the individual; it was the other way around – the individual existed to continue the group. In this sense, there was no individual identity because the individual only existed in relation to and for the sake of social groups, such as the family, lineage, or a network of ranked social relations (Fei 1992 [1947]; Baker 1979). At the turn of the twentieth century, however, many Chinese intellectuals identified the prolonged oppression of the individual to be one of the major causes of China's decline and thus called for the liberation of the individual from her traditional bondage. They hoped to recast the individual into a new type of responsible and competitive citizen who devotes herself/himself to the great goal of building a strong and modern China. This was both part of the modernization dream and at the same time a key strategy to modernize (Schwarcz 1986). Liang Qichao, the enlightenment figure of modern China, was among the most influential to advocate tirelessly for the making of the new individual. He also claimed that the individual has a dual self: the small self centered on personal interest and the great self based on the interest of the nation; when the two are in conflict, the small self must submit to the great self (Liang 1998 [1906]; Chang 1971). Liang's theory of the new individual, especially his notion of the dual self, was widely accepted by intellectuals and reform-minded political elites of different ideological persuasions and by different political powers because it continued the traditional supremacy of the collective over the individual, while, at the same time, calling on the individual to strive for the sake of modernity and nation-building. However, the theory remained primarily at the level of discourse among the educated elite prior to the 1949 Communist revolution. With respect to actual changes in the social structure and their impact on the individual, the Maoist era of radical socialism was the first stage in the Chinese path to individualization.

As I document elsewhere (Yan 2010), after the 1949 revolution, the party-state gradually established a comprehensive system of production, redistribution, and social control through four mechanisms: the class label system classifying Chinese people into different status groups, the household registration system regulating people's residence and travel, the work-unit system enabling the party-state to monopolize employment opportunities, and the political dossier system controlling chances for upward mobility. These four mechanisms, which in practice fixed the individual to an almost immutable position with a standard biography, resulted from a series of ideological, political, and economic projects of social engineering that aimed to transform China into a strong and wealthy modern nation-state. Through land reform and the nationalization of industry and commerce, the party-state eliminated private ownership of the means of production as well as, to a great extent, the free market. Individuals first were mobilized to break away from the former all-encompassing social categories of the extended family, kinship organization, and local community, and then were organized to join the newly established rural collectives and urban work units as members of the new socialist society. Old patterns of interpersonal relations that centered on the family were denounced as feudalistic, and a new universalistic comradeship was created to guide interactions among individuals as well as the relationship between the individual and the state (Vogel 1965). The socialist transformation project penetrated the private life sphere through the women's liberation movement, new laws and regulations on sex and marriage, and new patterns of consumption and lifestyle. Romantic love, gender equality, freedom of marriage, and independence were promoted by state-sponsored projects of social transformation (Yan 2003). Accompanying these institutional changes, endless ideological campaigns attacked the traditional cultural values such as Confucian ethics and promoted the Maoist morality of class struggle, revolution, and self-sacrifice for the sake of the Communist utopia (Ci 1994; Madson 1984; Cheng 2009: 48 ff.).

Measured by the tripartite yardstick of liberation, loss of stability, and re-integration (or, disembedment, detraditionalization, and re-embedment) in the theorem of individualization (Beck 1992: 128), it is plausible to argue that under China's radical Maoist socialism a partial individualization occurred. The various practices of Maoist socialism were nothing less than a process of de-traditonalizing, disembeding, and re-embedding the individual, shifting the individual from an individual-ancestor (read: family) axis in social relations to a new axis based on the party-state. For generations of youth and women, this was particularly liberating as they had existed on the margins in traditional society where the individual lived under the shadow of his ancestors throughout his life course (Hsu 1948). Yet, we must also keep in mind that, paradoxically, all of these changes of partial individualization were carried out by the collectives led by the party-state, and the individual had to submit his/her small self to the great self represented by the party-state.

The individualization process in post-Mao China first emerged as a reflexive correction of the most radical mistakes of Maoist socialism, but it gradually went on to negate the Maoist path to modernity and became a full-blown market-oriented developmental strategy of the party-state as well as a life-changing social transformation. By the turn of the new century, it had led to the rise of the individual on the one hand and the individualization of the social structure on the other. Whereas the rise of the individual is primarily reflected in the changing patterns of individual biographies, the structural changes mostly result from institutional reforms, policy changes, and the impact of the market economy (Yan 2009, 2010).

It is impossible to briefly review this ongoing three-decade-long process; instead, I will highlight the role of the individual in this process. In retrospect, it becomes clear that during the 1980s many important reform initiatives were initiated by individuals against political-ideological pressures; but since the mid-1990s, most reform initiatives were promoted by the party-state against resistance by individuals. For example, in the late 1970s individual villagers boldly attempted to contract collective land to private households in order to boost agricultural productivity, eventually leading to the dismantling of the rural collectives; individual managers initiated new models of management and responsibility in the early 1980s, a first step that developed into the dramatic privatization of state enterprises in the early 1990s; and individual vendors and peddlers broke the ice by selling foods, clothing, and services on the streets, producing the booming private sector that accounted for almost half of China's GDP in 2006. By 2005, the total number of private business people reached almost 30 million, who in turn employed more than 96 million workers (see Tsai 2007: 51 ff.). Considering that there had been virtually no labor market under radical Maoist socialism and, at least in theory, no one worked outside the socialist planned economy until the late 1970s, this steady and rapid growth of a private labor market from zero to the 126 million individuals in the urban private sector plus the millions of peasants engaged in private farming constitute the most radical shift leading to the individualization of Chinese society. To take these initiatives, individuals had to face the political risks of being labeled anti-socialist and to run the risks of severe punishment. For example, many of the first generation of private business people were jailed for subverting the collective economy; even moonlighting during one's spare time could result in imprisonment because one's time still belonged to the party-state (Wu 2007: 86 f.).

During the 1980s the party-state was cautious about any changes in individualization and privatization because it remained under the spell of the Communist ideology and the planned economy. What it did was to gradually loosen up its control over the economy, selectively tolerating bold individual attempts to reform from below, making policy adjustments to accommodate successful local experiments, and calling for nation-wide institutional changes after local experiments were repeatedly tested on larger scales (White 1993: 21 ff.). This is known as *songbang* in Chinese, meaning to untie the individual from the socialist redistributive system. Most individuals in China welcomed this pattern of institutional change and actively participated in the process. At the same time, a consensus in favor of a market economy as a modernization strategy was formed among Chinese leaders, culminating in the formal decision at the 1992 Fourteenth Party Congress to build a socialist market economy, which was then written into the Chinese state Constitution in 1993.

After the 1992–93 turning point, the party-state completed its ideological reorientation and began aggressively promoting in a top-down fashion a series of marketization and privatization reforms aimed at cutting social welfare and shifting more responsibilities to the individual, such as the large-scale downsizing and privatization of state-owned enterprises (SOEs). This was accomplished between 1998 and 2003 through bankruptcies, sales and auctions, mergers, and acquisitions. Chinese official data reveal that between 1998 and 2003 more than 30 million workers were laid off from the SOEs, representing a 40 percent cut in the SOE work force (see Hurst 2009: 16). Unlike their rural counterparts, SOE workers did not have many incentives to leave the work-unit system which provided them with life-time employment, housing, medical care, pensions, and other benefits. Thus, the dramatic cuts and lay-offs in the public sector did not originate with individual initiative and support from below; in fact, throughout the second half of the 1990s, laid-off workers strongly resisted the institutional changes by taking to the streets, petitioning to upper-levels of government, and participating in other forms of resistance (Hurst 2009; Lee 2007).

In a similar vein, the three major reform projects since the late 1990s, namely, the privatization of housing and the marketization of education and medical care are all institutional changes launched by the state to force individuals to take more responsibilities, to more actively engage in market-based competition, and to take more risks and be more reflexive. These institutional and policy changes have eliminated most of the responsibilities of the state; local government agencies have become increasingly developmental at best and predatory at worst. Therefore, these institutional changes toward individualization have been referred to as »*xieze*« (meaning for the party-state to be »rid of responsibilities«).

At the level of ideology, the discourse on *suzhi* and the rise of consumerism played a crucial role in shaping the mentality of the individual. The Chinese term *suzhi* refers to the innate and nurtured physical, psychological, intellectual, and moral qualities of a human being, a group, or an entire population. In the early 1980s, the term was primarily used by government officials to carry out population-planning policies. Thereafter, it was frequently used in terms of education reform, governance of migrant workers, and the construction of civility among citizens. Most importantly, as many scholars point out, the *suzhi* discourse requires the individual to constantly improve and develop herself and obligates the individual to be self-motivated, self-disciplined, and self-reliant (see, e.g., Anagnost 2004; Kipnis 2006; Tomba 2009). Whereas the *suzhi* discourse encourages the individual to run faster, consumerism serves as a moving carrot hanging in front of the running individual. To distract public attention from political issues in the aftermath of the 1989 pro-democracy social movement and to stimulate the domestic market, in the early 1990s the party-state suddenly shifted course from its previous anti-consumerism stance to become a powerful advocate of mass consumption and consumerism and since then it has continued to grant more consumer rights and choices to Chinese individuals (Davis 2000; Palmer 2006; Yan 2009). As a result, by the turn of the 21st century material and sexual desires were celebrated through public culture and commercial outlets, individual freedom and choice had developed widely and rapidly in the sphere of private life, and instant gratification by way of materialism was dominating the moral landscape of China (Rofel 2007). Working together but in different ways, the *suzhi* discourse and the ideology of consumerism formed the push-and-pull forces that compelled the individual to take on more responsibilities and to work harder.

In short, the relationship between the Chinese individual and individualization is dynamic and interactive. Overall, from the late 1970s to the mid-1990s most individuals welcomed individualization; in fact many were the initiators or catalysts of individualization because of their sufferings under the stagnant planned economy and their yearnings for freedom, choice, and prosperity. After the mid-1990s, however, a many ordinary people, especially workers in state-owned enterprises, became the victims of individualization because they lost the social safety net that had previously provided by the socialist planned economy and because the departmental state had retreated from its former responsibilities. The shift from enthusiastic participation to passive resistance took place among the winners from these changes as well. During the 1980s and 1990s, the newly emerging white-collar class of well-educated and young professionals was the poster child of the market economy and the most proactive force for individualization. Yet, along with the sky-high housing prices, rising costs of child rearing, and increasingly cut-throat job competition in the new century, the upwardly mobile young professionals also found themselves struggling to cope with the challenges and risks generated by the escalating market-oriented individualization as well as by their inner fears of insecurity (Xu 2011). Although a few with special political capital could resist the trend by playing the politics of identity and patriotism (see Li 2010), most individuals had to internalize the negative impacts of individualization by taking on more responsibilities and working harder, leading to the emergence of a new type of self – which I call the »striving individual.«

A SKETCH OF THE STRIVING INDIVIDUAL IN CHINA

Let me start with a particular individual who goes all out to strive for a hard-to-reach goal. When I revisited Xiajia village in 2008 for the tenth time, a rural community in northeast China where I lived as a farmer in the 1970s and have been conducting longitudinal fieldwork since 1989, Mr. Wang, the son of an old friend of mine, agreed to talk with me for no more than one hour out of his busy schedule. In his late thirties, Mr. Wang looked at least 10 years older – his hands were rough, his face wrinkled, and his voice revealed anxiety and emptiness. ›I am exhausted and scared,‹ he told me matter of factually. To make a long story short, growing up in a poor family, he quit school after eighth grade to work full-time on a farm but he soon joined other villagers seeking temporary jobs in the cities. Like most migrant workers in urban areas, Wang endured long hours of heavy manual labor, lengthy separations from his family, and several debilitating work injuries; but, above all, as a member of the lowest ranked social group in urban China he also suffered from various types of open discrimination from government officials, work bosses, and ordinary urban residents. He worked extremely hard, and together with his wife, who suffered from a birth deformity on her right leg, saved every penny for one goal – to send their son to elite schools so that the son would not face a life similar to theirs and would be accorded respect and status in village society. He considered himself lucky because his son had done well in primary and junior high school, and by the time I met Mr. Wang, his son was attending a highly competitive high school in the county seat located 50 kilometers away from Xiajia village. To take care of their child, he and his wife moved to the county seat, where Mr. Wang accepted odd jobs as a temporary laborer and his wife shifted between cleaning rooms at a cheap hotel and taking care of the family. Mr. Wang had to return to Xiajia village to borrow money from relatives because they had not saved enough to pay for their son's tuition which was four times higher than that of a regular middle school. He told me that their debt was already more than seven times their annual income. When I expressed some concern, he said that he had no choice but to continue investing in his son's education: ›If he can get into Peking University like you did in 1978, he will make a lot of money, all our efforts will be worth it, and I will be somebody in the village.‹

Looking into Wang's hopeful eyes during our conversation, I could not bear the thought that each year only a few thousand high school graduates from throughout the country are admitted to Peking University, and, based on what I had heard from local teachers, his son had almost no chance to be accepted even at a second-tier university, much less the top one. Meanwhile, because of the marketization of education, enrollment in Chinese universities has increased drastically, admitting 4.5 million in 2007, 5.3 million in 2008 and 6.1 million in 2009, even though in 2008 and 2009 only 68 percent of college graduates could find employment upon graduation according to the government statistics. By the time Wang's son will graduate from a college, it is very unclear whether he will be able to find a job, and even more so whether he will be able to make the big money that was the dream of his parents. Obviously, Wang and his wife proactively took a DIY biographic approach to solve their problems of poverty, low social status, and lack of upward mobility. But, as Beck points out, the biographic approach can hardly solve systemic problems, an inherent dilemma in individualization.

Mr. Wang is by no means alone; in fact, all villagers in this community did exactly the same, and many strived even harder. More than a dozen parents sent their toddlers to kindergarten in the county seat, and about 11 percent of the village households sent their children to the county seat for education. Nearly 150 young villagers worked in cities all over China for six months or longer, repeating Mr. Wang's dream of twenty years ago, and elderly men and women farmed the land and took care of their grandchildren in the village because the young and able-bodied had all left to work in the cities. Regardless of what they do and where they are, these villagers all share the same determination to work hard, to move up the social ladder, and to create a life of their own.

Looking beyond Xiajia village, we find the same biographic approach being adopted by Chinese individuals in both cities and countryside. According to conservative estimations, the number of rural migrant workers in the cities reached 76 million in 2000, over 100 million in 2005, and close to 150 million in 2010. The majority of these migrant workers do not live with their family members, who are either left behind in the village or who working in other locales, thus creating new social sufferings of individual isolation and estrangement of family ties (see Ye et al. 2005). Workers in factories are under tremendous stress to work harder, faster, and often to work overtime because the wages are too low to have any savings for the future. In 2009, *Time* magazine chose the Chinese worker as the runner-up »person of the year,« recognizing that it was due to the extraordinary hard work of the striving Chinese worker that China had been able to maintain an 8 percent annual rate of economic growth in the aftermath of the global economic crisis, thus helping to stabilize the global economy, and praised the Chinese worker as ›leading the world to economic recovery‹ (Ramzy 2009). It may come as surprising that of the four female workers whose photo is featured by *Time*, one left home to work in a factory at age 16; two left home at age 17; and two had to leave behind their young children when they migrated to find work. Only a few months after the *Time* feature article, thirteen young workers in the giant electronic company Foxconn, which employs 400,000 people in the city of Shenzhen, committed suicide over a span of five months. Follow-up investigations show that although work conditions in this company met most official standards, the Foxconn workers compete with one another to apply for over-time work to receive extra pay and they endure long, monotonous, and boring work on assembly lines. As a labor analysis notes, ›They feel a sense of pressure – pressure to make more money, pressure to work harder, pressure from family or difficulties in personal relationships‹ (quoted in Ramzy 2010).

Workers are certainly not the only striving individuals under pressure; those at higher levels of the pyramid, e.g., the overworked white-collar professionals (Hanser 2001; Hoffman 2010), who must work extra hard to compete with the younger cohort, or the private entrepreneurs who are walking a thin line between economic freedom and political control (Delman and Yin 2008), are all under the same, if not more, pressures and feel the same types of anxiety. Among others, the over-striving and thus overstressed Chinese students have received the most public attention. It can be said that Chinese children are born into a society full of pressures to strive and to succeed, as most parents begin to invest in their child's education shortly after they are conceived, based on the prevailing wisdom that »we cannot afford to let our child fall behind at the departure point.« Starting from kindergarten and all the way to the last year of high school, children are forced by their parents and teachers to focus on only one thing in their learning – obtaining the highest possible test scores – and to reach only one goal in their life – earning admissions to the best universities. This is so much the case that studying hard and testing well have come to define life for most Chinese students (Fong 2004: 31 ff.). This is particularly true for rural students: they have much less access to learning resources yet much more at stake because education is the only way for them to change their social status from rural to urban residents (Kipnis 2001). In one case reported by the media in 2002, a 9-year-old girl in a southern city earned more than a dozen certificates of qualification, covering a wide range of subjects from mathematics, history, and computer science, to English and piano. To obtain these certificates on top of keeping up with her regular school work, she had to sacrifice all her play time, including weekends. When asked why, she calmly told the reporter that she was working for the future because some of the certificates would help her be successful on the job market (Yan 2006).

When almost everyone in the society, from children to adults to the elderly, tries so hard to strive for success, the aggregated competitive pressures drive them to strive even harder. This creates a vicious circle that produces serious mental and physical problems among Chinese individuals. According to a 2004 research report by the Institute of Psychology of the Chinese Academy of Science, psychological pressures on Chinese individuals began to rise in 2000; among others, pressures caused by the lack of a social safety net, to perform well at work, and to make individual achievements are the greatest (Huo 2004). The Regus Business Tracker Survey (2010) confirms this overall trend of increased pressures on Chinese individuals, showing 86 percent of employees in Chinese companies reported an increase in pressure during the past two years, making such pressure in China the highest among the 11,000 companies across thirteen countries in this survey. A 2005 survey shows that more than 65 percent of the respondents worked more than 8 hours per day and more than 20 percent worked more than 10 hours per day. In answering the hypothetical question ›if the bonus is high enough, how many hours per day are you willing to work?‹ 82 percent of the respondents chose ›15 hours or more.‹ (Cheng 2005). According to a number of surveys and media reports, there seems to be connection between striving and early death, which is referred to as »death from overworking«; it is estimated that nearly 600,000 deaths per year are caused by overworking (Xinhua News Agency 2006). A journalist has documented the early deaths of several top CEOs in the Chinese IT sector, whose ages range from 26 to 34 (Shi 2005). Research in 2009 found that the average life expectancy of well-educated professionals in Beijing in 2006 had been reduced by five years, to 53–54, nearly 20 years less than the average life expectancy among all Beijing residents (Pan et al. 2009).

Although motivations to achieve have never been in short supply in Chinese culture, the drive for success has never been as strong and as widespread as it is today. But there are at least two features that set the present striving individual apart from the hard-working person in traditional China. First, the individualization process that I outline above liberated Chinese individuals from the constraints of the previous all-encompassing social categories of the family, kinship, and socialist work unit. Virtually all institutional changes in the reform era were designed to encourage, push, or even force the individual to be more self-reliant and proactive. Throughout its long history, individual agency was never so cherished in the collectivist society as it is today. Second, and more importantly, the meaning of personal achievement has also shifted to the individual. Until the 1980s, a cultural imperative to curb self-interest and submit the ego to a collectivity – be it family, kinship, community, or the state – served as the guiding principle in the cultural construction of the person. Thus, the Chinese individual worked hard first and foremost for the interest of the family group (Harrell 1985). In the post-Mao era, however, the market-oriented reforms effectively made the individual, instead of a collective entity, the new unit of policy making, resource distribution, and social mobilization. Consequently, to strive for self-interest and happiness, the long-condemned corrupt values of the petty bourgeoisie all of a sudden became not only a legitimate goal but also a preferred new spirit of the reform era (Wang 2002). By the late 1990s, the zeal to make it big was further crystallized in new imagery of successful individuals (*chenggong renshi* in Chinese), who often appeared in commercials and the mass media as fashionable, rich, and confident individuals – mostly men but occasionally women as well (Wang 1998). The new role model of successful and self-serving people replaced the former socialist morality that stressed sacrificing oneself for communism and implicitly further negated the traditional ethic of glorifying one's ancestors that had already been attacked by Communist ethics. Thus, the moral meanings of working hard were also individualized.

VARIETIES OF INDIVIDUALIZATION: THE STRIVING INDIVIDUAL VS. THE ENTERPRISING SELF

Elsewhere I examine the mentality changes of the Chinese individual in post-Mao China and refer to the new type of individual emerging out of the individualization process as »the striving individual« (Yan 2012). The striving individual is driven by an urge to succeed or a fear of failure, or a combination of both; in order to succeed and to avoid losing out, the individual must be industrious, self-disciplined, calculating, and pragmatic. Yet, because of the entanglement of different value systems and the Chinese path to individualization (Yan 2010), to a great extent the striving individual is confined to the sphere of private life and to economic activities in the public sphere; success is mainly defined in materialistic terms, namely, income, accumulated wealth, and purchasing power. One of the most recent material indicators of success is home ownership, which has gained the moral meaning of defining one's personhood, as young people, especially young men, are not regarded as adults unless they own a private flat (Zhang 2010). Individual autonomy and freedom have not developed much beyond the pursuit of personal interest and the striving individual has become increasingly apolitical and devoid of civic obligations (Yan 2012, 2003). By being part of the consequences of individualization, the striving individual in China differs from her counterparts in contemporary Western societies, which Nikolas Rose refers to as the »enterprising self.«

Based on Foucault's notions of governmentality and the technologies of the self, Rose claims that the liberal-democratic polities in Western societies have helped to produce a new type of individual:

›The enterprising self will make an enterprise of its life, seek to maximize its own human capital, project itself a future, and seek to shape itself in order to become that which it wishes to be. The enterprising self is thus both an active self and a calculating self, a self that calculates *about* itself and that acts *upon* itself in order to better itself‹ (1998: 154; italics in original).

It is noteworthy that when analyzing the social causes for the making of the enterprise self, Rose refers to the same economic and political regimes featured in Beck's individualization thesis. Whereas Beck chooses to focus on the objective dimensions of individualization, such as the changing patterns of employment, education, and family laws, Rose turns his attention to the role of psychology in the individualization process and therefore by default studies the subjective dimensions of individualization. In an interesting way, Rose answers the question about how the individual deals with individualization in Western European societies – a missing link in Beck's theory – and goes further to explore the subjective consequences of objective individualization, that is, the making of the enterprising self.

On the surface, the striving individual in contemporary China resembles Rose's enterprising self because the Chinese individual is also experiencing patterns of social change similar to the individualization process in Western Europe. Like the enterprising self, the striving individual in China is a self-driven, calculating, and determined subject who wants to better her life in accordance with individual plans, seeking to live »a life of one's own« or a »do-it-yourself biography« (see Beck 1992; Beck and Beck-Gernsheim 2002).

Yet, there are also deeply rooted differences between the Chinese case and its counterpart in Western societies, chief among which is the absence of classical liberalism in the Chinese polity and consequently the unfinished task of emancipation politics. This remains the greatest challenge for the striving individual in China. In contrast, the enterprising self is born out of the presupposition about the individual's natural rights of autonomy, freedom, choice, liberty, and identity, which ›underpinning and legitimating political activity imbues the political mentalities of the modern West‹ (Rose 1998: 151). Similarly, Beck's individualization thesis identifies three preconditions for the wave of individualization in second modernity, namely, cultural democracy, the welfare state, and classic individualism (see Bauman 2001; Beck 1992; Beck and Beck-Gernsheim 2002). To my mind, these are two sides of the same coin of the liberal-democratic polity that has been succinctly described by Charles Taylor as a gradual yet consistent growth of a new moral order concerning how human beings should live together in a given society (Taylor 2004). This is also what Bauman refers to as the individual *de jure*; what he is mostly concerned with is how the individual *de jure* can become the individual *de facto* by way of the realization of all legal rights among citizens (2001: 105 ff.). In contrast, the individual *de jure* has yet come close to the Chinese landscape of political morality.

This fundamental difference not only sets the Chinese variety of individualization apart from its counterparts in the UK or Germany, or any Western society (see Yan 2010), it also determines that the relationship between the individual and individualization in China is entangled with the political agenda of the party-state and the particular features of the striving individual arising out of this process. Briefly, the striving individual in China differs from the enterprising self in three specific ways. First, the Chinese individual strives for the goals of first modernity which are almost entirely defined in China in materialistic terms; in contrast both Beck and Rose recognize that during the second wave of individualization in Western Europe, emancipation politics and economic development are no longer the main goals and consequently the enterprising self shows a strong tendency of post-materialism. Second, although the materialistic orientation of the striving individual can in part explain the economic miracle in China during the last three decades, it also further minimizes the scope of choices that an individual can make in applying the biographic approach to solve real-life problems. Due to the overwhelming pressures to make money, the striving individual cannot be enterprising about any other pursuits and must only focus on working hard and earning more money. Third, because of the lack of liberal politics and a moral order of the individual as the bearer of natural rights, in all important areas of public life, such as free speech or self-organized collective action, the striving individual is still tightly controlled and regulated by the party-state. There is no legal basis for individualization but there is also no shortage of gray areas for the striving individual to map out and take advantage of. Being unable to claim and defend one's rights against the powerful party-state, the striving individual can only increase her/his compatibility against that of fellow individuals, deepening the imbalance of rights and duties between the individual and the state. This feature is noted by Rose when he attempts to apply his theory of bio-citizenship to China:

›It seemed that in China, at the start of the new millennium, while there was no »right to health« there was nonetheless a growing individual »duty to be well« – or rather, an obligation to seek to maximize one's quality in all ways possible‹ (2011: 251).

Finally, my research on the Chinese case shows that how the individual deals with individualization may vary from one society to another, one social group to another, and one temporal context to another. As indicated above, in Western European societies, women and their supporters have long been proactively pushing for the individualization of family law and the family institution, albeit with the individualization imposed on individuals in other areas of social life. In China, the most striking variation lies in the temporal context, as most individuals actively embraced individualization in the first stage of the post-Mao reform but turned to either resist or to involuntarily cope with it since 1992-93. Variations in individual responses to individualization in China also occurred across social groups and gender lines, but they are not as remarkable as those across the temporal divide. Unlike in Western Europe where individualization results from the radicalization of modernity itself, Chinese individualization remains a developmental strategy under the direction and management of the powerful party-state.

The Chinese case is by no means an exception. Once the individualization thesis, alone or together with other theses in the theory of second modernity, is applied to non-European societies that are in different stages of development and modernization, the result of empirical research is bound to be rich and rewarding (see case studies in Beck and Grande 2010). The debates on whether the agency of the individual matters in the process of individualization, to what extent the concept of class has become a zombie category, and in what sense the subjective dimension of individualization can be delinked from the objective dimension of the same process (Atkinson 2007; Beck 2007; de Beer 2007; Howard 2007; Roberts 2010; Woodman 2009) have also opened up new horizons in further developing the theory that catches the essence of modern changes in all types of societies in our time, that is, the re-formation of the relationship between the individual and society. An important implication arises: how the individual deals with individualization is both path-dependent and path-constitutive; consequently, there will be different varieties of the new individual emerging out of the differing varieties of individualization.

References

Anagnost, Ann (2004). The Corporeal Politics of Quality (*Suzhi*). In: *Public Culture*, 16 (2): 189–208

Atkinson, Will (2007). Beck, Individualization and the Death of Class: A Critique. In: *British Journal of Sociology*, 58(3): 349–365

Baker, Hugh (1979). *Chinese Family and Kinship*. New York: Columbia University Press

Bauman, Zygmunt (2001). *The Individualized Society*. Cambridge: Polity Press

Beck, Ulrich (1992). *Risk Society: Towards a New Modernity*. Trans. Mark Ritter. London and Thousand Oaks: Sage Publications

Beck, Ulrich (2007). Beyond Class and Nation: Reframing Social Inequalities in a Globalizing World. In: *British Journal of Sociology*, 58(4): 679–705

Beck, Ulrich and Elisabeth Beck-Gernsheim (1995). *The Normal Chaos of Love*. Cambridge: Polity Press

Beck, Ulrich and Elisabeth Beck-Gernsheim (2002). *Individualization: Institutionalized Individualism and its Social and Political Consequences*. London and Thousand Oaks: Sage Publications

Beck, Ulrich and Elisabeth Beck-Gernsheim (2010). Foreword: Varieties of Individualization. In: Mette Halskov Hansen and Rune Svarverud (eds.). *iChina: The Rise of the Individual in Modern Chinese Society*. Copenhagen: NIAS Press

Beck, Ulrich and Edgar Grande (eds.) (2010). Special Issue: Varieties of Second Modernity: Extra European and European Experiences and Perspectives. In: *The British Journal of Sociology*, 61(3): 409–596

Chang, Hao (1971). *Liang Ch'i-ch'ao and Intellectual Transition in China, 1890–1927*. Cambridge: Harvard University Press

Cheng Mei (2005). Zhongqingnian guolaozi xianxiang (The phenomenon of death caused by overworking among young and mid-aged Chinese). In: *Zhongguo Qingnianbao*, April 18

Cheng, Yinghong (2009). *Creating the »New Man«: From Enlightenment Ideals to Socialist Realities*. Honolulu: University of Hawai'i Press

Ci, Jiwei (1994). *Dialectic of the Chinese Revolution: From Utopianism to Hedonism*. Stanford: Stanford University Press

Davis, Deborah S. (ed.) (2000). *The Consumer Revolution in Urban China*. Berkeley: University of California Press

De Beer, Paul (2007). How Individualized Are the Dutch? In: *Current Sociology*, 55(3): 389–413

Delman, Jørgen and Xiaoqing Yin (2008). Individualization and Politics in China: The Political Identity and Agency of Private Business People. In: *European Journal of East Asian Studies*, 7(1): 39–73

Fei Xiaotong (1992 [1947]). *From the Soil: The Foundations of Chinese Society (Xiangtu Zhongguo)*, trans. by Gary Hamilton and Wang Zheng. Berkeley: University of California Press

Fong, Vanessa L. (2004). *Only Hope: Coming of Age Under China's One-Child Policy*. Stanford: Stanford University Press.

Hanser, Amy (2001). The Chinese Enterprising Self: Young, Educated Urbanites and the Search for Work. In: Perry Link, Richard P. Madsen and Paul G. Pickowicz (eds.). *Popular China: Unofficial Culture in a Globalizing Society*. Lanham: Rowman & Littlefield

Harrell, Stevan (1985). Why Do the Chinese Work So Hard? Reflections on an Entrepreneurial Ethic. In: *Modern China*, 11(2): 203–226

Howard, Cosmo (ed.) (2007). *Contested Individualization: Debates about Contemporary Personhood*. New York: Palgrave Macmillan

Hoffman, Lisa M. (2010). *Patriotic Professionalism in Urban China: Fostering Talent*. Philadelphia: Temple University Press

Hsu, Francis L. K. (1948). *Under the Ancestors' Shadow: Kinship, Personality, and Social Mobility in Village China*. New York: Columbia University Press

Huo Xia (2004). Zhongguo ren xinli yali da diaocha (Large survey on psychological pressures on Chinese individuals). In: *Beijing Kejibao*, December 24

Hurst, William (2009). *The Chinese Worker after Socialism.* Cambridge: Cambridge University Press
Kipnis, Andrew (2001). The Disturbing Educational Discipline of ›Peasants‹. In: *The China Journal,* no. 46: 1–24
Kipnis, Andrew (2006). Suzhi: A Keyword Approach. In: *The China Quarterly,* no. 186: 295–313
Lee, Ching Kwan (2007). *Against the Law: Labour Protests in China's Rustbelt and Sunbelt.* Berkeley: University of California Press
Li, Minghuan (2010). Collective Symbols and Individual Options: Life on a State Farm for Returned Overseas Chinese after Decollectivization. In: Mette Halskov Hansen and Rune Svarverud (eds.). *iChina: The Rise of the Individual in Modern Chinese Society.* Copenhagen: NIAS Press
Liang Qichao (1998 [1906]). *Xinmin shuo* (On the new individual). Zhengzhou: Zhongzhou Guji Chubanshe
Madsen, Richard (1984). *Morality and Power in a Chinese Village.* Berkeley: University of California Press
Palmer, Michael (2006). The Emergence of Consumer Rights: Legal Protection of the Consumer in the PRC. In: Kevin Latham, Stuart Thompson and Jakob Klein (eds.). *Consuming China: Approaches to Cultural Change in Contemporary China.* London: Routledge
Pan Qiwen, Li Chunyan, and Chen Jing (2009). Zhishi fenzi xinli jiankang jiedu (Unpacking the psychological health of Chinese professionals). *Zhongguo Shehui Kexue Wenzhai.* http://qk.cass.cn/zgshkxwz/zdtj/200906/t20090617_10467.htm, accessed February 10, 2011
Ramzy, Austin (2009). The Chinese Worker. In: *Time,* December 16
Ramzy, Austin (2010). Chinese Factory under Scrutiny as Suicides Mount. In: *Time,* May 26
Regus Business Tracker Survey (2010). http://www.regus.presscentre.com/imagelibrary/downloadMedia.ashx?MediaDetailsID=520, accessed March 12, 2011
Roberts, Steven (2010). Misrepresenting ›Choice Biographies‹?: A Reply to Woodman. In: *Journal of Youth Studies,* 13(1): 137–149
Rofel, Lisa (2007). *Desiring China: Experiments in Neoliberalism, Sexuality, and Public Culture.* Durham: Duke University Press
Rose, Nikolas (1998). *Inventing Our Selves: Psychology, Power, and Personhood.* Cambridge: Cambridge University Press
Rose, Nikolas (2011). Biological Citizenship and Its Forms. In: Everett Zhang, Arthur Kleinman and Tu Weiming (eds.). *Governance of Life in Chinese Moral Experience: The Quest for an Adequate Life.* London: Routledge
Schwarcz, Vera (1986). *The Chinese Enlightenment: Intellectuals and the Legacy of the May Fourth Movement of 1919.* Berkeley: University of California Press
Shi Yaping (2005). IT ren shengcun zhuangtai diaocha (Investigation of living conditions among IT people). In: *Caijing Shibao,* October 7

Taylor, Charles (2004). *Modern Social Imaginaries*. Durham: Duke University Press

Tomba, Luigi (2009). Of Quality, Harmony, and Community: Civilization and the Middle Class in Urban China. In: *Positions*, 17(3): 592–616

Tsai, Kellee S. (2007). *Capitalism Without Democracy: The Private Sector in Contemporary China*. Ithaca: Cornell University Press

Vogel, Ezra F. (1965). From Friendship to Comradeship: The Change in Personal Relations in Communist China. In: *The China Quarterly*, (21): 46–60

Wang Xiaoming (1998). Banzhanglian de xiaoxiang« (A half-faced portrait). Reprinted in Wang Xiaoming (2003). *Banzhanglian de shenhua* (The half-faced myth). Guilin: Guangxi Shifan Daxue Chubanshe

Wang, Xiaoying (2002). The Post-Communist Personality: The Spectre of China's Capitalist Market Reforms. *The China Journal*, no. 47: 1–17

White, Gordon (1993). *Riding the Tiger: The Politics of Economic Reform in Post-Mao China*. Stanford: Stanford University Press

Woodman, Dan (2009). The Mysterious Case of the Pervasive Choice Biography: Ulrich Beck, Structure/Agency and the Middling State of Theory in the Sociology of Youth. In: *Journal of Youth Studies*, 12(3): 243–256

Wu Xiaobo (2007). *Jidang sanshinian: Zhongguo qiye 1978–2008* (The vibrant thirty years: Enterprises in China 1978–2008), Volume 1. Beijing: Zhongxin Chubanshe

Xinhua News Agency (2006). *Zhongguo ren gongzuo shijian quanshijie zuichang* (Chinese have the longest working hours in the world). June 26, http://news.qq.com/a/20060628/001399.htm, accessed February 16, 2011

Xu Linling (2011). Yige zhongchanzhe de shinian (A middle-class man's decade). In: *Nanfang Renwu Zhoukan*, no. 5: 90–92

Yan, Yunxiang (2003). *Private Life under Socialism: Love, Intimacy, and Family Change in a Chinese Village, 1949–1999*. Stanford: Stanford University Press

Yan, Yunxiang (2006). Little Emperors or Frail Pragmatists? China's '8oers Generation. In: *Current History: A Journal of Contemporary World Affairs*, 105 (692): 255–262

Yan, Yunxiang (2009). *The Individualization of Chinese Society*. Oxford: Berg

Yan, Yunxiang (2010). The Chinese Path to Individualization. In: *British Journal of Sociology*, 61(3): 489–512

Yan, Yunxiang (2012). Afterword: The Drive for Success and the Ethics of the Striving Individual. In: Charles Stafford (ed.). *Ordinary Ethics in China Today*. Oxford: Berg Publishers

Ye Jingzhong, James Murray, and Wang Yihuan (eds.) (2005). *Guanzhu liushou ertong* (Left-behind Children in Rural China). Beijing: Shehui kexue wenxian chubanshe

Zhang, Li (2010). *In Search of Paradise: Middle-Class Living in a Chinese Metropolis*. Ithaca: Cornell University Press

Individualisation, Migration and Gender Relations

ELISABETH BECK-GERNSHEIM

INTRODUCTION

Immigrants scarcely featured in the German sociology of the 1970s and 1980s. They counted as a »marginal social group«, as a »special case«, not as actually part of our society. In accounts of the social structure they merited at best a couple of sentences, but more often were omitted entirely. For a long time, the discussion of individualisation also remained captive to this restriction of the field of vision; it also had its gaze firmly fixed on the mainstream society (this also holds for the texts of Beck and Beck-Gernsheim on this topic, e.g. Beck and Beck-Gernsheim 1994). The German federal government's Sixth Family Report, which appeared in 2000, rightly criticised that:

›The research on individualisation and pluralisation in modern societies has [...] never taken into account the ways of life of the resident immigrant population‹ (Sechster Familienbericht 2000: 24f.).

This deficiency is clearly bound up with prescientific images and stereotypes which influence science in subliminal and unreflected ways.

The following reflections are an attempt to rectify this deficiency. They are specifically intended to address the topic which at the time remained a blank spot, namely, the connection between migration and individualisation. This will be accomplished briefly in the form of two theses. The first provides an outline of the general framework, namely, the relation between migration and the experience of individualisation. The second goes on to address gender relations more specifically and enquiries into the different forms assumed by the relation between migration and the experience of individualisation in the case of men as opposed to women.

First Thesis:
Migration is a Motor of Individualisation Processes

It is generally taken for granted that individualisation is a process that takes place in the mainstream society. Immigrants, by contrast, live within the rigid constraints of the tradition they brought with them from their country of origin and now continue in their new surroundings.

That, at any rate, is the cliché. However, migration studies reveal time and again that migration processes are bound up with a biographical turning point. Through the »migration« event, the unquestioning integration into the culture of origin becomes ruptured. Migration means being cast out of the familiar world and thrust into an unfamiliar world; it means a confrontation with different rules, expectations and customs. Moreover, this is especially true of the large groups of immigrant workers, a majority of whom come from societies with patriarchal structures and are now confronted with the ways of life and norms of modern secularised Western societies. Through this confrontation the ways of life which had been accepted unquestioningly until then become conscious to a certain degree and an object of comparison and of individual choice (e.g. Baumann 2002). Immigrants are continually faced with decisions: What do I want to preserve? What is important to me? Where do I want to leave the old behind? Where do I want to try out the new?

Thus, one could say that immigrants are involuntary biographical tinkerers. Each seeks an individual answer according to their personality, social origin, education, age and gender. In what follows, I would like to show this in greater detail using the example of gender relations.

Second Thesis:
In piecing together their biographies, immigrants exhibit typically male and typically female approaches

As the American sociologist Jessie Bernard put it, ›marriage‹ as such does not exist but instead *his marriage* and *her marriage*, the marriage of the husband and the marriage of the wife (Bernard 1976). This statement can also be transferred to the experience of migration: There is *his migration* and *her migration*. This this is especially true when it comes to paid work, marital relations and the intention to return.

Paid work

Immigrant workers are generally located on the lower rungs of the occupational ladder, which means scant money, scant job security and scant respect. This is bound up with different forms of discrimination, but also with lack of training, poor language skills and uncertain resident status.

Many male immigrants experience this situation as humiliating, as a loss of status and as degrading. This is different in the case of women, the *female* immigrants. They also have to perform menial, badly paid jobs. But at the same time new opportunities become tangible. Paid work opens the door to the world outside the family. This takes place under the pressure of the new living conditions (because money is scarce among immigrants). Nevertheless, this is potentially bound up with additional opportunities: money of one's own, more negotiation power in marriage, more independence, more personal contacts beyond the radius of the family. This is why, in spite of all of the impositions, gainful employment often means a certain gain in freedom for female immigrants. Thus, for example, Karen Pyke writes in a study on immigrant families in the USA:

›The movement of women into the labor force [...] is one of the most dramatic changes impacting upon immigrant families [...] The greater economic resources, self-esteem, and independence that work provides immigrant wives results in a decline of patriarchal arrangements and male dominance [...]‹ (Pyke 2004: 260).

Marriage and family

Men who have grown up in patriarchal structures often experience the gain in freedom of women as a threat and a loss and as a challenge to their rightful privileges and authority.

This is shown, for example, by studies on the choice of partners among second-generation immigrants (summary in Beck-Gernsheim 2007). According to these studies, a significant number of the young men of the second generation, hence those who were born in the West, want a wife who comes directly from the country of origin. For the hope is that she has not yet been contaminated by Western culture but has grown up in the traditional manner and is willing to obey. Or, as a young Pakistani immigrant put it in an interview: ›She knows the customs. She doesn't stand up to you‹ (Shaw 2001:330).

Quite often the *daughters* from immigrant families are also willing to marry a man from the country of origin. For then they have the ›home advantage', as it were, having grown up in the global West: They are versed in the language, customs and rules of the host country. The bridegroom, by contrast, fresh from a village in India or Pakistan, first has a lot to learn. But it is gradually becoming apparent that the men are not prepared for this kind of role reversal – for them the gender relation is out of balance. It is not by chance that a relevant study by Katharine Charsley bears the distinctive title *Unhappy Husbands*. Tensions and physical violence occur strikingly often among such couples, and often the marriages also fail (Charsley 2005).

Intention to return

Here, too, studies on migration point to pronounced differences between men and women. Boiled down to its essence, many men want to return to the homeland once circumstances permit. The women, by contrast, are much more likely to want to stay in the new country because they fear that otherwise they will once again lose their increased personal freedom (summary in Beck and Beck-Gernsheim 2011) . Patricia R. Pessar, for example, writes along these lines on female immigrants from the Dominican Republic in the USA:

›Because wage work has brought immigrant women many personal gains [...] they are much more active agents than men in prolonging the household's stay in the United States [...] When they left the Dominican Republic, most women looked forward to going back to live. This orientation has changed in New York. Women realize that if they returned to the Dominican Republic they might well end up cloistered in the home [...]‹ (Pessar 1987: 123).

Conclusion

I have attempted to show that migration involves a form of individualisation of its own which assumes different forms according to gender. To summarise briefly: What women experience as a gain in freedom is a threat in the eyes of many men.

With reference to the framing topic, this means that, as regards the connection between migration and individualisation, we do not find a uniform pattern but instead characteristic differences between men and women. On the other hand, however, we also find a surprising commonality – namely, between immigrants and the mainstream society. This is the surprising point: Immigrants and mainstream society are not as far apart as is generally thought. In both cases it is women who are today changing more rapidly than men. In both cases there exists a ›contemporaneous non-contemporaneity‹, an ›incomplete social revolution‹ (Hochschild 1989) in relations between the sexes.

Translation by Ciaran Cronin

References

Baumann, Martin (2002). Migrant Settlement, Religion, and Phases of Diaspora, Exemplified by Hindu Traditions Stepping on European Shores. In: *Migration*, 33/34/35: 93–117

Beck, Ulrich and Elisabeth Beck-Gernsheim (1994) (eds.). *Riskante Freiheiten. Individualisierung in modernen Gesellschaften.* Frankfurt/M.: Suhrkamp

Beck, Ulrich and Elisabeth Beck-Gernsheim (2011). *Fernliebe. Zusammen aber getrennt – Lebens- und Liebesformen im globalen Zeitalter.* Berlin: Suhrkamp

Beck-Gernsheim, Elisabeth (2007). Transnational Lives, Transnational Marriages: A Review of the Evidence from Migrant Communities in Europe. In: *Global Networks,* 7 (3): 271–288

Bernard, Jessie (1976). *The Future of Marriage.* Harmondsworth: Pelican

Bundesministerium für Familie, Senioren, Frauen und Jugend (2000). *Sechster Familienbericht: Familien ausländischer Herkunft in Deutschland. Leistungen, Belastungen, Herausforderungen.* Bonn: Bundesanzeiger Verlagsgesellschaft

Charsley, Katharine (2005). Unhappy Husbands: Masculinity and Migration in Transnational Pakistani Marriages. In: *Journal of the Royal Anthropological Institute,* 11 (1): 85–105

Hochschild, Arlie (1989). *The Second Shift. Working Parents and the Revolution at Home.* New York: Viking

Pessar, Patricia R. (1987). The Dominicans: Women in the Household and the Garment Industry. In: Nancy Foner (ed.). *New Immigrants in New York.* New York: Columbia University Press

Pyke, Karen (2004). Immigrant Families in the US. In: Jacqueline Scott, Judith Treas and Martin Richards (eds.). *The Blackwell Companion to the Sociology of Families.* Malden: Blackwell

Shaw, Alison (2001). Kinship, Cultural Preference and Immigration: Consanguineous Marriage Among British Pakistanis. In: *Journal of the Royal Anthropological Institute,* 7 (2): 315–334

Shaw, Alison (2004). Immigrant Families in the UK. In: Jacqueline Scott, Judith Treas and Martin Richards (eds). *The Blackwell Companion to the Sociology of Families.* Malden: Blackwell

Inequality: From Natural »Facts« to Injustice
On the Political Sensibility of the Individualized Human

RONALD HITZLER

Across an ongoing debate about plausible *explanations* for the causes, emergence and cessation of social inequalities, there has for some time also been discussion in the social sciences about appropriate *descriptions* of society with regard to social inequalities which are relevant to order. This means, then, that most discussion centres on whether we still, or no longer, or once again live in a society which can be adequately portrayed by the traditional models of classes and strata. Both the class model and the stratification model have been linked with ideas about overcoming the inequalities observed in each case. At present, however, it looks more as though social inequalities do not disappear »beyond« the class society or stratified society, but, on the contrary, grow and multiply (cf. Beck and Sopp 1997). At the same time more recent debates about phenomena of exclusion (cf. e.g. Bude and Willisch 2006) report a radicalization and exacerbation of social inequality.

INEQUALITY AS A NATURAL »FACT«

One of the things which again needs explanation here, or which needs a new explanation, is the old question of where the multifarious inequalities actually come from. Our everyday experience already teaches us that people are undoubtedly diverse. They differ in all kinds of respects – and so markedly that we can distinguish every single one as an unmistakable individual.

Jean-Jacques Rousseau, in his *Discours sur l'Origine et les Fondements de l'Inegalité parmi les Hommes* (1754/1910), was only willing to acknowledge natural differences between humans with regard to age, health, physical strength, and strength of mind and spirit; apart from this, he painted an influential picture of prehistoric man as noble and solitary but otherwise not unequal to his own kind. A good hundred years ago, however, the English researcher Francis Galton, a distant relation of Charles Darwin, began to examine the question of inequality between humans empirically, rather than just reflecting on it in a philosophical and speculative manner. Galton in fact studied the most diverse forms of *difference* between humans (e.g. body size, sporting ability, but also intellectual performance). In doing so he evoked the question of the influence of *hereditary* factors on social inequality – highly controversial, then as now – and developed this into the research field of eugenics, which would, politically, entail some disastrous consequences (Galton 1865, 1869).

This interest was connected to the research of Darwin, the »father« of the theory of evolution. Darwin, as we know, had been looking for a scientific theory for the diversity of vegetable and animal life forms. In the process he resorted to older, speculative ideas (e.g. those of Johann Wolfgang von Goethe), positing that the species had developed gradually, i.e. that nature was changeable. Darwin realized that the development of living beings could be explained *purely* by natural processes. A basic assumption of his theory here is that members of the same species differ to a greater or lesser extent, and that these differences are in part hereditary. Most of these qualities, partly random, partly inherited, are unimportant for the individual's chances of survival and particularly of reproduction, many are detrimental to its survival or that of its possible descendants, but a small number of them improve the relative chances of surviving and in particular of reproducing successfully. Thus qualities which reduce the chances of reproduction disappear rapidly, or gradually, from populations, whereas characteristics which increase the chances of reproduction obviously become more and more widespread. Some populations also develop divergently. New characteristics lead, for example, to the exploration of new ecological niches, or natural disasters cause the extinction of populations in some areas, perhaps with the exception of an (initially) small number of specimens with special biological features etc. Thus new species, races and types keep emerging, in the interplay between environmental conditions and the natural diversity of the individual organisms.

A key factor here is the phenomenon of the so-called mutation, the erratic, undirected, i.e. random modification of the genetic material. This is where the famous process of natural selection begins, following the simple criteria of harmfulness, irrelevance, and advantage – always with reference to the mutant's chances of survival and reproduction, it should be noted. A further factor in the Darwinist scenario is *sexual* reproduction, which – due to the principles of heredity – inevitably leads to the mixing of characteristics in the offspring. So if, more or less by chance, two individuals with different advantageous characteristics mate, then these particular characteristics may perhaps be united in their offspring, making them particularly capable of surviving and/or reproducing. This could also be expressed differently: Darwinistically speaking, the first thing indispensable for the development of the species is difference. But in these terms the individual organisms belonging to a species are no longer just different, but actually *unequal* with regard to their respective chances of life, and here this refers particularly to their chances of reproduction. The chances of survival of a species in competition with other species and in a changing environment thus correlate not only with biological differences, but also very much with the natural inequality between individuals of this species.

Individuals of the same species not only *are* (genetically and phenotypically) diverse, their inequality is also – if they belong to a species which lives socially – recognized and acknowledged by members of the same species: mates are selected according to externally perceptible indicators of the differing reproductive fitness of the »candidates«.[1] Understood in this way, i.e. with a view to individual chances of life and reproduction, inequality stabilizes social orders in populations. The best-known case is probably the pecking order in the chicken run. Of course there are occasionally (or repeatedly) not only changes in the social order – e.g. because of aging processes or status transitions (female with and without young) or because of environmental influences, etc. – but also what might be called »revolutions«. But however changes take place: the positions in the structure are merely redistributed, not abolished altogether.

POLITICAL IMPLICATIONS OF SCIENTIFIC POSITIONS

As mentioned, Francis Galton investigated the natural inequality resulting from genotypic and phenotypic differences, specifically between humans. That is, he examined both how biological differences are processed socially (e.g. differences in appearance, age, gender etc.) and to what extent social inequalities can be explained as »natural«. This formed the essential basis for the exploration of presocial conditions of social inequalities; this in turn brought forth theories whose quintessential nature is probably most concisely and clearly expressed in what is known as »Herrnstein's Syllogism« (named after the psychologist Richard J. Herrnstein, who taught at Harvard):

›1. If differences in mental abilities are inherited, and 2. if success requires those abilities, and 3. if earnings and prestige depend on success, 4. then social standing [...] will be based to some extent on inherited differences among people‹ (Herrnstein 1971; also Herrnstein and Murray 1994).

---

1 | Many animals, furthermore, know each other individually and their behaviour towards one another reflects this familiarity. This has been observed in apes, particularly by Frans de Waal, Jane (Lawick-)Goodall, Diane Fossey, Barbara Harrison and Birute Galdikas. There are also, however, corresponding accounts, e.g. from Konrad Lorenz, Nico Tinbergen and other ethologists (dogs, cats, but also songbirds, seem to have *individual* voices, by which members of the same species identify them).

To sum it up even more briefly: according to theories of natural inequality, the social opportunities of individuals are already unequally distributed because of their genetic make-up. Karl Marx, incidentally, saw it the same way; in justification of his maxim »From each according to his abilities, to each according to his needs!« he observed in the *Kritik des Gothaer Programms*: ›The one, however, is mentally or intellectually superior to the other [...]‹ (1962). »Innate«, strictly speaking, refers to everything an individual is born with. But not everything is determined by heredity. Prenatal injuries, whatever may have caused them, are innate, but are not the result of defective genetic material. Irrespective of this, the issue of innate qualities is essentially about genetically inherited qualities which continue to significantly influence or determine individual life processes after birth (e.g. numerous physical characteristics which only develop over the years).

In particular, the question of whether *mental* or *intellectual* differences between humans have only social or also or even primarily presocial causes is still a constant point of contention between human ethologists and behaviourist milieu theorists. In 1969 Arthur R. Jensen exposed himself not only to massive criticism but also to a number of personal attacks when he asked, in the *Harvard Educational* Review, ›How Much Can We Boost IQ and Achievement?‹ (Jensen 1969), and answered to the effect that compensatory education programmes did not significantly improve levels of intelligence, since differences in intelligence were mainly genetically and not socially determined. This was particularly sensitive because Jensen looked at the statistically significant differences in intelligence between »black« and »white« U.S. recruits, as established by representative surveys, and suggested that they might be based on genetic differences between the races.

What is uncontroversial so far is that *if* differences in intelligence are determined by heredity, they are certainly not just controlled by *one* gene, but are caused by a complex interplay of a number of genes. Staunch proponents of the theory of environmental influence, however, argue that the genes which create the prerequisites for intellectual performance are the same for all humans, and that if there are differences in intelligence, then these can be ascribed to the fact that humans are exposed to different environmental influences. Beyond such diametrically opposed positions – which continue to exist – experts in the field today tend to regard humans as *biosocial* beings, i.e. as determined by their genes *and* their environment. It then follows that both genetic defects and harmful environmental conditions have a detrimental effect on the way an individual lives his or her life. And consequently, the »nature«/«nurture« controversy (Pastore 1949), which reached its peak in the 1970s, and of which traces are still in evidence today, has for some time been considered obsolete (Ingold 2001).

Neither the genetic disposition nor factors of social environment *explain* individual behaviour, but both obviously explain the *boundary conditions* of individual behaviour. And both *together* must presumably »somehow« explain the inequalities between individuals. The most simplistic calculation here is *addition*: i.e. it is assumed that hereditary and environmental components can be clearly separated, and that when they are simply put together they will add up to 100 per cent of the existing differences. And yet the calculation does not seem to work out quite so simply after all: certain genes, for example, react differently to the same environmental variables; certain environmental conditions, for example, clearly show up the difference between two genotypes, while others attenuate these differences or level them out altogether (e.g. muscles in various body types, in active bodybuilders and »couch potatoes«). This means that hereditary dispositions and environmental conditions »somehow« interact. This relationship cannot, in any case, be represented as a simple matter of addition.

Another non-additive component which is particularly significant in intelligence research is what is known as *covariance*. That is, genotype and environment vary together (television makes the »stupid« stupider and the »clever« even cleverer. In more general terms: an intelligent person will derive more intellectual stimulation and challenges from the environment than a less intelligent person). It then becomes impossible to determine for certain where the actual intelligence ultimately comes from. But all these theories are based on the assumption that differences in intelligence are always, whatever the extent, *partly determined* by genes. A representative example is the position advocated by the geneticist Theodosius Dobzhansky in *Genetic Diversity and Human Equality* (1973), that hereditary dispositions shape IQ to such an extent that the IQs of monozygotic twins brought up separately correlate more strongly than those of dizygotic twins brought up together. Studies of this kind are highly controversial today; the discussion on the influence of »the genes« points less to unambiguous knowledge than to a highly complex set of interrelationships (and similar tendencies can be seen, for example, in developments in neuroscience). It is obvious, however, that these different »assets« do not simply mark biological differences, but that they »naturally« also find expression in various forms of social inequality (e.g. in the different distribution of responsibilities and thus of hierarchies).

The conclusion to be drawn from such theories of natural inequality, a problematic conclusion, particularly for intellectuals trained in the social sciences, is – to put it in simplified terms – that it is fundamentally impossible to train up a whole population of intellectuals, and that every scheme aimed in this direction is »naturally« doomed to failure. And of course the acceptance or denial of innate differences in ability has grave political consequences: if humans are, by nature, equal, then existing differences are the effects of different living conditions and will disappear when these conditions are equalized. In the context of social problem-solving, this has led to the well-known policies of compensation and adjustment, focused on the semantics of »equal opportunities« or »justice«. If, however, humans are unequal – in part – by nature, then egalitarian conditions will only further reinforce the existing differences.

SOCIAL INEQUALITIES AND INDIVIDUALIZATION

The usual *sociological* approaches to explaining social inequalities are »scattered« from theories of class struggle to organic metaphors about the »social body«. Class antagonisms in particular have always occupied a central position in theories formed within in the social sciences (to mention only Karl Marx, Max Weber and, among the more recent classics, Pierre Bourdieu 1982). Even in gender studies, the class model is still important; theses positing a »dual« and »triple« socialization and oppression (Becker-Schmidt 1987; Lenz 1996) make reference to it, and the current discussion on intersectionality (cf. e.g. Klinger and Knapp 2008) also persists in working over the relationship of »class«, »race«, and »gender«.

The most important alternative to class theories is undoubtedly the organic model of social strata developed in structural functionalism. According to this model, the inequalities present in a society are functionally necessary to preserve this society's »balance«. The model assumes that the resolving of functionally significant problems must be appropriately rewarded, so that enough »talented« people are prepared to taken on the roles and positions which have to be filled (cf. Davis and Moore 1945). According to this, social inequalities arise and achieve stability by way of a market of supply and demand, so to speak. For some time, however, there have been considerable, mainly empirical objections to these structural/functionalist assumptions (cf. e.g. Mayntz 1961; Solga 2009). In particular Ralf Dahrendorf (1957) once again connected the model of social stratification with a conflict-based approach inspired by the old theory of class struggle. One of the tenets of this conflict theory is that the main way in which social orders are stabilized is that dominant groupings impose norms and thus legitimate the given hierarchy.

In relation to the »new social inequalities«, however, all these attempts at explanation appear too *static*: they are exclusively limited to large, stable groups, they only register *vertical* inequalities, and they concentrate entirely on positionings and conflicts related to the profit-oriented economy. In other words: theories of class and stratification are by no means *false* as models, but they seem insufficient for the description of or misleading in the analysis of the post-industrial multi-option risk society which currently exists (and shows no signs of departing). In this post-industrial multi-option risk society (Gross 1994; Beck 1986, 2007), a number of inequalities which cannot or can *no longer* be captured with and in the traditional models of vertical stratification become relevant to everyday experience and to description by the social sciences. This by no means implies the assertion that »objective« social strata no longer exist. On the contrary, it can be assumed that class affiliation still has a huge influence on the individual's opportunities in life. At the same time, this affiliation goes hand in hand with multiple other relevant experiences of inequality – at least in people's conscious biographical orientation. These other recently perceived inequalities are evidently connected with something which, since 1983, has been discussed using the term ›individualization‹ or ›process of individualization‹ (Beck 1983; cf. also Beck and Beck-Gernsheim 1994, 2002).

The protagonists of this approach do not understand the process of individualization as a (dramatic) phenomenon of self-realization aiming at »individualism« or »individuality«, but essentially as a functional consequence of changes in the social structure of modern societies – such as: universalization of the principle of equality, juridification of ever more areas of life, expansion and devaluation of education, dissolution of normal working hours, increase in the average level of prosperity (»elevator effect«), erosion of the model of the nuclear family as a relatively binding element of culture etc. – especially after and since the Second World War. The main phenomena considered to be effects of the process of individualization include loss or renunciation of lasting normative ties, release from internalized roles, increased mobility, transfer of meaning from the professional to the private sphere, dissolution of the remnants of »feudal« relationships (especially between man and woman), more frequent changes in partner, focus on self-help groups or interest groups. To quote Ulrich Beck and Elisabeth Beck-Gernsheim (1990: 12 f.):

›The proportion of life possibilities which are fundamentally closed to decision-making is decreasing, and the proportion of the biography which is open to decision-making and can be created by the individual is increasing‹.

And, according to Jürgen Habermas (1988: 238), ›this individual, who is simultaneously set free and isolated, has no other criteria at his disposal than his own individual preferences‹. The crucially *new* thing about this is that something which has always applied to a few people is increasingly required of *more* people, i.e. that they lead and structure their own lives without reliable directions.

AN AMBIGUOUS TREND

This individualized human is a person who is released from traditional ties to a milieu, but also from the care of a milieu: a person who no longer sees himself as being in a relationship of direct responsibility towards others, but who is directly connected, so to speak, to the omnipresent but barely tangible entity of society as a whole, or to its economic, political, judicial, medical institutions etc. He is involved in a number of relationships which he himself has created and can dissolve, is confronted with different situations, and must therefore constantly deal with diverse, non-coordinated schemes of interpretation and action. Being-able-to-choose *and* having-to-choose thus seems to have become a standard problem in his way of life. Of course this individualized human is a »homunculus«, a theoretical construct, a one-sided, exaggerated portrait of us all – we who continue to cultivate and put up with our little family, local and class ties. But the juridification of interpersonal relationships on all levels, for example, is making perceptible progress, since anything that is not juridified does not seem or no longer seems to have »binding« force for the individualized human. Social stratifications in fact seem less and less to be predetermined by fate, and instead increasingly arise from *temporary* involvement in some associative structures or other (see contributions in Hitzler et al. 2008).

In contrast to this finding on the situation of »modern man«, sections of gender studies are now ascertaining that the concept of individualization is essentially only conceived in terms of the standard male biography, and that the liberation from traditional ties and the margins of freedom thus opened up are much greater for men than for women. They argue, for example, that the typical reality of a woman's life is still shaped by the double burden of family and career. Despite these surviving traditional ties, however, there has undoubtedly been a push towards individualization in the context of the typical female life as well – and this is attended by new uncertainties and inequalities (even between women). Women's levels of educational certification, for example, have risen considerably, and their participation in the labour market is not simply »stabilizing«; rather, paid employment is becoming an increasingly self-evident component of the typical female lifestyle.

In contrast to the assumption, still cultivated in the more traditionalist areas of sociology, that humans still typically live in stable relationships, the theory of individualization states that we are *fundamentally* subject to existential uncertainty today. And that means: even if our current situation in life appears stable on the outside, we are, on a near-permanent basis, not just placed in positions where we have to choose and decide, but also confronted with new plans, schemes and decisions of other people, which surprise us to varying degrees. And in the resulting unstable situation (unstable in terms of social structure, amongst other things), a confusing multitude of *new* inequalities develops. Analysts of social structure and inequality researchers have thus been trying hard for some time to penetrate this »new complexity« of social phenomena of individualization, particularly with recourse to concepts of order such as situation in life, life course and lifestyle, and to reconstruct it by means of adequate models.

Now one may categorize many of the new antagonisms as luxury conflicts under the conditions of what Ulrich Beck has termed »Vollkasko-Individualisierung« (»fully ensured individualization«) (as was perhaps symptomatic of West Germany in the 1980s). But it is hard to overlook the fact that where the traditional *direct* disputes over the allocation of resources are losing their importance or are highly ritualized (as the collective bargaining between unions and employers traditionally is), other, more indirect, more unregulated disputes over the allocation of resources are breaking out: e.g. in the form of covert discrimination or open violence against foreigners, against people with disabilities, old people, and also against members of the opposite sex. All this is of course further exacerbated when a long period of economic prosperity gives way to a phase of recession. That is, it appears that the advent of new inequalities (again) reinforces the need to mark belonging and non-belonging, familiarity and foreignness, civilization and barbarity, and to undertake processes of inclusion and exclusion along social demarcation lines of this kind.

DIFFERENCE – INEQUALITIY – CONFLICT

Thus at first glance it looks as though social inequality is already the key to analysing the dynamics of *political* conflicts in our society as well. That is and is not true: human diversity does not in itself imply social inequality, and nor does social inequality generate social or political conflict merely by its existence. In both cases, there must be another element: diversity *alone* – e.g. with regard to eye or hair colour, weight, shoe size, age, leisure pursuits, but also with regard to personal opinions, skin colour or gender – does not explain different situations in life or opportunities in life. In order for diversity to become social inequality, it must be unequally *evaluated*, and entail consequences for a person's positioning in social space. This positioning is based on cultural attributions and social definitions and – analytically speaking – directs attention towards *empirical* processes of differentiating, classifying, valorizing or devalorizing, overglorification and stigmatization in all facets and nuances of social relationships and forms of social intercourse.

In this way the »new inequalities« broaden the palette of the old inequalities rather than replacing them: health, for example, is no longer seen as natural or God-given, as a matter of fate, but as a manufacturable commodity which should in principle be equally accessible to every human. Similar ideas apply to cultural resources of every kind. And with the new social inequalities, in a trend which has clearly been increasing again of late, the »classical« *social question* (the question of the just distribution of social wealth) is supplemented or even (e.g. in phases of prosperity) supplanted by the so-called *ecological question* (the question of the just distribution of the risks and hazardous situations produced by industry and technology). We therefore speak of *»social inequality«* when individuals and groups, or aggregations of individuals, have different opportunities in life because of qualities ascribed to them or acquired by them, or when they are allocated unequal proportions of social budgets because of their position in the social structure. The mere existence of social inequality, on the other hand, by no means signifies in itself the existence of a social or political *conflict*. This can perhaps be best illustrated by the relationship between the sexes: we all know that the undoubted bio-sexual diversity of men and women has led to very different opportunities in life for the two sexes in most cultures – stabilized by »gendering«, i.e. by constructions of binary concepts of gender which lead to hierarchic gender orders. But in most cultures the generally striking *inequality* of men and women has *not* led, over the millennia, to collective conflicts between the sexes. The inequality between the sexes has only been politically virulent in the industrialized societies for about a hundred years. And it was only in the second half of the last century that this inequality developed into a potentially explosive conflict which (so far) shows no signs of abating.

This can be explained by the fact that, as explanations for the inequality between the sexes with reference to orders transcending society (God, nature etc.) have become subject to doubt, this inequality has come to be seen (with a sufficient degree of consensus) as *unjust*, with reference to the political and moral ideals of modern, bourgeois societies, particularly the ideals of freedom and equality. Technological progress, war and post-war periods and labour requirements, as well as better education, new methods of contraception and higher levels of professional activity have gradually increased women's potential for conflict. The inequality of the sexes was (and is) *politicized* as discrimination against women or as an emancipatory struggle *against* this discrimination. At present, however, the clash between women and men seems to be shifting again, towards a conflict between more family-oriented and more career-oriented people of *both* sexes. That is, in the relevant discourse the so-called »issue of women« is increasingly turning into the issue of mothers, and in general social discourse it is gradually turning into the issue of parents. The simple difference between people who are raising children and those who are not entails quite different opportunities in life in different cultures: in premodern societies, especially simple ones with subsistence economies, children are an economic resource for their parents, and an important provision for old age. In simplified terms: in premodern societies, children make parents *richer*, so to speak. In welfare-state conditions, on the other hand, as we all know, children become a *luxury* for parents, diminishing their individual resources and – at least for one parent, usually still the woman – hampering or thwarting their professional careers. At present this inequality between people who are bringing up children and people who are not is also increasingly being defined as *unjust* – and mainly, as we all know, with reference to aspects of *demographic* policy (e.g. pension security and the intergenerational contract).

The upshot of all this is that the *political* aspect of social inequality lies in the issue of social *justice*. In other words: the potential of any social inequality to cause conflict results from questioning of its legitimacy. So: not every difference automatically causes social inequality. And not every social inequality is felt to be unjust. Many differences, however, lead to social inequalities. And these days more and more social inequalities or their consequences are defined as

»unjust«, making them – in a broad sense – politically virulent. For nearly everything which impinges noticeably on the ideals of freedom and equality seems »unjust« to us as modern people. This fundamental fact is also being studied at present in new approaches to a ›cosmopolitan‹ sociology of social inequality (Beck 2008; Poferl 2012).

Thus it is primarily the ideal of justice cultivated in modern societies which tends to lead to the problematization of every form of social inequality. The ideal of justice turns inequalities into political grievances which can flare up into conflicts at any time, and generalizes the social struggle for resources and opportunities in life. As a result the traditional lines of conflict between classes and strata are in part replaced, in part supplemented by various short-lived, scattered, interwoven antagonisms. This in turn destabilizes traditional habits of interaction, and means that the forms of social intercourse have to be renegotiated and reorganized. One question which is at present unresolved is whether, in these ongoing processes of transformation, »we« as a society can bear to consider (with renewed intensity) the *possibility* of natural inequality – and the political direction this might entail – rather than excluding this possibility from the outset. Of course we would also have to bear in mind that, under the conditions of reflexive modernization, it is becoming more and more difficult to distinguish what is given by nature from what can be created or achieved in or by society – especially when we are dealing with ever more extreme forms of manipulative intervention in human life, based on medical technology, medication and therapy, and with other culturally available practices by which people produce their own »outer« appearance and »inner« state, physical and mental competence and performance – in short, a vast range of optimization programmes (cf., in the context of reflexive research on modernization, Lau and Keller 2001; Viehöver et al. 2004).

Translation by Nicola Barfoot on behalf of Textworks Translations

REFERENCES

Beck, Ulrich (1983). Jenseits von Klasse und Stand? Soziale Ungleichheiten, gesellschaftliche Individualisierungsprozesse und die Entstehung neuer sozialer Formationen und Identitäten. In: Reinhard Kreckel (ed.). *Soziale Ungleichheiten*. Soziale Welt, Sonderband 2. Göttingen: Schwartz

Beck, Ulrich (1986). *Risikogesellschaft. Auf dem Weg in eine andere Moderne*. Frankfurt/M.: Suhrkamp

Beck, Ulrich (2007). *Weltrisikogesellschaft. Auf der Suche nach der verlorenen Sicherheit*. Frankfurt/M.: Suhrkamp

Beck, Ulrich (2008). *Die Neuvermessung der Ungleichheit unter den Menschen.* Frankfurt/M.: Suhrkamp

Beck, Ulrich and Elisabeth Beck-Gernsheim (1990). *Das ganz normale Chaos der Liebe.* Frankfurt/M.: Suhrkamp

Beck, Ulrich and Elisabeth Beck-Gernsheim (eds.) (1994). *Riskante Freiheiten. Individualisierung in modernen Gesellschaften.* Frankfurt/M.: Suhrkamp

Beck, Ulrich and Elisabeth Beck-Gernsheim (2002). *Individualization. Institutionalized Individualism and its Social and Political Consequences.* London: Sage

Beck, Ulrich and Peter Sopp (eds.) (1997). *Individualisierung und Integration: Neue Konfliktlinien und neuer Integrationsmodus?* Opladen: Leske + Budrich

Becker-Schmidt, Regina (1987). Die doppelte Vergesellschaftung – die doppelte Unterdrückung. Besonderheiten der Frauenforschung in den Sozialwissenschaften. In: Lilo Unterkirchner and Ina Wagner (eds.). *Die andere Hälfte der Gesellschaft. Österreichischer Soziologentag 1985.* Wien: Verlag des Österreichischen Gewerkschaftsbundes

Bourdieu, Pierre (1982). *Die feinen Unterschiede. Kritik der gesellschaftlichen Urteilskraft.* Frankfurt/M.: Suhrkamp

Bude, Heinz and Andreas Willisch (eds.) (2006). *Das Problem der Exklusion. Ausgegrenzte, Entbehrliche, Überflüssige.* Hamburg: Hamburger Edition

Dahrendorf, Ralf (1957). *Soziale Klassen und Klassenkonflikt in der industriellen Gesellschaft.* Stuttgart: Ferdinand Enke

Davis, Kingsley and Wilbert E. Moore (1945). Some Principles of Stratification. In: *American Sociological Review*, 10 (2): 242–249

Dobzhansky, Theodosius (1973). *Genetic Diversity and Human Equality.* New York: Basic Books

Galton, Francis (1865). Heredity Talent and Character. In: *Macmillan's Magazine* 12: 157–166, 318–327

Galton, Francis (1869). *Hereditary Genius.* London: Macmillan

Gross, Peter (1994). *Die Multioptionsgesellschaft.* Frankfurt/M.: Suhrkamp

Habermas, Jürgen (1988). Individuierung durch Vergesellschaftung. In: Jürgen Habermas. *Nachmetaphysisches Denken.* Frankfurt/M.: Suhrkamp

Herrnstein, Richard J. (1971). IQ. In: *Atlantic Monthly* (September): 43–64

Herrnstein, Richard and Charles Murray (1994). *The Bell Curve: Intelligence and Class Structure in American Life.* New York: The Free Press

Hitzler, Ronald; Anne Honer, and Michaela Pfadenhauer (eds.) (2008). *Posttraditionale Gemeinschaften.* Wiesbaden: VS Verlag für Sozialwissenschaften

Ingold, Tim (2001). From Complementarity to Obviation. In: Susan Oyama, Paul Griffiths, and Gray Russel (eds.). *Cycles of Contingency. Developmental Systems and Evolution.* Cambridge: MIT Press

Jensen, Arthur (1969). How much can we boost IQ and Scholastic Achievement? In: *Harvard Educational Review* 39 (1): 1–123

Klinger, Cornelia and Gudrun-Axeli Knapp (eds.) (2008). *Überkreuzungen. Fremdheit, Ungleichheit, Differenz.* Westfälisches Dampfboot: Münster

Lau, Christoph and Reiner Keller (2001). Zur Politisierung gesellschaftlicher Naturabgrenzungen. In: Ulrich Beck and Wolfgang Bonß (eds.). *Die Modernisierung der Moderne.* Frankfurt/M.: Suhrkamp

Lenz, Ilse (1996). Grenzziehungen und Öffnungen: Zum Verhältnis von Geschlecht und Ethnizität zu Zeiten der Globalisierung. In: Ilse Lenz and Andrea Germer (eds.). *Wechselnde Blicke. Frauenforschung in internationaler Perspektive.* Opladen: Leske + Budrich

Marx, Karl (1962). Kritik des Gothaer Programms. In: *Marx-Engels-Werke,* Band 19. Berlin: Karl Dietz

Mayntz, Renate (1961). Kritische Bemerkungen zur funktionalistischen Schichtungstheorie. In: David Glass and René König (eds.). *Soziale Schichtung und soziale Mobilität.* Kölner Zeitschrift für Soziologie und Sozialpsychologie, Sonderheft 5. Opladen, Wiesbaden: Westdeutscher Verlag

Pastore, Nicholas (1949). *The Nature-Nurture Controversy.* New York: King's Crown Press

Poferl, Angelika (forthcoming in 2012). ›Gender‹ und die Soziologie der Kosmopolitisierung. In: Heike Kahlert und Christine Weinbach (eds.). *Zeitgenössische Gesellschaftstheorien und Genderforschung. Einladung zum Dialog.* Wiesbaden: VS Verlag für Sozialwissenschaften

Rousseau, Jean-Jacques (1910 [1754]): *Discours sur l'Origine et les Fondements de l'Inegalité parmi les Hommes. Discourse in the Origin and Basis of Inequality among Men.* Auckland: Floating Press

Solga, Heike (2009). Meritokratie – die moderne Legitimation ungleicher Bildungschancen. In: Heike Solga, Justin Powell and Peter A. Berger (eds.): *Soziale Ungleichheit. Klassische Texte der Sozialstrukturanalyse.* Frankfurt/M.: Campus

Viehöver, Willy; Robert Gugutzer, Reiner Keller and Christoph. Lau (2004). Vergesellschaftung der Natur – Naturalisierung der Gesellschaft. In: Ulrich Beck and Christoph Lau (eds.). *Entgrenzung und Entscheidung: Was ist neu an der Theorie reflexiver Modernisierung?* Frankfurt/M. Suhrkamp

Cosmopolitan Individualization.
Twelve Theses on Ulrich Beck
A God of One's Own. Religion's Capacity for Peace
and Potential for Violence[1]

HANS-GEORG SOEFFNER

> *(1) The anthropological foundation: the finiteness, »halfness« (Plessner), neediness and contingency of human life on the one hand and on the other hand man's capacity to think beyond his[2] death and to design ideal worlds in which finiteness and contingency are apparently overcome, is the origin of human religiosity. The latter in turn underlies the design and formulation of religions.*

Georg Simmel's pointed statement that there are ›religious natures that have no religion‹ (Simmel 1912: 38), is underlain by the supposition that ultimately all human beings are »religious natures«. The human disposition to religiosity thus appears, on the one hand, as the force that helps to bring religions to life and is always presupposed whenever we speak of the influence and effect of religion on human life. On the other hand, we have to ask on what the human disposition toward religiosity itself rests and whether it is possible to imagine a »religious nature« that has »no religion«.

For Kant, the desire »to be happy« arises necessarily from the »finite nature« of man: finiteness and neediness permit neither »satisfaction« with one's entire being nor a complacent state of »bliss«. To be finitely needy and *at the same time* rational is a »problem thrust upon us by nature« that we cannot escape.[3] It is expressed in the boundaries that we experience in fact, but which we can vault over in our imagination. We can imagine a world in which we are not yet or are no longer: a world before our birth and after our death, a world of the »beyond«,

---

1 | Beck (2008)
2 | For purely stylistic reasons, the translation has put ›he‹, ›his‹ etc. rather than ›he/she‹, ›his/her‹ throughout.
3 | Kant (1788)

in other words, one which does not (yet) derive from the transcendent concept of religion: We can overcome the equally fundamental boundary between »ego« and »alter«, between one individual and other individuals or between one individual and a community – in everyday life and in general – through the »fundamental assumption« of the reciprocity of perspectives and an interchangeability of points of view that is, in principle, always possible.

The interplay of boundary experiences and designs for overcoming boundaries is the legacy of the interconnectedness of finiteness, neediness and rationality. The place where this interplay that is forced upon us occurs is the *individual* human being, which is constantly thrown back on its »halfness« and contingency, thanks to its comprehensive, irreversible boundary situation and the boundary situations that follow from it and are concretely experienced. From this anthropologically based starting situation, because we must live in and with it on a daily basis, there arises for us a paradox: On the one hand, it is pointless to ask about the »meaning« of this anthropological destiny, while on the other hand, as fallible beings [Mängelwesen] endowed with reason, we are compelled to give meaning to our actions – despite the finiteness, contingency and fragmentation of our life.

Religiosity owes its existence to this paradox. It arises from the need for meaning-conferral [Sinngebung] that cannot support itself and therefore points to something beyond itself. But it cannot derive any certain counterpart from this reaching-beyond-itself. Instead, however, it can both design a counterpart and imagine a »comforting no-place«, a utopia, if it does not want to lose itself in the nowhere. In short, as involuntary constructors of meaning, obeying »anthropological need«, ultimately all human beings are religious, even when they do not succeed in having a religion.

(2) It is therefore necessary to distinguish between religiosity and religion. (1) Religiosity arises from the structurally given and always possible experience of complete isolation, of »being solitary«. In this the individual experiences himself as a socially »excommunicated«, isolated being, at the mercy of his own diseases, pain, passions and emotions and his own death – a being that seeks help that others/ society, cannot give him. (2) By contrast, religion/religions are socially communicated, traditional and collectively believed ideas and guidelines, claiming to be experience-based, that enable the individual to fit into a socially and historically »heightened« reality.

When in extreme situations the individual at last discovers himself to be the sole measure of experience, knowledge, decision and legitimation, and when he has to understand that it ›is his own final position‹, a position in which ›everyone finds and obeys the daemon that holds the threads of *his* life‹ (Weber 1973: 613), at that moment he experiences the limits of communication and the ability to

Klinger, Cornelia and Gudrun-Axeli Knapp (eds.) (2008). *Überkreuzungen. Fremdheit, Ungleichheit, Differenz.* Westfälisches Dampfboot: Münster

Lau, Christoph and Reiner Keller (2001). Zur Politisierung gesellschaftlicher Naturabgrenzungen. In: Ulrich Beck and Wolfgang Bonß (eds.). *Die Modernisierung der Moderne.* Frankfurt/M.: Suhrkamp

Lenz, Ilse (1996). Grenzziehungen und Öffnungen: Zum Verhältnis von Geschlecht und Ethnizität zu Zeiten der Globalisierung. In: Ilse Lenz and Andrea Germer (eds.). *Wechselnde Blicke. Frauenforschung in internationaler Perspektive.* Opladen: Leske + Budrich

Marx, Karl (1962). Kritik des Gothaer Programms. In: *Marx-Engels-Werke,* Band 19. Berlin: Karl Dietz

Mayntz, Renate (1961). Kritische Bemerkungen zur funktionalistischen Schichtungstheorie. In: David Glass and René König (eds.). *Soziale Schichtung und soziale Mobilität.* Kölner Zeitschrift für Soziologie und Sozialpsychologie, Sonderheft 5. Opladen, Wiesbaden: Westdeutscher Verlag

Pastore, Nicholas (1949). *The Nature-Nurture Controversy.* New York: King's Crown Press

Poferl, Angelika (forthcoming in 2012). ›Gender‹ und die Soziologie der Kosmopolitisierung. In: Heike Kahlert und Christine Weinbach (eds.). *Zeitgenössische Gesellschaftstheorien und Genderforschung. Einladung zum Dialog.* Wiesbaden: VS Verlag für Sozialwissenschaften

Rousseau, Jean-Jacques (1910 [1754]): *Discours sur l'Origine et les Fondements de l'Inegalité parmi les Hommes. Discourse in the Origin and Basis of Inequality among Men.* Auckland: Floating Press

Solga, Heike (2009). Meritokratie – die moderne Legitimation ungleicher Bildungschancen. In: Heike Solga, Justin Powell and Peter A. Berger (eds.): *Soziale Ungleichheit. Klassische Texte der Sozialstrukturanalyse.* Frankfurt/M.: Campus

Viehöver, Willy; Robert Gugutzer, Reiner Keller and Christoph. Lau (2004). Vergesellschaftung der Natur – Naturalisierung der Gesellschaft. In: Ulrich Beck and Christoph Lau (eds.). *Entgrenzung und Entscheidung: Was ist neu an der Theorie reflexiver Modernisierung?* Frankfurt/M. Suhrkamp

Cosmopolitan Individualization.
Twelve Theses on Ulrich Beck
A God of One's Own. Religion's Capacity for Peace
and Potential for Violence[1]

HANS-GEORG SOEFFNER

> *(1) The anthropological foundation: the finiteness, »halfness« (Plessner), neediness and contingency of human life on the one hand and on the other hand man's capacity to think beyond his[2] death and to design ideal worlds in which finiteness and contingency are apparently overcome, is the origin of human religiosity. The latter in turn underlies the design and formulation of religions.*

Georg Simmel's pointed statement that there are ›religious natures that have no religion‹ (Simmel 1912: 38), is underlain by the supposition that ultimately all human beings are »religious natures«. The human disposition to religiosity thus appears, on the one hand, as the force that helps to bring religions to life and is always presupposed whenever we speak of the influence and effect of religion on human life. On the other hand, we have to ask on what the human disposition toward religiosity itself rests and whether it is possible to imagine a »religious nature« that has »no religion«.

For Kant, the desire »to be happy« arises necessarily from the »finite nature« of man: finiteness and neediness permit neither »satisfaction« with one's entire being nor a complacent state of »bliss«. To be finitely needy and *at the same time* rational is a »problem thrust upon us by nature« that we cannot escape.[3] It is expressed in the boundaries that we experience in fact, but which we can vault over in our imagination. We can imagine a world in which we are not yet or are no longer: a world before our birth and after our death, a world of the »beyond«,

---

1 | Beck (2008)
2 | For purely stylistic reasons, the translation has put ›he‹, ›his‹ etc. rather than ›he/she‹, ›his/her‹ throughout.
3 | Kant (1788)

in other words, one which does not (yet) derive from the transcendent concept of religion: We can overcome the equally fundamental boundary between »ego« and »alter«, between one individual and other individuals or between one individual and a community – in everyday life and in general – through the »fundamental assumption« of the reciprocity of perspectives and an interchangeability of points of view that is, in principle, always possible.

The interplay of boundary experiences and designs for overcoming boundaries is the legacy of the interconnectedness of finiteness, neediness and rationality. The place where this interplay that is forced upon us occurs is the *individual* human being, which is constantly thrown back on its »halfness« and contingency, thanks to its comprehensive, irreversible boundary situation and the boundary situations that follow from it and are concretely experienced. From this anthropologically based starting situation, because we must live in and with it on a daily basis, there arises for us a paradox: On the one hand, it is pointless to ask about the »meaning« of this anthropological destiny, while on the other hand, as fallible beings [Mängelwesen] endowed with reason, we are compelled to give meaning to our actions – despite the finiteness, contingency and fragmentation of our life.

Religiosity owes its existence to this paradox. It arises from the need for meaning-conferral [Sinngebung] that cannot support itself and therefore points to something beyond itself. But it cannot derive any certain counterpart from this reaching-beyond-itself. Instead, however, it can both design a counterpart and imagine a »comforting no-place«, a utopia, if it does not want to lose itself in the nowhere. In short, as involuntary constructors of meaning, obeying »anthropological need«, ultimately all human beings are religious, even when they do not succeed in having a religion.

(2) It is therefore necessary to distinguish between religiosity and religion. (1) Religiosity arises from the structurally given and always possible experience of complete isolation, of »being solitary«. In this the individual experiences himself as a socially »excommunicated«, isolated being, at the mercy of his own diseases, pain, passions and emotions and his own death – a being that seeks help that others/ society, cannot give him. (2) By contrast, religion/religions are socially communicated, traditional and collectively believed ideas and guidelines, claiming to be experience-based, that enable the individual to fit into a socially and historically »heightened« reality.

When in extreme situations the individual at last discovers himself to be the sole measure of experience, knowledge, decision and legitimation, and when he has to understand that it ›is his own final position‹, a position in which ›everyone finds and obeys the daemon that holds the threads of *his* life‹ (Weber 1973: 613), at that moment he experiences the limits of communication and the ability to communicate. Not only can the isolated individual, communicating exclusively with himself in extreme situations, find himself, as a solitary and because of his »unique« experiences, compelled to turn against a collective and thereby also against its culture and religion, but he will also have to discover that for his solitary world of perception and experience he can find no collectively safeguarded language: Thus the solitary human struggles with the unsayable that he himself is, lives and designs, but which at the last he cannot communicate.

The limits of *religion* as a ›communicative construct‹ (Knoblauch 1991: 14; cf. also Krech 2011: 32 ff.) become evident when the individual, in a state of ›total solitariness‹ not shared by the collective, ›stands before his God‹ as an individual (Simmel 1912: 78). But even *religiosity*, as a disposition embedded in the individual, fundamentally holds the danger that he cannot communicate the materiality and foundation of his religious world of feeling, and experiences himself as thereby excommunicated. This experience is constitutive for both the religious and the aesthetic consciousness and sensitivity: Through the »revelation« of a fundamental difference between the solitary individual being and a collective, between what is communicable through collective coding and what has not (yet) been coded, it opens up an area of possibility that the community cannot canonize and close off. This is the meeting point of heresy and art, the heretic and the artist. Their common basis is the individual experience, which cannot at first be collectivized.

Religions react to the risk of isolation and the boundary experiences connected with it with a system of safeguards. The founders of religions and the great prophets themselves are, of course, usually great individuals, social outsiders, who owe their solitary experiences of God or visions to exposure to the risk of boundary experience and the – often extreme – danger from an encounter with the ›numinous‹ (cf. Rudolf 1963 [1917]). For in almost every case there is a manifestation of sublime majesty (lat. maiestas) in a ›moment of [...] sheer overwhelming power‹, which neither the individual nor a community can withstand (ibid.: 6ff). Thereby the *extraordinary* individual becomes the representative of a community that is afraid of being exposed to such a threat itself. The book of Genesis describes this representative function in exemplary fashion: In order to avoid an encounter between the God and the people, who fear they might die (cf. Exodus 20, 19), the individual, here Moses, ›drew near unto the thick darkness where God was‹ (Exodus, 20,21).

After this, however, the chosen one reports back and preaches about his experiences. And so the social machinery of communication begins to work. It transforms the individual experience into a community experience, the visions into the community's beliefs and the collective belief into a system of meaning that permits »normal« members of society to fit into a pre-ordained order without having again and again to expose themselves to the boundary experiences that threaten isolation and the social excommunication that it brings.

(3) It is only when a religion is safeguarded by special social institutions that a distinction can be created between »religion« and »society«, or between individual religiosity and religion. The institutional establishment of a religion is the necessary condition of an independent history of religious dogmas, organisations and expert expositors – beyond social and non-religious institutions.

The problem of the chosen, the prophets, the founders of religions and their disciples consists in their having to perpetuate both their personal charisma and the extraordinary charismatic experience – they must give the extraordinary a »place in the life« of the community. If a newly founded religious community wishes to safeguard itself for the future, it must not only carry out the transformation of the personal, prophetic or »divine« charisma into the charisma of office of the successors of those chosen ones, as described by Max Weber, but must also ensure that the charismatic experiences are established communicatively.

The institutionalization of religion is due to these efforts. But unlike the rise of other social institutions (cf. Berger and Luckmann 1970 [1966], esp. chap. II) the special feature of religious institutions is that they must represent and assert their extraordinary character and their specific world of experience to distinguish them from other institutions. For this reason they distinguish themselves, on the one hand, from non-religious institutions by particular »other-worldly« rites, buildings, training, dress, and experts, and, on the other hand, from other religions by specific ritual precepts – pertaining to ceremonial actions, food, clothing etc. – and by their own sacred writings, »distinctive« dogmas and their own dogmatic history. Only through such demarcations, sanctioned by institutions and institutionally safeguarded, can important contrasts come into being: Contrasts between »religion« and society, between the religiosity of an individual and the religion of a community, between different religions and – not least – between religion and science.

Where a religion dominates both everyday life and the life of the society it tends to blend social and religious institutions, legal provisions and religious precepts, everyday customs and religious rituals, patterns of thought or analysis and religious beliefs, in such a way that the »social construction of reality« and societal action become subsumed by the cosmology of this religion. Each one of these dichotomies is felt to be a direct threat to the religious consensus, an offence to religion and an insult to God or the gods. Thus a growing and often high level of internal differentiation within the religion (e.g. through the increase in religious orders) contrasts with minimal external differentiation – if any – and even that which does exist is seen as a violation of »community spirit«: Community spirit and religion are one.

Pluralist societies, on the other hand – where there is competition between religions, institutions, traditions, customs and models of action – represent, per se, a threat both to a religion's claim to represent the one true faith and to a smooth incorporation of individuals into a society and thus also to an individual's »ideological certainty« [Sinngewissheit].

(4) The more firmly individuals are embedded in relatively homogeneous communities, clans or groups, the more seldom – apart from direct existential crises – does the danger arise of their being exposed to the experience of being isolated. Individuality is certainly present in the structure here, but it is relatively unproblematic because it is not experienced as a difference from the community. In proportion as societies become more complex and »differentiated«, so individuals become increasingly detached from firm social ties, and their own individuality and thus also their own living and dying become more problematic (cf. Ulrich Beck's ›individualization‹).

The transition from closed to open societies, from »mechanical to organic solidarity« (Emile Durkheim) represents a threat not only to individuals but also to the entire community. When a society that experiences itself as *one* community becomes a society of *many different* communities, almost inevitably there is a desire to return to the »original« secure and protective network. An alliance – now reflexive in character – between individual and community is formed. But since the earlier closed society/community has become transformed into a society of different communities, it remains possible for an individual to bind himself to a community, although he cannot now return to the »original unity« of the *one* big community that embraces the whole society.

The individual's desire to return becomes allied with his self-binding to *one* of the many, now rival, communities to create an illusion of return, an illusion which draws strength from individuals‹ deliberate self-binding. Here lie the roots of fundamentalism. This is a *modern* phenomenon and converts the – realistic – fear of the failure of the illusion of return into a lasting and deep-seated resentment toward a society that can no longer be »mine«, because it is made up of a variety of communities and associations. All of them can equally well offer me multiple membership or deny me membership.

Whereas previously the other person was a fellow resident of the heaven of a common society, now the others are, to the individual, the hell of an anonymous society. Accordingly, fundamentalism based on religion seeks its salvation in the cosmos, which exalts and transcends the community, whereas secular radicalism tries to find it in the pipe-dream of the »collective identity« of a people, a nation or an idea.

(5) Analogous to the dual aspect of culture, which on the one hand arises from subjective »cultural work« and is experienced as an expression of freedom, but on the other hand can appear as an alien and threatening object to the person who is born into a culture or has been moved into it – Simmel's »tragedy of culture« – there is

also the »tragedy of religion«: On the one hand religion arises from the religiosity of the individual and lives from it. On the other hand, religions, as doctrinal systems of established constructions of meaning and systems of norms, tend to be perceived by the individual believer as alien and as an authority demanding subjection. In Christian history, for example, the »individual believer's direct access to God«, as postulated by Luther, was a reaction to this constraint to subject oneself to the church as an institution.

Nevertheless, such »direct access to God by the individual« carries a high risk. It makes every individual a divinely chosen person, who must stand before a sovereign and omnipotent God. The consoling recourse to the »means of grace« of the institutional church is replaced by the responsibility of the individual and the knowledge that this responsibility must be accepted without it being ultimately capable of fulfilment. Whereas previously religion could promise security to the anxious believer with its treasury of experience garnered over many generations and guaranteed by the »saints«, now the individual must seek answers to his questions directly from his God.

In the latter part of the 18th century and the start of the 19th, this – for many individuals insoluble – problem situation in both philosophy and literature, is not only articulated, but also reformulated in exemplary fashion in the *The Nightwatches of Bonaventura* (1970 [1805]) and in the *Speech of the dead Christ from the edifice of the world that there is no God* (Jean Paul 1975 [1795]: 270 ff.) so that it becomes applicable to the emancipation of culture from religion.

(6) For European modernism (especially since the Enlightenment) both culture and religion can be seen to be creatures of, and an expression of, human religiosity: Culture can be viewed as a secular religion and an attempt to provide a ›finite section of the world‹ with ›sense and meaning‹ from the human point of view and so redeem it from the ›meaningless infinity of world history‹ (Max Weber); religion, by contrast, as ›the last attachment and ordering [...], reconciliation with fate, [final] interpretation of reality and home‹ (Helmuth Plessner).

For anyone interested in a history of subjectivity, the myths and religions (ancient or Jewish) of the »Christian« West and the philosophies and world views derived from them[4] read like a *Bildungsroman* or coming-of-age novel branching off into an unending number of episodes. The story of the hero (or subject), who

---

4 | On the continuity and discontinuity of images, symbols and »moulds« for the gods and their successors cf. especially Seznec (1990) and Starobinski (1990). There are few comparable historical works on Judaeo-Christian imagery. A notable exception is Gutzen's essay (Gutzen 1991), entitled: ›Und ich sah den Himmel aufgetan [...]‹ (Offb. 19, 11). Zur Poesie der Offenbarung des Johannes [›And I saw heaven opened‹ (Rev.

goes through ever-changing metamorphoses, at first moves very slowly but then in the course of the last three hundred years speeds up more and more. In this story the tragic and the comic, the heroic and the pragmatic, the unusual and the banal, succeed one another in quick succession. Finally, in various different costumes and roles, a »figure« comes into view – to borrow the language of Goethe and of the early 19th century: a (pre)-shaped form that lives and develops; in the abstract and etiolated synthetic language favoured by contemporary social science: a generative structure.

In their rational thought experiments, the philosophers of the Enlightenment and their successors produced, in the abstract, what had already been lavishly depicted in symbolic shapes and images. The question concerning the »rootedness« or »justification« of »sociality« (state, social contract, the body politic) leads them to that element that constitutes the heart of the »social« and at the same time its limits – the individual as isolated and simultaneously socialized. The structurally designed isolation of individuals, as opposed to communities or societies, which is potentially actualizable in any age, is now comprehended as a threat *and* an opportunity for both individual and societies. As an opportunity for the enlargement of individuals' space it drives the development forward. As a threat to the community and out of fear of the detachment of the individual it becomes the motive for binding the society to enduring, fixed forms.

Both religion and culture, which without any distinction between them for long held together a socially constructed plexus of meaning, respond in a reassuring, protective and comforting tone to man's »eccentric personality«. Even where a contrast between religion and society emerges or many relationships and possible »models« compete with each other, there is no antithesis in principle between culture and religion. An antithesis of this kind can only be felt and formulated if – as in Plessner – culture is set up, in the »spirit of the Enlightenment«, as a religion of reason in opposition to religion as an illusory yearning for home (Plessner 1975 [1929]: 342): culture and religion as rivals in the conferral of meaning and interpretation as they struggle for primacy in the social construction of views of reality.

The philosophers and protagonists of the Enlightenment tell us the story of the children who set out to grow up. In humanity's infancy, so the story goes, culture was first promoted through religion. But then, enlightened reason, having grown up, detached itself from the fairy tales of its childhood, which were »unmasked« as illusions. Culture and science took the place of religion. – There is much to be said for the view that we should rewrite this story and should see a »scientifically grounded« culture not merely as a grown-up descendant of

---

19,11). On the poetry of the Revelation of John] (a title which only at second glance strikes one as odd).

the ancient myths but also as a successor religion to the Judaeo-Christian and ancient world views.

In terms of the history of ideas, Plessner himself has described a shift of emphasis in the desire for salvation: from the hope for redemption in the next world to the yearning for fulfilment in this world, a shift in which the ›lost other world‹ is replaced by a ›hidden this world‹ (Plessner 1982 [1935] [1959]: 19). Here, belief has changed direction: from the next world to this world. It remains what it was, however: a belief, a religious idea, even if this now presents itself in an innerworldly desire for redemption. Looking at »culture« as an embedding of »true nature« (now »second nature«) *in* the world – rather than in opposition to it – is part of this belief: a newly ordered religious process.

True, through belief the individual is also fitted into ›a socially and historically transcendent reality‹ (Luckmann 1991: 165) but this belief is based on a model that is organized in a new way. It is now a »scientifically grounded« culture, which, as an earthly religion, must achieve the self-transcendence of man. This innerworldly transcendence must, on the one hand, take place *in* society and history, on the other hand it faces these as a heightened form of the everyday and as factually superimposed upon it:[5] culture as a gilded background, the reflection of which bathes everyday constraints in the warm light of liberty, play and art.

In culture we venerate both our possibilities and fantasies and a world that we have designed, in which we could feel at home if we did not know that a last attachment to something that we ourselves have built – and by means whose limitations we know – stands on shaky ground (Plessner 1975 [1929]: 342). Worldly piety (cf. Plessner 1982 [1935] [1959]: 73 ff.) replaces other-worldly piety and becomes the expression of culture as a this-worldly religion.[6]

It is clear from this that there is not such an ›absolute antagonism‹ as Plessner (1975 [1929]: 42) assumes between religion and a culture that has been split off from religion in the modernist period. The security in the ›definitivum‹ (ibid.) that is sought and found by the former, and the latter's knowledge that human reason is always forced to overlay its own products with criticism and doubt and is thereby itself inevitably forced into »homelessness« if it does not ›offer itself as a sacrifice to faith‹ (ibid.) admittedly differ fundamentally in their security policy, but not in their religious function. Both religion and the »culture« of humanity and worldly piety transform ›members of a natural species into actors within a social order with historical origins‹ (Luckmann 1991: 165), and both fit the individual into ›a socially and historically transcendent reality‹ (ibid.).

---

5 | On the concept of »culture« employed here cf. Soeffner 2000.

6 | A not-insignificant feature of »earthly religions« is that, alongside other-worldly heavens and paradises, hells and purgatories are also transferred to this world: utopias and apocalypses.

(7) In modern, differentiated and pluralist societies a structurally problematic individuality is imposed on individuals. Modernism reacts against this »constraint« with an ideological consolation: with the enhancement of the single person to the status of the »autonomous«, »free« and »self-realizing« individual. Thus something that cannot be an institution, namely the individual, the smallest element in society, is to be raised to the level of an institution. The reaction of modern constitutions to this paradox is to strengthen the weakest member of the community by protecting and placing supreme value upon the »dignity of the individual person«.

Now, in addition to the functional affinity between traditional religion and its earthly religious heirs a structural affinity also becomes evident. Enlightenment – reason's and culture's self-enlightenment – (Kant, Plessner) touches the same basic element, the same driving force, from which myths, other-worldly and earthly paradises and homelands, hells and apocalypses, other-worldly and earthly pieties are produced and on which they are founded: it touches the individual as the ultimate measure of experience, knowledge, decision and legitimation.[7]

This basic element, however, is not only the foundation, but also the boundary that marks off religion and culture, both community products. However »barbarically« societies as a whole may again and again conduct themselves, and however lacking in »culture« or »religion« they may be, the true counterpart of religion and culture as collective figures is the individual, just as the religiosity of the individual stands simultaneously both on this side of and beyond all religions and cultures. Society's tireless work and effort in fitting and inserting the individual into a social world and its orders arises from this fundamental, irrevocable constellation.

The isolation of the individual vis-à-vis society, Durkheim's innerworldly god, does not, however, lead to that fathomless depth that is ascribed to the experience of the numinous. The individual does not yet sink into the void in the face of society. He is preserved from this by an almost elemental belief in himself, ›a fundamental calmness and assurance in the ultimate feeling of the self, expressed in the idea that he will victoriously preserve this self and bring it through in every situation‹ (Simmel 1912: 46). It is precisely this calmness and assurance that are the preconditions for the individual to succeed, even if only

---

7 | It is in this context that Max Weber, representative and analyst of the thought of his time, traces the boundary line separating individual decisions from every kind of collective claim to legitimation – including the scientific: Neither science nor any other institution decides on what the individual binds himself to. It is ›his own final position‹, that in which ›everyone finds and obeys the daemon that holds the threads of his life‹ (Weber 1973: 613).

rarely, in confronting a society – and a community, which is even harder. They are also the preconditions for the individual, in his particularity and uniqueness, to be made responsible for his actions and for ensuring that he cannot either hide in the collective or appeal to experienced predecessors.

(8) *Thus, in a »saving translation« the secular religion of modernism has linked the »image and likeness of God in which all men are made« (Jürgen Habermas) with general attributes that in monotheistic religions belonged to God alone: autarchy, autonomy and freedom. In the secular religion of modernism the individual's own god is the individual himself. The god of society is no longer society (Emile Durkheim); society becomes the polytheistic Olympia of individual gods, who are conscious of their sovereignty.*

It is part of modernism's belief in the individual that a uniqueness is attributed to the individual person which, although it strengthens his resistance to complete socialization, also, due to his experience of solitariness, detaches him from all the societal security and embeddedness on which he was accustomed to rely. In this detachment, the self – as the counterpart of society – is the *tendentially* absolute: an absolute based on innerworldliness. It is this innerworldly absolute that is the essential counterpart of the absolute of the »beyond« – God. The innerworldly absolute, the solitary self, is the foundation of religiosity. This (religiosity) is the ground over which religions stretch the canopy of heaven and the various gods set up their thrones in lofty heights until such time as religions and the gods take their seats in *this* world: in the faith that individuals have in individuals and in the possibility of happiness in this world.

The human disposition to the possibility of being solitary, the disposition to religiosity, activates all these different developments, which history has clothed again and again in new ways. Whether the individual »consciously« wants to be alone with himself for his own sake or not is, admittedly, an important question for ethics and moral philosophy. What is structurally more significant, however, is that the individual can be compelled to be alone with himself, even though – as a social being – he is incapable of existing on his own. However he may define himself, he is an incomplete subject, an invalid monarch of his autonomy, harnessed to two transcendental movements that simultaneously resist and complement each other. In one of these, this monadic torso takes a step forward toward other individuals or communities, while in the other he takes a step back as a social being and experiences himself as a tendentially solitary monad.

In fact, man, inasmuch as ›the personal identity‹ appears ›as a universal form of individual religiosity‹ (Luckmann 1991: 109) builds up a religious relationship (not just any relationship) with himself and *his* ideas, worlds and gods. This relationship, however, no matter how visible it may be in its forms of expression, must, in its concrete and singular (solitary) core, and in the world of ideas and experience that builds on it, be hidden from others and remain so.

Religiosity, the disposition that precedes religion and holds the individual in tension between solitariness and sociality, is the basis of this relationship. It is the place where the non-mundane occurs, the »inexpressible«, which is not »adequately« communicable to others and is »invisible« to others – and therefore also the precondition for what presently is termed »invisible religion«. And it marks the boundary which sociological analyses in the fields of knowledge and religion, analyses that represent intersubjectivity and rationality, prefer, for good reasons, not to cross.

(9) In contemporary societies, thanks to the pluralism of the religions that compete with each other, we have a ›heretical imperative‹ (Berger 1980) an individual deciding to bind himself to a particular religion and its truth or to the »god of his own choosing« (Ulrich Beck) – the god that he himself has found and experienced – and his very own truth. The first type of self-binding tends toward fundamentalism, the second to an extremely precarious form of permanent self-reassurance; the first is anti-cosmopolitan, the second produces a free-floating, socially unattached, cosmopolitan atom.

In contrast to what the phrase »heretical imperative« suggests, there is, as empirical studies of religiosity in the USA show (cf. Matter 2007), a convenient third way, which is chosen by the pragmatic, conventionally religious person (a type representative of the majority), namely a temporary polyheresy. Unlike the emotionally charged decision in favour of a lasting self-binding to a once-only choice and the »leap« into »absolute faith« (Kierkegaard 1960 [1844]), the conventionally religious person makes a number of pragmatic decisions: a move to another city, for instance, is often followed – in the USA at least – by a »change of mind« in favour of a different congregation or set of beliefs.

The decisive factor when making a new decision is not a particular doctrine or dogma but the social functioning and attractiveness of the new fellowship you are proposing to join. In an extreme case, you can pass through a series of heresies, beginning as a Baptist, and ending up, via Methodism and Catholicism or the Russian Orthodox Church, as a Buddhist. Each choice is based, not on any profound existential decision, but on social opportunism. Above all, it is observable that the social risks that a socially detached, cosmopolitan atom must take upon itself is felt to be almost impossible to cope with. By contrast, the choice of either fundamentalist attachment to a faith community or pragmatic membership of one successful congregation after another is seen as considerably less risky.

In pluralist societies the pragmatic, conventionally religious person benefits from the relatively peaceful co-existence of the different religions. In the places where, with relatively few problems, it currently obtains, however, this co-existence of people of differing world views owes its existence to its institutional safeguarding by a political system that has emerged in a relatively small part of the world out of a specific, historical development: The interplay of Greek antiquity, Judaeo-Christian traditions of faith and thought, the separation of church and state that began with the Investiture Controversy, the experience of bloody religions wars and the »modernist project« that began with the Enlightenment – all these have led, in a long development process, to the point where state and society are no longer understood as the expression of the divine will but as the result of social contracts.

The purpose of these contracts is to maintain a precarious balance between the state's claim to power on the one hand and civil liberty on the other and between the will of the majority and protection of minorities, and, not least, it is to safeguard the individual, who (see above) is seen as the weakest member of society and yet also as a responsible citizen on whom the community is founded and who should be not only protected but also strengthened. Consequently, modern constitutions ensure that freedom of decision, choice, speech and religion or creed are all jointly guaranteed: It is not only peaceful co-existence of religions that is made possible by this joint guarantee, but also the »heretical imperative«, temporary polyheresy, and the inevitable result, the ever-present possibility of conversion.

A person's decision to choose a »god of his own« outside established religions here represents an extreme enhancement of individualization: it represents the unity of individual religiosity and fully privatized religion. In this respect the adherent of his own god is seen by a collective religion as a solipsistic convert, by Christian theology as a practical example of the direct access of the believer to God and by sociology as someone making a structural, systematic attempt, in pluralist *and* individualized societies, to replace institutionalized religions by a religious authority established within and sustained by the individual. Pluralist societies give this risky attempt at religious self-institutionalization a chance.

(10) *From Herodotus (490–42 BC), Kublai Khan in China (13th century), Akbar the Great in India (16th century) and the Renaissance utopias, in whose »reflexively broken« tradition Ulrich Beck stands, right through to the present, the mutual recognition of religions has been called for and attempted. The constitutions of modern nation-states have created a legal framework for religions to live together by excluding the problem of truth and leaving the decision for or against (a) religion to individuals. The – still rudimentary – institutions of the international community try to encourage cultures and religions, if not yet to live together, at least to live alongside one another in a relatively conflict-free relationship. In doing so they have not yet succeeded in reconciling the canon of values enshrined in the »universal declaration of human rights« with the system of »absolute« truths, rights and duties of the world religions.*

Here too the combination of the free democratic constitutional state and the pluralist society offers a way out. But it is one that makes the assumption that representatives of »absolute truths« are prepared to renounce the right of a religion or world view to primacy over all areas of the life of society and of the individual – and they are not prepared to do this. Indeed, where religions compete with each other within a society it is inevitable that there will be great potential for conflict. On the other hand, precisely the proximity alongside one another of mutually exclusive and antithetical »absolute truths« offers the opportunity not only to draw comparisons and change one's perspective, but also to arrive, if not at a religious model of the »social market economy«, at least at a legally and institutionally backed balance of assertions and claims to disputed territory.

Here again, modern democratic constitutions lay stress on the freedom of choice of the individual, of the competent (or so it is claimed) citizen. However, every citizen should use the freedom of choice that is not only given to him but imposed upon him, to show loyalty to the constitution and the laws that protect him (cf. Soeffner 2011: 144 ff.). Toward the end of the 1960s, the constitutional lawyer Ernst-Wolfgang Böckenförde pointed to the circularity and the hidden assumptions in this constitutional idea with his pertinent and provocative assertion that the freedom-based secular state lived from assumptions that it could not itself guarantee without calling its freedom-based character into question (cf. Böckenförde 1967).

Böckenförde provides an illustration of the paradoxes thereby arising by the example of the law of religious freedom in the heterogeneous modern constitutional state. In sharp contrast to the confusing mishmash of opinion so often heard in political debates and TV talkshows, Böckenförde asserts: ›The degree of religious freedom achieved is in proportion to the degree of secularity of the state‹ (ibid.: 57).

What is at stake here is the freedom of the individual to decide on his own – in this case religious – values and to venerate his own god. Conversely, the freedom-based state, says Böckenförde, cannot and ought not to demand *any* profession of values as a condition of citizen status – as overt or veiled talk of an obligation on the citizen to observe a »dominant culture« seems to suggest. The citizen must, however, accept the constitution and abide by the laws of the state (cf. Böckenförde 1978). In short, the citizen owes allegiance to the law, *not* to an ideology. The contrast is between, on the one hand, heterogeneity and pluralism as the fundamental structure of modern states, and, on the other hand, the imposition of common agreement on matters of faith or ideology.

(11) *As far as the problem of truth is concerned, the Christian religion, if we take seriously the account of the »divine founder of religion« doubting his God (›My God, my God, why hast Thou forsaken me‹, Matthew, 7, 46), has confronted its own truth with a fundamental doubt. Certainty of belief and truth are extremely*

> rare, and the reaction of Dietrich Bonhoeffer to the notion that the existence of
> God was beyond doubt was: ›God has nothing to do with a god as we imagine
> him‹ (cf. Bonhoeffer 1997¹⁶: 210).

However theological source criticism may evaluate the historical attribution of the above-mentioned cry »quoted« in Matthew's gospel, this does not alter the uniqueness and tremendous provocation of this lament, as the »divine founder of religion« calls into question a truth that had hitherto been beyond question by uttering an unheard-of doubt. Because it is documented in a »sacred book«, this doubt still remains an intellectual thorn in the flesh of Christianity's vision of God – and at the same time remains not only a profoundly anti-fundamentalist element in the attitude of faith, but also, despite the wars of religion fought and the Crusades undertaken in the name of Christianity, a unique feature of this religion that distinguishes it from other world religions: In no other religion do we find a god who, in the form of his human incarnation, has doubts about himself.

In the »Occident«, this existential doubt finds an ally who at an early stage articulates the relationship between reason and faith, certainty and doubt. It is true that Socrates, with his pronouncement »I know that I do not know« is regarded as the progenitor of the principle of the pre-eminence of doubt and criticism in the face of apparent certainties, but what is crucial is that this foundation stone of Western philosophizing and of the understanding of science that followed from it has endured and grown stronger over the centuries, until it formed an alliance with the existential doubt of the Christian faith, which, finally, led Georg Simmel to make his insightful comment that the ›Christ God‹, unlike other godheads, is ›the God of the individual‹ (Simmel 1912: 89).

So it was that with the god of the Gospel of Matthew and of the individual – alongside the philosophical god – a fundamental religious doubt became entrenched in our culture. The occidental understanding of science is based on both: this is shown in exemplary fashion firstly in the attempt rationally and »scientifically« to construct proofs of the existence of God and secondly, and inevitably, in the subsequent »rational« destruction of those very proofs. Max Weber's statement that ›belief in the value of scientific truth is not derived from nature but is a product of definite cultures‹ (Weber 1973: 213) applies particularly to the theory of doubt and falsification in the modern understanding of science, as articulated by Descartes, Kant, Husserl and Popper right up to the present day. Fundamentally, anyone who lives with a world view like this can only be said to inhabit a »society of limited hope«.[8] Accordingly, even the individual's »own

---

8 | The wordplay in the German source text defies translation, it refers to »Gesellschaft mit beschränkter Hoffnung« and Monty Python's *The Meaning of Life* [*Der Sinn des Lebens*] from 1983 (Dir. Terry Jones).

god« is confronted by unresolvable doubts, and this only gets worse in proportion as reason and faith search for a balance within individuals.

(12) *The hope for a »god of one's own«, and thus the hope that the many »own gods« of cosmopolitan individuals can live together under a polytheist canopy, therefore appears – and not only from the viewpoint of cultural and religious sociology – as a cherished utopia of an admittedly reflective but nevertheless heroically optimistic modernist age. If it were true, as Kant expressed it with evident self-irony, that the god of religion is the god in us and at the same time ›is himself the interpreter, because we understand no one but him who speaks with us through our own understanding and our own reason‹ (Kant 1971 [1798]: 315), the god of enlightenment and reason of the first modernism would long since have led us to a secular rational cosmopolitanism. The frequently irrational motives of reason (Max Weber) and the ambivalence of the modern age (cf. Baumann 1992) have prevented this. As to whether or not in the second modernism each individual's own god, »invoked« by Ulrich Beck, will be any more successful through the exclusion of the problem of truth (but what would a religion be without its truth?) and through the maxims enjoining a duty of peace across all conflicts – not merely in modern constitutional states but throughout the world – we must await (but for how long?) »the verdict of history« (Gadamer).*

Translation by Gordon Wells on behalf of Textworks Translations

REFERENCES

Anonymous (1970 [1805]). *Die Nachtwachen des Bonaventura*. Stuttgart: Reclam
Baumann, Zygmunt (1992). *Moderne und Ambivalenz. Das Ende der Eindeutigkeit*. Hamburg: Hamburger Edition
Beck, Ulrich (2008). *Der eigene Gott. Friedensfähigkeit und Gewaltpotenzial der Religionen*. Frankfurt/M.: Verlag der Weltreligionen
Berger, Peter L. (1980). *Der Zwang zur Häresie. Religion in der pluralistischen Gesellschaft*. Frankfurt/M.: Fischer
Berger, Peter L. and Thomas Luckmann (1970 [1966]). *Die gesellschaftliche Konstruktion der Wirklichkeit. Eine Theorie der Wissenssoziologie*. Frankfurt/M.: Fischer
Böckenförde, Ernst-Wolfgang (1967). Die Entstehung des Staates als Vorgang der Säkularisierung. In: ibid. *Staat, Gesellschaft, Freiheit*. Frankfurt/M.: Suhrkamp
Böckenförde, Ernst-Wolfgang (1978). *Der Staat als sittlicher Staat*. Berlin: Duncker & Humblot

Bonhoeffer, Dietrich (1997). *Widerstand und Ergebung. Briefe und Aufzeichnungen aus der Haft.* Gütersloh: Gütersloher Verlagshaus

Gutzen, Dieter (1991). ›Und ich sah den Himmel aufgetan [...]‹ (Offb. 19, 1 1). Zur Poesie der Offenbarung des Johannes. In: Gerhard R. Kaiser (ed.). *Poesie der Apokalypse.* Würzburg: Königshausen & Neumann

Jean Paul (1975 [1795]). Rede des toten Christus vom Weltgebäude herab, dass kein Gott sei. In: *Siebenkäs. Jean Paul.* Works in Twelve Volumes. Vol. 3. München, Wien: Carl Hanser

Kant, Immanuel (1788). Kritik der praktischen Vernunft. In: ibid. *Complete Works in Ten Volumes,* ed. Wilhelm Weischedel. Vol. 6. Darmstadt: Wissenschaftliche Buchgesellschaft

Kant, Immanuel (1971 [1798]). Der Streit der Fakultäten. In: ibid. *Works in Ten Volumes,* ed. Wilhelm Weischedel. Vol. 9. Darmstadt: Wissenschaftliche Buchgesellschaft

Knoblauch, Hubert (1991). Vorwort. In: Thomas Luckmann: *Die unsichtbare Religion.* Frankfurt/M.

Krech, Volker (2011). *Wo bleibt die Religion? Zur Ambivalenz der Religion in der modernen Gesellschaft.* Bielefeld: transcript

Luckmann, Thomas (1991). *Die unsichtbare Religion.* Frankfurt/M.: Suhrkamp

Matter, Christine (2007). *»New World Horizon«. Religion, Moderne und amerikanische Individualität.* Bielefeld: transcript

Otto, Rudolf (1963 [1917]). *Das Heilige. Über das Irrationale in der Idee des Göttlichen und sein Verhältnis zum Rationalen.* München: C.H. Beck

Plessner, Helmuth (1975 [1929]). *Die Stufen des Organischen und der Mensch.* Berlin, New York: de Gruyter

Plessner, Helmuth (1982 [1935] [1959]). *Die verspätete Nation.* Collected writings. Vol. V. Frankfurt/M.: Suhrkamp

Seznec, Jean (1990). *Das Fortleben der antiken Götter. Die mythologische Tradition im Humanismus und in der Kunst der Renaissance.* München: Fink

Simmel, Georg (1912). *Die Religion.* Frankfurt/M.: Loening.

Soeffner, Hans-Georg (2000). Kulturmythos und kulturelle Realität(en). In: ibid. *Gesellschaft ohne Baldachin.* Weilerswist: Velbrück

Soeffner, Hans-Georg (2011). Die Zukunft der Soziologie. In: *Soziologie,* 40 (2): 137–150

Starobinski, Jean (1990). *1789. Die Embleme der Vernunft.* München: Fink

Weber, Max (1973). *Gesammelte Aufsätze zur Wissenschaftslehre. Wissenschaft als Beruf.* Tübingen: Mohr

Notes on Editors and Contributors

Arjun Appadurai is Paulette Goddard Professor of Media, Culture, and Communication at the New York University, Steinhardt School of Culture, Education, and Human Development. Selected publications: *Modernity at Large: Cultural Dimensions of Globalization* (1996), Minneapolis: University of Minnesota Press; *Fear of Small Numbers: An Essay on the Geography of Anger* (2006), Durham: Duke University Press.

Zygmunt Bauman is Professor emerit. of Sociology at the University of Leeds. Selected publications: *Liquid Times: Living in an Age of Uncertainty* (2007), Cambridge: Polity Press; *Collateral Damage: Social Inequalities in a Global Age* (2011); Cambridge: Polity Press.

Ulrich Beck is Professor of Sociology at the Ludwig Maximilians University of Munich, British Journal of Sociology Visiting Centennial Professor at the London School of Economics and Political Science, and Professor at the Fondation Maison des Sciences de l'Homme, Paris. Selected publications: *Twenty Observations on a World in Turmoil* (2012), Cambridge: Polity Press; forthcoming: *Distant Love* (2013), Cambridge: Polity Press (with Elisabeth Beck-Gernsheim).

Elisabeth Beck-Gernsheim is Professor of Sociology at the Norwegian University of Science and Technology / Universität Trondheim. Selected Publications: *Wir und die Anderen. Kopftuch, Zwangsheirat und andere Missverständnisse* (2007), Frankfurt/M.: Suhrkamp; forthcoming: *Distant Love* (2013), Cambridge: Polity Press (with Ulrich Beck).

Edgar Grande is Professor of Comparative Politics at the Ludwig Maximilians University of Munich, and representative of the Munich Center on Governance, Communication, Public Policy and Law. Selected Publications: *Cosmopolitan Europe* (2007), Cambridge, Malden: Polity Press (with Ulrich Beck); *West European Politics in the Age of Globalization* (2008), Cambridge: Cambridge University Press (co-edited with Hanspeter Kriesi, Romain Lachat, Martin Dolezal, Simon Bornschier and Timotheos Frey).

Maarten Hajer is Professor of Public Policy at the University of Amsterdam, and Director of the Netherlands Environmental Assessment Agency (PBL – Planbureau voor de Leefomgeving). Selected publications: *Deliberative Policy Analysis. Understanding Governance in the Network Society* (2003), Cambridge: Cambridge University Press (with Hendrik Wagenaar); *Authoritative Governance. Policy Making in the Age of Mediatization* (2009), Oxford: Oxford University Press.

Michael Heinlein is a senior lecturer at the Ludwig Maximilians University of Munich. Selected publications: *Die Erfindung der Erinnerung: Deutsche Kriegskindheiten im Gedächtnis der Gegenwart* (2010), Bielefeld: transcript; *Reflexive Particularism and Cosmopolitanization: The Reconfiguration of the National in Europe* (2010), in: Global Networks, 11(2) (with Daniel Levy and Lars Breuer).

Ronald Hitzler is Professor of Sociology at the TU Dortmund University. Selected Publications: *Individualisierungen. Ein Vierteljahrhundert »jenseits von Stand und Klasse«?* (2010), Wiesbaden: VS Verlag (co-edited with Peter Berger); *Posttraditionale Gemeinschaften. Theoretische und ethnografische Bestimmungen* (2008), Wiesbaden: VS Verlag (co-edited with Anne Honer and Michaela Pfadenhauer).

Cordula Kropp is Professor of Innovation and Futures Studies at the University of Applied Sciences, München, and Research Director at the Munich Group for Social Research and Sustainable Development (MPS). Selected Publications: *Beyond Speaking Truth? Institutional Responses to Uncertainty in Scientific Governance* (2010), In: Science, Technology, & Human Values (Special Issue) (with Kathrin Braun); *Gesellschaft innovativ – Wer sind die Akteure* (2011), Wiesbaden: VS Verlag (with Gerald Beck).

Bruno Latour is Professor and Scientific Director at Sciences Po, Paris, and visiting Professor at the University of California, San Diego, the London School of Economics, and the History of Science Department of Harvard University. Selected Publications: *Reassembling the Social. An Introduction to Actor-Network-Theory* (2005), Oxford: Oxford University Press; *An Inquiry into Modes of Existence* (2012), Cambridge: Harvard University Press.

Wolf Lepenies is Professor emerit. of Sociology at the Department of Political and Social Science at Freie Universität Berlin, and at the Wissenschaftskolleg zu Berlin. Selected publications: *Toleration in the New Europe: Three Tales* (1993), Wassenaar: NIAS; *Entangled Histories and Negotiated Universals* (2003), Frankfurt/M.: Campus.

Angela McRobbie is Professor of Communications at Goldsmiths, University of London. Selected Publications: *The Aftermath of Feminism* (2009), London:

Sage, also in German as *Top Girls* (2010), Wiesbaden: VS Verlag; forthcoming: *Be Creative? Making a Living in the New Culture Industries* (2013), Cambridge: Polity Press.

Judith Neumer is a research assistant at the Institute for Social Science Research in Munich (ISF München). Selected Publications: Die Kosmopolitisierung der Arbeit: Vom methodologischen Nationalismus zum kosmopolitischen Blick (2010), in: Götz et al. (eds.), *Mobilität und Mobilisierung*, Frankfurt/M.: Campus (with Ulrich Beck and Michael Heinlein); Management of the Informal by Decisions Within the Work Process (2012), in: Böhle et al. (eds.), *Innovation Management by Promoting the Informal*, Berlin, Heidelberg: Springer.

Ted Nordhaus is Chairman at the Breakthrough Institute, Oakland California. Selected Publications: *Break Through: From the Death of Environmentalism to the Politics of Possibility* (2007), New York: Houghton Mifflin Comp.; *Break Through: Why We Can't Leave Saving the Planet to Environmentalists* (2009), New York: Mariner Books (both with Michael Shellenberger).

Angelika Poferl is Professor of Sociology at the Department of Social Sciences and Cultural Studies, University of Applied Sciences Fulda. Selected Publications: *Große Armut, großer Reichtum. Zur Transnationalisierung sozialer Ungleichheit* (2010), Berlin: Suhrkamp (co-edited with Ulrich Beck); *Lebenswelt und Ethnographie* (2012), oldib: Essen (co-edited with Norbert Schröer, Volker Hinnenkamp and Simone Kreher).

Regina Römhild is Professor at the Department of European Ethnology, Humboldt Universität zu Berlin. Selected publications: *Turbulente Ränder. Neue Perspektiven auf Migration an den Grenzen Europas* (2007), Bielefeld: transcript (with Transit Migration Forschungsgruppe); The Art of Governance (2009), in: Ina-Maria Greverus (ed.), *Aesthetics and Anthropology*, Münster, Berlin: Lit (with Sabine Hess and Peter Spillmann).

Michael Shellenberger is President at the Breakthrough Institute, Oakland California. Selected Publications: *Break Through: From the Death of Environmentalism to the Politics of Possibility* (2007), New York: Houghton Mifflin Comp.; *Break Through: Why We Can't Leave Saving the Planet to Environmentalists* (2009), New York: Mariner Books (both with Ted Nordhaus).

Hans-Georg Soeffner is Professor Emeritus for Sociology at the University of Konstanz, Senior Fellow and Member of the Board of Directors at the Institute for Advanced Studies in the Humanities, Essen. Selected Publications: *Symbolische Formung. Eine Soziologie des Symbols und des Rituals* (2010), Weilerswist: Velbrück Wissenschaft; *Zeitbilder. Versuche über Glück, Lebensstil, Gewalt und Schuld* (2005), Frankfurt/M., New York: Campus.

Natan Sznaider is Professor of Sociology at the Academic College, Tel-Aviv Yaffo. Selected publications: *Human Rights and Memory* (2010), University Park: Pennsylvania State University Press (with Daniel Levy); *Jewish Memory and the Cosmopolitan Order* (2011), Cambridge et al: Polity Press.

Anna Tsing is Professor of Anthropology at the University of California, Santa Cruz. Selected Publications: *Nature in the Global South: Environmental Projects in South and Southeast Asia* (2003), Durham: Duke University Press (with Paul Greenough); *Friction. An Ethnography of Global Connection* (2005), Princeton: Princeton University Press.

Anja Weiß is Professor of Sociology at the University of Duisburg-Essen. Selected Publications: Overcoming Methodological Nationalism in Migration Studies (2012), in: Anna Amelina et al. (eds.), *Beyond Methodological Nationalism*, London: Routledge, (with Arnd-Michael Nohl); The Transnationalization of Social Inequality. Conceptualizing Social Positions on a World Scale (2005), in: *Current Sociology*, 53(4).

Yunxiang Yan is Professor of Socio-Cultural Anthropology at the University of California Los Angeles. Selected Publications: *The Individualization of Chinese Society* (2009), Oxford: Berg; *Private Life under Socialism: Love, Intimacy, and Family Change in a Chinese Village 1949–1999* (2003), Stanford: Stanford University Press.